PHILOSOP
THE TWILIGHT ZONE

PHILOSOPHY IN
THE TWILIGHT ZONE

EDITED BY

NOËL CARROLL AND
LESTER H. HUNT

WILEY-BLACKWELL

A John Wiley & Sons, Ltd., Publication

This edition first published 2009
© 2009 Blackwell Publishing Ltd

Blackwell Publishing was acquired by John Wiley & Sons in February 2007. Blackwell's publishing program has been merged with Wiley's global Scientific, Technical, and Medical business to form Wiley-Blackwell.

Registered Office
John Wiley & Sons Ltd, The Atrium, Southern Gate, Chichester, West Sussex, PO19 8SQ, United Kingdom

Editorial Offices
350 Main Street, Malden, MA 02148-5020, USA
9600 Garsington Road, Oxford, OX4 2DQ, UK
The Atrium, Southern Gate, Chichester, West Sussex, PO19 8SQ, UK

For details of our global editorial offices, for customer services, and for information about how to apply for permission to reuse the copyright material in this book please see our website at www.wiley.com/wiley-blackwell.

The right of Noël Carroll and Lester Hunt to be identified as the authors of the editorial material in this work has been asserted in accordance with the Copyright, Designs and Patents Act 1988.

Wiley also publishes its books in a variety of electronic formats. Some content that appears in print may not be available in electronic books.

Designations used by companies to distinguish their products are often claimed as trademarks. All brand names and product names used in this book are trade names, service marks, trademarks or registered trademarks of their respective owners. The publisher is not associated with any product or vendor mentioned in this book. This publication is designed to provide accurate and authoritative information in regard to the subject matter covered. It is sold on the understanding that the publisher is not engaged in rendering professional services. If professional advice or other expert assistance is required, the services of a competent professional should be sought.

Library of Congress Cataloging-in-Publication Data

Philosophy in the Twilight zone / edited by Noël Carroll and Lester H. Hunt.
　　p. cm.
　Includes bibliographical references and index.
　ISBN 978-1-4051-4904-4 (hardcover : alk. paper) — ISBN 978-1-4051-4905-1 (pbk. : alk. paper)
　1. Twilight zone (Television program : 1959–1964)　2. Philosophy.　I. Carroll, Noël, 1947–
II. Hunt, Lester H., 1946–
　PN1992.77.T87P45 2009
　791.45′72—dc22

                                                                                            2008041556

A catalogue record for this book is available from the British Library.

Set in 11/13pt Dante by Graphicraft Limited, Hong Kong
Printed in Singapore by Ho Printing Pte Ltd

01　2009

CONTENTS

CONTENTS

NOTES ON CONTRIBUTORS

Noël Carroll is a Distinguished Professor of Philosophy at the Graduate Center of the City University of New York. His most recent books are *The Philosophy of Motion Pictures* (2008) and *On Criticism* (2008). He is presently working on *A Short Introduction to Humour* for Oxford University Press.

Susan L. Feagin is Visiting Research Professor of Philosophy at Temple University and editor of *The Journal of Aesthetics and Art Criticism*. She is the author of *Reading with Feeling: The Aesthetics of Appreciation* (1996), co-editor of *Aesthetics* (1997), and editor of *Global Theories of the Arts and Aesthetics* (2007). Her recent work has focused mainly on emotion, fiction, and narrative, and on philosophy of the visual arts.

Lewis R. Gordon is the Laura H. Carnell Professor of Philosophy, Religion, and Judaic Studies at Temple University, where he also is Director of the Institute for the Study of Race and Social Thought and the Center for Afro-Jewish Studies. His many books include, more recently, *Disciplinary Decadence: Living Thought in Trying Times* (2006), *An Introduction to Africana Philosophy* (2008), and, with Jane Anna Gordon, *Of Divine Warning: Reading Disaster in the Modern Age* (2008).

Richard Hanley philosophizes at the University of Delaware. He is the author of *The Metaphysics of Star Trek* (1997), as well as several articles on philosophy and popular culture, and is the main author of *South Park and Philosophy: Bigger, Longer, and More Penetrating* (2007). His next book is on time travel.

NOTES ON CONTRIBUTORS

Lester H. Hunt is Professor of Philosophy at the University of Wisconsin, Madison. He has also taught at Carnegie-Mellon University, University of Pittsburgh, and The Johns Hopkins University. He is the author of *Nietzsche and the Origins of Virtue* (1990) and *Character and Culture* (1998). Most recently, he was editor and a principal contributor to *Grade Inflation: Academic Standards in Higher Education* (2008). His current research is taking him into fundamental issues in the aesthetics of film.

Sheila Lintott is Assistant Professor of Philosophy at Bucknell University (Lewisburg). Her research interests include aesthetics and the philosophy of art, environmental philosophy, and feminist philosophy. In addition to a number of articles in these and related areas, she is co-editor (with Allen Carlson) of *Nature, Aesthetics, and Environmentalism: From Beauty to Duty* (2008).

Carl Plantinga is a Professor of Film Studies in the Communication Arts and Sciences Department at Calvin College. Recently he has authored *Moving Viewers: American Film and the Spectator's Experience* (2009) and co-edited (with Paisley Livingston) *The Routledge Companion to Philosophy and Film* (2008). He is also associate editor of *Projections: The Journal for Movies and Mind*.

Mary Sirridge is Professor of Philosophy at Louisiana State University, Baton Rouge. She has also taught at the University of Massachusetts, Amherst, and at the University of Wisconsin, Madison. She has written on philosophy of art, philosophy in literature, and ancient and medieval philosophy. She is currently co-editing the *Abstractiones* by Richard the Sophist, a work in thirteenth-century medieval logic.

Aeon J. Skoble is Professor of Philosophy and Chair of the Philosophy Department at Bridgewater State College in Massachusetts. He is the co-editor of *Political Philosophy: Essential Selections* (1999), author of *Deleting the State: An Argument about Government* (2008), and editor of *Reading Rasmussen and Den Uyl: Critical Essays on Norms of Liberty* (2008), and has written many essays in both scholarly and popular journals. In addition, he writes widely on the intersection of philosophy and popular culture.

Aaron Smuts is Visiting Assistant Professor in the Department of Philosophy at Temple University. He works in a variety of areas in the philosophy of art and ethics, and his articles have appeared in *American Philosophical Quarterly, Asian Cinema Journal, Contemporary Aesthetics, Film and Philosophy*, the *Journal of Aesthetic Education*, the *Journal of Aesthetics* *and Art Criticism, Philosophy and Literature,* and the *Stanford Encyclopedia of Philosophy.*

James Stacey Taylor is an Assistant Professor of Philosophy at the College of New Jersey. He is the author of *Stakes and Kidneys: Why Markets in Human Body Parts are Morally Imperative* (2005), as well as numerous articles on ethics, applied ethics, and action theory. He is also the editor of *Personal Autonomy: New Essays on Personal Autonomy and Its Roles in Contemporary Moral Philosophy* (2005). He is currently completing a monograph defending an Epicurean metaphysics of death.

Thomas E. Wartenberg is Professor of Philosophy at Mount Holyoke College where he also teaches in the Film Studies Program. He is the author of, among other works, *Unlikely Couples: Movie Romance as Social Criticism* (1999) and *Thinking On Screen: Film as Philosophy* (2007), and the editor of a number of anthologies on the philosophy of film, most recently, *Thinking Through Cinema: Film as Philosophy* (2006) with Murray Smith.

Introduction

LESTER H. HUNT

The 156 episodes of the original *Twilight Zone* series (1959–64) constitute by far one of the most influential and enduringly popular of all dramatic series. It has been revived twice, and has served as the basis for a feature film, books of short stories, and a comic book. It has introduced many catch-phrases and mythic images into our culture. All five seasons are available on DVD.

The episodes were often quite consciously intended to provoke thought and argument about philosophical issues and ideas, and were very effective at doing so. The issues it treated included, for instance, those of skepticism in its various forms, the ethics of war and peace, the nature and value of privacy and personal dignity, the nature and value of knowledge (and of ignorance), the nature of love, the objectivity of judgments of value, the nature of happiness, of freedom, and of justice. In addition, some episodes just *are*, you might say, philosophical problems in themselves. They often violated the conventions of classical narration. They often committed spectacular violations of explanatory closure. As everyone knows, story lines would often include impossible events. An airliner flies through time. A man "overhears" the thoughts of others. A woman does not realize that she is dead. In a great many cases, as everyone knows,

I

the script makes no attempt to explain why or how they happened. The series required a generation of viewers to revise the expectations that guided them in interpreting and appreciating narratives, and challenged them to think about fundamental issues.

This book is for people who want to take up this challenge and reflect on these revised expectations. One's thinking on any issue is apt to be most effective if done together with a companion who can help one to identify and clarify issues. It can also help, though of course in a different way, if they take provocative positions on the issues involved, positions to which one might be inspired to respond. The essays in this volume are meant to provide such help and stimulus.

Except for the first chapter, which is biographical, these essays fall into three different groups: 1. Essays that use a single episode or pair of episodes as the basis for a discussion of some philosophical question. In effect, the events in the episode function as examples illustrating or otherwise shedding light on the ideas discussed in the essay; 2. Essays interpreting the series as a whole, or some episode or cycle or sub-genre of episodes; 3. Essays on aesthetic issues raised by distinctive features of the series, such as issues about genres, or about modernist narrational strategies.

The following is a rough guide to the content and purpose of each of the essays, and to a few of the connections between them.

Lester Hunt leads off with a chapter explaining how series creator Rod Serling became the philosophically interesting author he was in *The Twilight Zone.* He began his distinguished career as a writer of quite a different kind. That he became associated in the public mind with the narratives of such a fanciful or fantastic sort was the unpredictable result of a collision between talent, temperament, and circumstances that proved to be well beyond the author's control.

Noël Carroll discusses a large sub-genre of episodes, which he calls the Tales of Dread. Tales of dread are narrative fantasies in which a character is punished in a way that is both appropriate and mordantly humorous or ironic. Though the punishment is not meted out by any character depicted in the story, it seems so appropriate that one is left with the feeling that it is somehow intentional. The dread induced by the stories comes from the feeling they give one of a universe in which judgment is meted out by unseen powers characterized by diabolical wit.

The sub-genre that Carl Plantinga treats is in some ways the opposite of the one that concerns Carroll. While Carroll is concerned with episodes that, in a way, have more coherence than life often has, in which our hankerings for meaning and justice are all-too-fully satisfied, Plantinga is

2

concerned with ones that, in a certain way, thwart our expectations and undermine our assumptions – namely, the ones with surprise endings. He is especially interested in the ones he calls "frame shifters," in which the viewer's frame of reference is somehow reversed in the end: the seemingly futuristic tale is actually set in the past, the tiny invading aliens are actually humans, and so forth. He argues that frame-shifting is a narrational strategy that enables the series to provoke thought even while using what is fundamentally traditionally entertaining Hollywood-style narration.

Mary Sirridge discusses a sub-genre that is subtly related to the one discussed by Plantinga: these are episodes in which the audience is fooled by "the treachery of the commonplace." The audience either wrongly accepts at face value what the problem is that the characters are facing (the problem seems to be the possibility that the aliens will colonize humans, whereas the real problem is that they will eat them), or they fail to question some commonplace idea that is so familiar that it does not even present itself to the human mind as an idea. The result of these episodes, she finds, is to show us the limits of our knowledge and, when they venture from the realm of epistemology into that of politics, the limits of authority.

The one essay in this volume that addresses a philosophical issue raised by the entire series, and not just by some of its episodes or narrational strategies, is Richard Hanley's "Where is the Twilight Zone?" He asks whether there could be such a place as "the twilight zone" and comes to the surprising conclusion that, yes, there probably could be, and that the idea of extra spatial dimensions offers the best possible hope of accounting for the goings-on in the Zone, and of its ability to interact with beings in our world.

Susan Feagin explores Sartrean existentialist themes and a critique of Cartesian certainties about personal identity in the episode "Five Characters in Search of an Exit," and although she does find un-existentialist hopes of redeeming contact with other people offered in "In His Image," the hopes, she points out, are not presented by a person, but by a machine. Overall, she says, though the series often does pursue existentialist themes, it is generally too optimistic to have an overall existentialist sensibility.

Lewis Gordon discusses the treatment of racial issues in the series. He points out that the indirect, ambiguous way in which it treats these issues is one strategy for dealing with such issues in the context of a racist society: it is a subject that the intended audience wishes to avoid. A viewer who sees the somewhat Caucasian-looking aliens, the Kanamits, in "To

Serve Man" is free to ignore the fact that their homicidal practices and indeed their very name associates them with a practice that white stereotypes associate with African races: namely, cannibalism.

The remaining essays focus on particular episodes of *The Twilight Zone*. Thomas Wartenberg discusses "The Odyssey of Flight 33." He takes an experience he had as a child – anxiously listening to an unseen plane overhead with the feeling that this might be flight 33, even though he knew that flight 33 was fictional – as emblematic of something the series very often did. In a number of ways, it would suggest the possibility of fictional worlds overlapping with the real world, thus opening up realms of disturbing possibilities for the viewer.

Sheila Lintott finds in "Nightmare at 20,000 Feet" an opportunity to reconsider and sharpen our views about the nature of truth. That episode, she maintains, illustrates a reason why the seemingly most intuitive theory of the nature of truth – the "correspondence theory," the view that a belief that a thing is so is true if and only if that thing is actually so – is actually an inadequate theory, at least if it is not supplemented somehow by one of this theory's main rivals: the so-called "coherence theory."

Aeon Skoble finds in "Nick of Time" some useful wisdom about the relationship between freedom and reason. Don, the character who seems to be threatened with enslavement by a devilish (in more senses than one) fortune-dispensing machine, is actually held in bondage by his own irrational thinking about it. This episode is in a way atypical of the series in that the plot turns out to include no supernatural or science fiction elements, but Skoble points out that situations in which a character's real problem is his or her own failures of rationality is a theme that recurs in other episodes as well.

Aaron Smuts consults the episode "The Little People," in which a space traveler forces tiny aliens to worship him, only to be accidentally crushed to death by voyagers larger than himself, for insight into the issue of what *would* make a being worthy of worship. He finds that the episode not only suggests but actually provides us with reason to think that mere awe-inspiring power no matter how great would be enough.

James S. Taylor defends the position taken by the episode "Nothing in the Dark" in which Wanda Dunn hides from the world, depriving herself of all the pleasures of life, in order to avoid fatal contact with "Mr. Death." When Mr. Death finally appears, he tells her that death is nothing to be afraid of. Taylor argues that this is quite right: to die is not to suffer a harm at all. Rather, as in the case of Wanda Dunn, it is the *fear* of death that is actually, seriously harmful.

I

"AND NOW, ROD SERLING, CREATOR OF THE TWILIGHT ZONE"

THE AUTHOR AS AUTEUR

LESTER H. HUNT

It has been said that the so-called *"auteur* theory," the idea that the director is the true "author" of a film is "probably the most widely shared assumption in film studies today."[1] Those who are tempted to find in this idea an immutable truth might do well to remember that, for a while during the sixties, there were several American television series in which the "author" in this sense, that is, the artistic personality who dominated the show and gave it its peculiar aesthetic, was a *literal* author: that is, a person who writes.[2] Examples included Stirling Silliphant's *Route 66* (1960–4) and Reginald Rose's *The Defenders* (1961–5). The last of them was *The Waltons* (1972–81), by *Twilight Zone* alumnus Earl Hamner, Jr. Probably the finest and surely the best-remembered of this distinguished company was Rod Serling's *The Twilight Zone*. It was very much a writer's show. In his on-screen introduction to each episode, Serling always named the author of the episode, if it was someone other than himself, and always named the author of the original story if it was an adaptation. This must have represented an all-time high in respect shown for writers on primetime, network television. Indeed, Serling's on-screen appearances soon made him the best known, most widely

5

recognized living writer in the world. Being a writer has never seemed so . . . well, so *cool*. In this chapter I would like to say a few words about how he came to be the writer we know, and how he came to create *The Twilight Zone*.[3]

Rodman Edward Serling was born on Christmas day in 1924 in Syracuse, New York, and grew up in the small southern tier town of Binghamton, where his father was the town butcher. There is a certain irony in this birth date, for Serling was Jewish, but his parents were assimilated Jews and the family always celebrated Christmas, as indeed Serling – who eventually converted to Unitarianism – did all his life. He graduated from Antioch College in Ohio, where he majored in creative writing. Antioch, one of the centers of "progressive education" earlier in the twentieth century, was a hotbed of liberal social idealism, a point of view that Serling absorbed and held as long as he lived. He also had a lifelong affinity for the academic ethos, and more than once he took a very large cut in pay in order to teach creative writing at his alma mater.

He wrote for radio stations in Ohio during the twilight years of that medium and, seeing the words of doom on the wall, began to write for the new medium of television. He sold his first script to network TV in 1950 for $100.[4] There could not have been a better time for a writer to enter any medium. It was the beginning of the age of live television drama, and the industry, then based in New York, was quickly developing a ravenous appetite for scripts. It also had an aching need for script writers who had two skills that Serling had developed in radio: the ability to write rapidly and copiously, and a knack for writing words that would take a specific number of minutes to say. Television, like radio and unlike movies and staged drama, was despotically ruled by the clock.

Serling thrived in this environment. Indeed several writers did. The writers who got their start writing for live TV included Paddy Chayefsky, Horton Foote, Reginald Rose, and Gore Vidal. For some reason that no one has explained, several of these people almost immediately became famous. Viewers recognized their names and the distinctive qualities of their work. Reviews of a show would to a considerable extent be reviews of the contribution of the writer, who would be mentioned by name. During these years, Serling won an Emmy for his teleplay "Patterns" (aired in 1955), and another for "Requiem for a Heavyweight" (1956). In 1956, Simon and Schuster published a book, titled *Patterns*, containing four of his teleplays and his "commentaries" on each one.[5] All this had happened by the time he was barely more than 30 years old.

I have suggested that early live TV was more like radio than film with respect to its being ruled by the clock. It had two other characteristics that are worth pausing to notice, because both carried over into the *Twilight Zone* aesthetic. First, they tended to convey narrative, as radio drama did, more by means of dialogue rather than depicted action. Second, they generally used few, often rather cramped, sets. Given that the genre category of *The Twilight Zone* – fantasy and science fiction – is one that we naturally associate with action and visual effects, it is really remarkable how many of the episodes consist mainly of two or three characters talking to each other. In addition, the shows typically use very few sets, sometimes one or two, very often no more that three. Some of the most memorable episodes take place virtually entirely within a single room (for instance, "A Game of Pool"). In several, the claustrophobia-inducing qualities of a single cramped set are actually part of the thematic content of the episode ("Six Characters in Search of an Exit," "Nervous Man in a Four Dollar Room," "The Last Night of a Jockey"). These characteristics of the series give it a certain quality, both cerebral and stylized, that seem to enhance its effectiveness as a means of communicating ideas.[6]

In several respects, though, the Rod Serling, who first achieved fame in the fifties, was a different sort of writer from the one that fans of *The Twilight Zone* know. In an article written while Serling's career was still soaring, Ayn Rand described the difference like this:

> Rod Serling, one of the most talented writers of television, started as a Naturalist, dramatizing controversial journalistic issues of the moment, never taking sides, conspicuously avoiding value-judgements, writing about ordinary people – except that these people spoke the most beautifully, eloquently romanticized dialogue, a purposeful, intellectual, sharply focused dialogue-by-essentials, of a kind that people do not speak in "real life," but should. Prompted, apparently, by the need to give full scope to his colorful imagination and brilliant sense of drama, Rod Serling turned to Romanticism – but placed his stories in another dimension, in *The Twilight Zone*.[7]

On at least one point, this is a penetrating description of the transformation that Serling underwent. Though I would rather say that the early Serling tended to conspicuously *appear* to avoid value-judgments, and prefer to call Serling's early style Realist rather than Naturalist, it is true that his work before *The Twilight Zone* was mainly in the aesthetic camp of Realists and Naturalists.[8] In 1949, Serling attended the first New York run of *Death of a Salesman*, with Lee J. Cobb as Willie Loman, and it seems to have made a powerful impression on him.[9] "Patterns" can be read as a sort of corporate *Death of a Salesman*, told from the point of view of one of the newcomers who are edging the Willie Loman character out. More generally, all of Serling's more ambitious early teleplays bear the most salient features of *Salesman*: they depict ordinary people dealing with today's problems and speaking today's language (or, more exactly, an idealized version of it). Their strongest emotional effects were achieved by setting these ordinary people on a collision-course with some sort of climactic result. It was the sort of thing that reviewers liked to describe as "gritty," "unsparing," and "hard-hitting."

His work in *The Twilight Zone* is not merely different from this; it is, as Rand suggests, in an altogether different aesthetic tradition. In *The Twilight Zone*, he is no longer in the Realist or Naturalist camp of writers like Arthur Miller and Frank Norris; he is in the Romantic, allegorical, or fantastical school of Edgar Allen Poe and Nathaniel Hawthorne. In Serling's life, the advent of *The Twilight Zone* was almost like one of the surprise endings that seemed typical of a *Twilight Zone* episode, those ironic twists that Serling sometimes called "the snappers." It was unpredictable and yet somehow logical after the fact. What was the nature of the logic that brought this transformation about? Rand speculates that he was driven in that direction by his own inner necessity. There I think she is simply wrong. Curiously enough, *The Twilight Zone*, probably Serling's most lasting achievement, was dragged out of him by circumstances beyond his control, almost against (as he saw it) his better judgment.

The origin of the transformation lay in a feature of early live television drama that I have not touched on yet, one that was not at all to Serling's liking. It is somewhat difficult for us to fully appreciate today, because it is somewhat alien to the nature of the mass media as they exist in our time. However, it is important for understanding the way Serling's career eventually developed. Everyone knows that network television gets its money from paid commercial announcements. In those days, this gave the sponsor a remarkable amount of control over program content. Sponsors often seemed to think of the shows as long, lavish, expensive ads for their products. Indeed, as in the days of radio, the name of the sponsor was often part of the title of the show. This was true, for instance, of the first of the hour-long live dramatic shows, *Kraft Television Theater* (premiered in 1947), and it was also true of the very last of them, *Bob Hope Presents the Chrysler Theater* (cancelled in 1965). Representatives of sponsoring companies, usually employees of their advertising agencies, actually read scripts before they were produced, and they often demanded changes. They nearly always got what they demanded. This influence took two forms, one of which was petty and the other potentially devastating.

In those days, the advertising industry was in the grip of a theory that held that consumer purchases are conditioned by factors that are a) extremely subtle, but b) identifiable by the clever people who work in the advertising industry. One practice that resulted from this curious theory was that of avoiding all mention of the competitor's product. In an early script for *The Twilight Zone*, a British navy officer orders a tray of tea to be brought up to the bridge. The sponsor, manufacturer of Sanka instant coffee, objected to the word "tea." The offending phrase, Serling tells us, was changed to "a tray."[10] Another practice, often just as silly as this one, was to avoid anything that would associate one's own product with something unpleasant. To give another of Serling's examples, in the original, *Playhouse 90* version of "Judgment at Nuremberg," one of the sponsors, a consortium of gas companies, had every mention of "gassing" and "gas ovens" expunged, evidently for fear that the viewers would unconsciously associate their product with Nazi genocide.

This sort of interference was annoying at best, degrading at worst, but Serling could put up with it when he had to. There was another sort of interference that was much deadlier, though evidently based on the same sort of thinking. The same instincts and assumptions that prompted advertisers to avoid associating their product with anything unpleasant also led them to avoid anything that might make anyone angry. The word that inevitably sprang up in these situations was "controversy." "Controversial" subjects tend to cause people to write angry letters to the network and threaten to do things like not buy the sponsor's product. Such subjects are therefore to be avoided altogether. Serling's early career, from its beginning up to the end of *The Twilight Zone*'s five-season run, can be seen as a series of responses to this practice.

One response was, quite simply, to argue against it. He was good at this and often did it in public. In the long introductory essay in the *Patterns* book, titled "About Writing for Television," Serling mounts his most sustained argument against television censorship on the part of sponsors. The core of his case consists of two narratives. These are the sad stories (sad as he tells them, at any rate) of two scripts of his that were produced in 1956. Both stories recounted events that were disappointing to him, one of them much more bitterly so than the other.

The first of these scripts was "The Arena" (directed by Franklin Schaffner), which aired on *Studio One* on Monday April 9 of that year. The title refers to the United States Senate, indicating that it will be treated as a place in which men meet to fight. Its central character is Jim Norton, an inexperienced young Senator, appointed by the governor when his predecessor died in office. Jim idolizes his father, Frank Norton, who was also a Senator. As a result of this, he harbors a bitter grudge against Rogers (the character is apparently never given a first name), the senior Senator from his state. Rogers had brought the elder Norton's political career to an ignominious end by leading a successful campaign to block his re-nomination some years earlier. He did so in spite of the fact that he is a member of the same party. It is clear that he thought him a bad Senator, mainly because of his over-indulgence in pork-barrel legislation. The younger Norton seems unable to control his temper and soon, first at a press conference and then on the floor of the Senate, launches intemperate verbal attacks on Rogers, who has no trouble provoking him to act like a hot-headed fool. Before long, Jim's reputation is in tatters, and it seems doubtful he will be able to accomplish anything of value in Washington. The real dramatic conflict in the story, one that occurs not between Rogers and Norton, but inside Norton's head, comes when his political advisor blurts out, while drunk and discouraged, something that very, very few people know: many years ago, Rogers was a member of a vicious group called "The Defenders," a thinly disguised version of the Ku Klux Klan. If Norton releases this information, Rogers will be ruined and his father avenged. In a climactic scene on the floor of the Senate, Rogers, who had figured out what Norton is planning to do, lets it be known that he will announce his resignation, but Norton heads him off, at the last possible minute, by indicating that he will not use his information.

Serling had high hopes for "The Arena," high enough to submit it to a major studio for consideration as a possible feature film. But its reception was disappointing. Serling clearly thought part of the blame belonged to the artificial restrictions built into the television medium by the producers and sponsors. In particular: "One of the edicts that comes down from the Mount Sinai of Advertisers Row is that at no time in a political drama must a speech or character be equated with an existing political party or current political problems." The object of this stricture was to avoid, at all costs, appearing to take sides on any current controversies, because that would have meant offending someone. This is workable enough in political dramas set in the distant past: he would have been permitted to depict, say, Lincoln and Douglas debating abolitionism because slavery is no longer controversial. There will not be any angry letters if *Studio One* comes out against slavery. But in a political drama set in the present, the characters would have to either avoid ever talking about politics, or talk about it in such a way that viewers could not tell what they were saying.

In "The Arena," according to Serling's account of it, he in effect took the latter course, with ridiculous results. Viewers who tuned in that April evening, he says,

> were treated to an incredible display on the floor of the United States Senate of groups of Senators shouting, gesticulating and talking in hieroglyphics about make-believe issues, using invented terminology, in a kind of prolonged, unbelievable double-talk. There were long and impassioned defenses of the principles involved in Bill H. R. 107803906 [actually, it was HR 1932: a little comic hyperbole here?] but the salient features of the bill were conveniently shoved off into a corner. . . .]

As a matter of fact, the existing script of "The Arena" is not nearly as bad, on these particular points, as Serling makes it sound.[11] In the scene in question, young Norton is claiming that his father deserves some of the credit for the passage of HR 1932, as it embodied principles for which he had long been fighting. Rogers replies that Norton had earlier inadvertently killed two very similar bills by attaching to them amendments "granting special privileges to interests in his home state" – measures, in other words, that constituted pure pork.[12] The charge is of course that his commitment to currying favor with his constituents at others' expense was stronger than the alleged political principle involved. The audience is never told what HR 1932 contained and is therefore in the dark about what the principle involved was. However, I would think that, for purposes of plot, characterization, and theme, it does not really matter very much what the principle is, and I don't think that the audience feels very confused about it.

Still, a case might well be made that the advertisers' ban on discussions of controversial issues did damage the script of "The Arena," and in a way that is actually more serious than the one Serling has alleged. After all, the ban means that, if Serling writes a script about contemporary politicians, he cannot clearly depict them *discussing politics*. Because of this stricture, he can only depict his principal character engaged in discussions on the Senate floor by depicting him as obsessed with the *purely personal* issue of Rogers' treatment of the character's father. But this motivation is really too petty and irrational for the viewer to feel a great deal of sympathy for his plight, or interest in how he resolves it. The fundamental point that Serling makes about the script of "The Arena" is I think correct: it is indeed a flawed script, and censorship on the part of advertisers is indeed part of the reason it is flawed.

The other script that Serling singled out as a case study for his indictment of television was "Noon on Doomsday," which aired on April 25, 1956 on the *United States Steel Hour* (produced by the Theater Guild and directed by Daniel Petrie). Here the story is a good deal more complicated than the story behind "The Arena," and it is also more interesting. The "Noon" script was inspired by Serling's anger over the notorious Emmett Till case, which had occurred the year before. Till, a young African-American from Chicago, was traveling in Mississippi, when he whistled at a white woman on the street. For this he was kidnapped, tortured, and murdered by white supremacists. The two men charged with the crime were tried in an atmosphere of intense media scrutiny, especially from the North. They were found not guilty on all counts. Serling believed that the disapproving attention they got from the North "was like a cold wind" that made the people in the Mississippi town "huddle together for protection against an outside force which they could equate with an adversary."[13] Thus, in his view, the whole town became complicit in the crime of the murderers.

The original version of his script for "Noon," Serling later said, followed the facts of the Till case "very closely."[14] However, Lawrence Langner, President of the Theater Guild, told Serling: "The only problem is that you can't make it [i.e., the conflict in the story] black and white."[15] Serling made the victim of the murder an elderly Jewish merchant. The killer was, as Serling later put it, a "neurotic malcontent" seeking a scapegoat for his own problems.

Somewhere during this course of events Serling mentioned to Dave Kaufman, a friend of his who wrote for *Variety*, that he was writing a show based on the Till case. Later (in a letter dated March 4) he asked Kaufman to mention the show in an article, but to report it as a rumor (i.e., not attributing it to him), as the network was not ready with an official press release. Kaufman did plug the show, but innocently added the earlier factoid, which was gradually becoming out of date, that the show was to be based on the Till case. What followed was an advertiser's worst nightmare. Across the South, White Citizen's Councils launched letter-writing campaigns. Southern branches of U.S. Steel, as Serling later told Kaufman, "bombarded" the network with telegrams demanding that "this here Till story" not be shown in the South.[16] Meanwhile, everything that could possibly suggest the South was removed from the "Noon" script.

The setting was moved to New England. Every word in the dialogue that could possibly have suggested a Southern accent or dialect was altered. Under no circumstances was the word *lynch* to be used. Bottles of Coca Cola were removed from the set (probably because Coke was originally a product of the state of Georgia). The murder victim was changed from a Jew to a non-specific "foreigner" (the victim's name eventually became Chinik). For some reason, Serling was also pressured to change the murderer from a neurotic malcontent to a decent kid who had momentarily gone wrong, a change that would probably have made the character unintelligible, but he put up what he called "a Pier 6 brawl" and blocked that particular revision.[17]

Despite the agony of creating it, Serling had high hopes for the "Noon" script, just as he had earlier had for "The Arena." During the month or so before airing, he repeatedly wrote to friends and acquaintances urging them to tune in when it aired, and he sent a copy of a draft of the script to United Artists, as a possible basis for a feature film.[18] After it was aired, however, he was rather taken aback by the mixed reaction to the show. Though it was praised elsewhere, it was panned in a brief review in the *New York Times*.[19]

He received a number of pieces of mail criticizing the show. One particularly acid-penned missive was a postcard from a stranger in the Bronx. Signed simply "A crank named M. Kroll," it said:

> May I congratulate you on your effort not to offend your sponsor, U.S. Steel.
>   I am sure if Emmett Till could, he would thank you for at least basing your drama on his murder.
>   Finally, may I congratulate you on your unimpeachable writer's integrity. I'm sure your script fee will be a soothing balm for your conscience.[20]

Remarkably, Serling wrote a reply that was well over a page long (single-spaced), and was, considering the provocative nature of Mr. Kroll's postcard, very well-reasoned. One reason for this, I think, was the fact that Kroll gave his name and address. Serling was by now well enough known to have received many letters from cranks, and the ones he really detested were those that were anonymously written. He thought of anonymous letters as attempts to intimidate and silence him, rather than efforts to open a dialogue. In addition, it is clear that Kroll's malicious little note had hit a tender spot. Serling replied: "Were I not to perform certain of the dilutions to my script, it would never have gone on [the air]." He continued:

I may be wrong, but I felt that NOON ON DOOMSDAY made itself heard. It did it obliquely and sometimes badly. But the words were there. And they stated quite clearly the extension of prejudice is violence; that prejudice is ugly, dirty and dangerous – no matter what level it exists on, or what group it aims at.

No, Mr. Kroll, probably the tragic figure of Emmett Till would hardly thank me for my efforts. But I wonder if, knowing the circumstances, he would accuse me of jobbing off an ideal for a script fee.

I worked almost a year on NOON. The last month before its production was a night and day job of trying to protect its basic premise, of trying to fight and scratch to just get it on. I can assure you that this wasn't done for a fee. I make a hundred grand a year and most of it comes without any altercations. For NOON ON DOOMSDAY I beat my brains in – and I do it knowing that whatever the end result, I'm going to get needled to death for my cowardice and my compromises.[21]

Some months later, when he was writing the introductory essay for the *Patterns* book, he had come to regard "Noon" as a failure. The main reason for this failure, as he saw it, was the restrictions that were part of the medium of television at the time:

What destroyed it as a piece of writing was the fact that when it was ultimately produced, its thesis had been diluted, and my characters had mounted a soap box to shout about something that had become too vague to warrant any shouting. The incident of violence that the play talked about should . . . have been treated as if a specific incident was symptomatic of a more general problem. But by the time "Noon on Doomsday" went in front of a camera, the only problem recognizable was that of a TV writer having to succumb to the ritual of track covering so characteristic of the medium he wrote for.[22]

This I think is an astute assessment of what went wrong with this script. Serling's strategy in "Noon" was to attack a general issue by narrating a single, concrete example of it. In order to work, a narrative of this sort must possess the virtue of *clarity*: the example, and the generalities in the speeches of the characters, should be handled in such a way that they shed light on each other. The concrete events put a human face on the generalities, while the generalities give the concretes universal relevance. In the "Noon" script, this fails to happen.

The events in the final script's narrative concern the aftermath of the trial of a character named Kattell, the nasty young malcontent I mentioned earlier. He has killed the "foreign" shopkeeper in a quarrel about whether he can have a bottle of wine on credit, but the jury finds him not guilty. The main action involves two characters who are appalled by the trial and its outcome: Frank, the father of the lawyer who successfully defended Kattell, and Lanier, the journalist who has been reporting the trial to a disapproving outside world. In the climactic scene, they confront Kattell in front of all the townspeople, who have gathered for a Founder's Day celebration. They provoke him into physically attacking both of them and to declaring that he did kill the old man, and that anyone would have done the same. At last, the people of the village are as appalled as Frank and Lanier are. He has lost the moral trial (as one of the characters calls it), despite having won the legal one. Then Frank berates the villagers:

> I call this boy [Kattell] a monster – because what he's done is the extension of your prejudice. He's the trigger finger for all your hatreds – for all your narrowness. He belongs to you and his crime belongs to you because you spawned it, and you spawned him.[23]

This of course is the point of view that the author wants to communicate. The trouble is that it does not clearly and convincingly refer to the events in the teleplay. The script is set in contemporary America. The setting licenses the audience to assume that the things that are true of contemporary America (all those things and only those things) are true of the story, except of course for all the details that are actually presented in the performance. And in contemporary America the audience knows of no social problem of hatred of European immigrants who speak English with an accent, on the massive sort of scale that could implicate a whole community in the act of one individual.

This problem is of course a direct result of the network's policy of controversy-avoidance. To effectively make the point he wants to make, in a realistic drama set in contemporary America, Serling would have to depict a minority group against whom many Americans really do have a virulent prejudice. But then the network could expect to get angry letters – from nativists, racists, and xenophobes, and possibly from minority group members as well. What can he do?

At this point in Serling's career, there has arisen a dramatic situation not unlike one that might hold at the outset of one of his early teleplays: there are conflicting forces afoot that combine to bring about an unstable situation. Something has got to give. Serling clearly wants to deal with issues that are important and relevant to the lives we are living today, which means that we do not agree about them. This would clearly require him to deal with controversial subjects. But on the other hand he is working in a medium that shrinks from controversy of any sort. Whatever happens next, it will have to be something new.

One direction in which events might develop was suggested in a letter Serling wrote soon after the exchange with Mr. Kroll, to Nolan Miller, his mentor and creative writing teacher at Antioch College. Noting that the Steel Hour version of "Noon" was "a greatly diluted and watered down version of the Till case," he says that he was now in the second draft of rewriting it as a stage play. Legitimate theater is far more accepting of controversy than the medium that was his current home:

> In its play form ["Noon"] doesn't futz around; it gets to the point in a hurry and it calls a spade a spade. I choose to think that I have sacrificed no drama in making it pretty sociologically telling.[24]

The play version was at the time being considered for summer production at the Playhouse in what was then Serling's home town, Westport, Connecticut.

The play version of "Noon" was indeed direct and blunt in all the ways in which the U.S. Steel Hour script was indirect and evasive. The town is identified as Southern in the very first line of the play. The murder is depicted on stage, and the victim is, like Till, a young black man. His killer is a white racist. The dialogue is peppered with nasty racial epithets. However, the play version was, curiously enough, not really an improvement over the Steel Hour script. It simply has the opposite sorts of flaws and shortcomings. Where the television show suffered from abstract speeches without adequate concrete events to which they can refer, the play presents lurid concretes without any universal point. In it, the fundamental conflict is not between different ideas, nor between rationality and prejudice, but simply between North and South. At one point in Act II of the play, in which a Southern segregationist is arguing with a Northern newspaper reporter, the Southerner throws out the then-familiar argument that, though we in the South are openly racist, you Northerners are covertly so, practicing de facto, unofficial segregation while hypocritically giving lip-service to justice and equality. Instead of saying that this is completely irrelevant to the principle involved, the Northerner says:

> If you tried to peddle Kattell [the murderer] up North all wrapped up with your little Southern legal refinements – take a cold-blooded killing, dress it

up with a joke prosecutor, comic witnesses, and a circus trial – you'd get results. You'd get mass vomiting from Los Angeles to Backbay Boston. I'll grant you something, Mr. Grinstead, sometimes when we point a finger at you, we're the pot and you're the kettle. But when you scratch through down to the bare rock and you come up with the one basic thing like human life – this we gotta butt in on.[25]

This, especially for Serling, is bad dialogue, but what I would like to point out is that the story, as reframed and retold in the play version, embodies a flawed rhetorical strategy. Serling is not writing the play merely to entertain, but to enlighten. He wants to convince people that the Southern system, as it existed in 1956, was unjust. But who is the intended audience, the would-be recipient of this enlightenment? The people of Westport, Connecticut are already aware of the simple truth he means to communicate. The racists of Alabama, on the other hand, would also fail to be enlightened by it – though for a different reason. In either case, Serling's argument will either induce yawns or fall on deaf ears. In the second telling of the "Noon" story, Serling wrote more or less directly about the specific event that inflamed his passionate concern: namely, the Till case. But this particular event, as interpreted by his anger, does not make a very good story. As far as I have been able to determine, the play has never been produced.

The story of the "Noon" script does not end here. Remarkably, Serling told the Till-based story one more time, and the last telling of it indicates the direction his work was soon to take, in *The Twilight Zone*. The third telling was a 90-minute teleplay that aired on *Playhouse 90* on June 19, 1958 (directed by John Frankenheimer), "A Town Has Turned to Dust." In this version of the story, he salvages the plot and a central character that he developed for the brutal, unpublished, and unperformed stage play version of "Noon." He also convincingly depicts real prejudice and vicious intergroup anger and hatred. How does he get away with it? By retelling the story *as a western*. In the new version, the story is set in the American Southwest in the nineteenth century. Racial tensions between the Anglo settlers and the indigenous Mexican population are inflamed by a long, cruel drought (hence the literal dust that is one of the title's meanings). In the jail is Pancho Rivera, a 16-year-old Mexican boy who, we are told, attempted to rob the local store and rape the wife of Jerry Paul, the storekeeper. Paul has been haranguing an angry mob, urging them to storm the jail and lynch the boy. When the mob storms the jail, Sheriff Denton's deputies all desert him and he eventually caves in and hands

Pancho over to the mob. The crowd lynches him by hanging him, just off screen, from a flagpole. After Pancho is buried, Ramon, his brother, enters the white-only saloon with a friend. Jerry Paul orders them to leave, but Sheriff Denton, who seems to be developing a backbone, declares that they are his guests and can stay. Paul lunges at Ramon, who stabs him in the shoulder with a knife. In the ensuing confusion, Ramon and his friend manage to get across the street and into the jail, bolting the door behind them. Faced with the inevitability of another lynching if he does nothing, the sheriff joins Ramon in the jail and passes out weapons and ammunition. When Ramon asks him if this is just "a grand gesture," he declares: "This is the one we go the route."

Once again, there is a vicious, angry mob at the door of the jail. This time, Paul's wife shows up and addresses the mob. She reveals to them something that the audience has already come to know in an earlier scene between her and her husband. The Mexican boy was actually innocent of the offense for which he was lynched. She had fallen in love with him, a fact that inspired jealousy and racist rage on the part of Paul. Just as Paul turns his gun on his wife to shoot her, Sheriff Denton shoots and kills him. Flagg, the town bartender, is surprised that Denton appears to be guilt-stricken at having to kill Paul: "You didn't have no choice," he says. Denton says: "We all had a choice. That was the one treasure we had – the privilege of choice. To live with what we've got – or try to blame someone for what we've got. That's why Jerry Paul is dead now."[26] He tells the village priest that he has a confession to make. He then reveals something crucial to understanding his earlier weakness in his handling of the Rivera lynching. At several points in the narrative, we have heard references to another lynching, a "migrant worker" who was dragged to death behind a wagon during another brutal drought 16 years ago. Denton was a member of the earlier lynch mob, in fact he was the leader. He has been weakened and compromised by guilt ever since. He then goes into the jail and closes the door. A long silence is broken at last by the roar of a gunshot from within the jail. A voice-over narration by Hannify, the reporter who has been telling the outside world of these events, rounds the narrative off with a comment that anticipates Serling's later Aesopian epilogues in The Twilight Zone:

> Dempseyville got rain tonight . . . for the first time in four months. But it came too late. The town had already turned to dust. It had taken a look at itself, crumbled and disintegrated. Because what it saw was the ugly picture of pre-judice and violence. Two men died within five minutes and fifty feet of each

other only because human beings have that perverse and strange way of not knowing how to live side by side. Until they do, this story that I am writing now will have no ending but must go on and on.[27]

The teleplay of "Dust" is as powerful and focused as that of "Noon" is weak and vague. Unlike the earlier script, "Dust" was praised in the *New York Times*, which spoke of its "vivid dialogue and sound situations."[28]

This, however, was not how Serling saw his performance in the "Dust" script at the time it was produced. In fact, he used "Dust" as an example of the damage done by censorship, as he had earlier used "The Arena" and "Noon." He made this bitter comment on it in the *Cincinnati Post*:

> By the time "A Town Has Turned to Dust" went before the cameras, my script had turned to dust. Emmett Till became a romantic Mexican. The setting was moved to the Southwest of the 1870s. The phrase "twenty men in hoods" became "twenty men in homemade masks." They chopped it up like a roomful of butchers at work on a steer.[29]

This, I probably should point out, might be another case of Serling exaggerating the damage done in order to make a point. There are two drafts of "Town" that are known to me, and neither contains the phrase "twenty men in homemade masks." The nearest approximation that I can find is in the later of the two, which is marked "REHEARSAL SCRIPT" on the title page, and there the phrase is "twenty men in sheets."[30] It replaces a phrase in the earlier draft, "six men in sheets."[31]

More important, for present purposes, is the fact that in these comments he seems to be expressing the view that a work of art that deals with the issues raised by the lynching of African-Americans is damaged, perhaps ruined, if it depicts some other minority in place of African-Americans. The same view is probably what prompted John Frankenheimer, director of "Dust" for *Playhouse 90*, to say in an interview many years later, that it represented "a terrible compromise, *terrible* compromise" with the censors.[32]

In an interview with Mike Wallace given just days before the air date (October 2, 1959) of the first episode of *The Twilight Zone*, Serling made some comments about his new series that have been quoted many times over the years. Wallace said to Serling that since he was "going to be obviously working so hard on *The Twilight Zone*" then "in essence, for the time being and for the foreseeable future," he must have "given up on writing anything important for television, right?" In response to this rather obnoxious question (it was at around this time that *Mad* Magazine parodied Wallace as "Mike Malice") the usually unflappable Serling seemed just a little flustered. He said:

> Yeah. Well, again, this is a semantic thing – important for television. I don't know. If by important you mean I'm not going to try to delve into current social problems dramatically, you're quite right. I'm not.[33]

I am sure many *Twilight Zone* fans have wondered what these two were talking about. *The Twilight Zone* not important? What do they mean by that? Decades later, Wallace explained Serling's answer like this: "At the time he did the interview, he'd just gotten through battling censorship and gotten through battling the system. So of course he was going to say, 'I'm not going to do anything controversial'."[34] In other words, Serling is telling a little white lie to avoid more self-defeating battles with bone-headed advertisers and their groveling network yes-men.

However, there is another way of reading these comments of his. If we look at them in the context of his remarks about the "Dust" teleplay, and more generally in his roots in aesthetic Realism, it is possible to see Serling's state of mind at the time of the Wallace interview as more complex than it seems at first. A minute or so after the above exchange with Wallace, Serling said:

> I stay in television because I think it's very possible to perform a function of providing adult, meaningful, exciting, challenging drama without dealing in controversy necessarily. This, of course, Mike, is not the best of all possible worlds. I am not suggesting that this is at the absolute millennium. I think it's criminal that we're not permitted to make dramatic note of social evils as they exist, of controversial themes as they are inherent in our society. I think it's ridiculous that drama, which by its very nature should make a comment on those things that affect our daily lives, is in the position, at least in terms of television drama, of not being able to take this stand. But these are the facts of life. This is the way it exists, and they can't look to me or Chayefsky or Rose or Gore Vidal or J. P. Miller or any of these guys as the precipitators of the big change. It's not for us to do it.

I hear in these words a sincere ambivalence about the *Twilight Zone* project, and it seems to be rooted in a line of reasoning that would come very naturally to one who is at the time still rooted in the Realist tradition. The underlying assumption behind all these comments – both what he is telling Wallace about *The Twilight Zone* and what he said earlier about

"Dust" – is the idea that art deals with the problems of the actual world, as it exists today, by depicting the actual world as it exists today. From this point of view, dealing with prejudice and mob violence as it exists in 1959 by depicting Mexicans in the 1870s is nearly as bad as depicting violence against a nondescript "foreigner." And, surely, dealing with it by depicting aliens or robots is incomparably worse. You either depict the problem in its actual, concrete specificity, or you water it down and compromise, or you do not deal with it at all.

Of course, other views are possible. An alternative view was suggested by the cranky Mr. Kroll of The Bronx, New York. In response to Serling's defense against his sarcastic post card, Martin Kroll (he signed his full name this time) had written back with a very intelligent observation. After thanking Serling for telling him of his struggles with the "Noon" script, he persists in disagreeing with him on his main contention, to the effect that in writing it he had taken the best of a stringently limited set of alternatives:

> You say that it is better to get something said than keep your principle and have nothing said. I believe you oversimpl[i]fy the case. There are numerous examples of television plays and motion picture scripts which deal with the indecency and injustice of mob violence and collusion that have come before the public. As an example may I cite *The Oxbow Incident*. The treatment was general and non-controversial, and yet it was a fine contribution as a drama and as a social document.[35]

Kroll is accusing Serling of having committed the fallacy of "false dichotomy": if he can't treat the contemporary problem of lynching by depicting lynching as it exists today, he can only treat it by presenting a watered-down, compromised depiction of what happens today, as he did in the "Noon" script. There is a third possibility: your treatment of the contemporary problem can be, to use Kroll's word, "general." This strategy, I take it, would mean presenting an image of a concrete, specific event in such a way that it presents the universal principles and ideas that these events illustrate: and doing so *in order to* present these principles and ideas.

Obviously, it was precisely this third route that Serling took in the "Dust" version of the Till story and later, brilliantly, in *The Twilight Zone*. He took it, not so much out of an inner artistic compulsion as much as as a way of responding to extrinsic circumstances. It was a way to evade the would-be censors and controversy-averse corporate cowards. As J. M. Coetzee pointed out a few years ago, censorship has always tended to prompt writers to express themselves in "allegorical modes, Aesopian language" and "implicit references."[36] As an attempt to evade censorship, the *Twilight Zone* strategy proved to be a great success. It is a curious fact, but undeniably true, that the same racists and segregationists who will write angry letters and organize boycotts if you produce a Realistic show that depicts the lynching of Emmett Till as a despicable atrocity, will be completely indifferent to a fantastic, allegorical show that says that *all* lynchings are despicable atrocities.

Beyond that, it is obvious to us now, as Serling probably eventually realized, that the allegorical or Aesopian mode he adopted in *The Twilight Zone* was not a dilution of his material at all. On this issue it is interesting to note that when, in 1998, "A Town Has Turned to Dust" was filmed for the Science Fiction Channel, the producers moved the tale from the 1870s to the distant, post-apocalyptic future, in which all of planet earth is a drought-parched desert and social conditions are those of the Wild West at its most anarchic. In other words, they moved it even further from the facts of the actual case that inspired it. And yet the effect is hardly one of dilution. Though the film is dedicated to the memory of Emmett Till, the remoteness of the film's setting serves, naturally enough, to emphasize the universality of its implications.

The emergence of the Rod Serling who created *The Twilight Zone* is a rather odd case of artistic evolution. He changed, rather abruptly and driven by the pressure of circumstance, from an artist who thought it was his highest calling to comment on the problems of the day by depicting them directly, to one who commented on principles and universals involved, not merely in the problems of the moment, but of human life itself. In so doing, he became just the sort of author who deserves the sort of treatment he is given in the essays in this volume. For to move from the concrete issues of the day to the principles that underlie them is to move from a journalistic approach to these problems to a philosophical one. Though concrete events, such as the Till case, can have philosophical interest or relevance, that is because they can illustrate, illuminate, or raise issues about general ideas and principles. One is not practicing philosophy until one is dealing with those ideas and principles themselves.

NOTES

1. The statement is from the 4th edition of David Bordwell and Kristin Thompson's *Film Art: An Introduction*, quoted in Berys Gaut, "Film

Authorship and Collaboration," in Richard Allen and Murray Smith's *Film Theory and Philosophy* (Oxford and New York: Oxford University Press, 1997), p. 169 fn. 1.

2. More recently, *The Sopranos* (1999–2007), created and dominated by writer David Chase, has brought this tradition back to life, at least for the length of eight years.

3. First, a brief comment on the nature of the approach I will take. Serling's career can easily be seen as a series of battles. His practice and convictions often put him at odds with others – with sponsors, with the advertising agencies who represented them, and with the network officials who usually took their side in a dispute – and he argued vigorously for his point of view. He was also a prolific raconteur and self-explainer who sometimes carried out his battles in the public press. To date, the published accounts of his career generally simply repeat his accounts as the unvarnished truth. This I think is a serious mistake. It is like basing a history of a war entirely on the propaganda statements of one of the combatants. In what follows I will, whenever I can, check Serling's self-explanations against other sources, and put them into context. The point of course is not to impugn his integrity. The point is that the purpose of my statements, made so long after the battles have been fought and their issues settled, is simply to achieve insight. The point of *his* statements was that of every act committed by a combatant: to win.

4. Rod Serling, *Patterns: Four Television Plays with the Author's Personal Commentaries* (New York: Bantam, 1958; orig. pub. Simon and Schuster, 1956), pp. 6 & 7. In what follows, details about Serling's life and career for which I cite no other source will be from the introductory essay in this book, "About Writing for Television."

5. See note 3 above.

6. As Noël Carroll has pointed out to me, there is another connection between *The Twilight Zone* and the radio medium. There had been several radio anthology series that involved horror or supernatural elements, including *Inner Sanctum, One Step Beyond*, and Arch Oboler's *Lights Out*. Serling was known to be a fan of *Lights Out*. He was also a great admirer of Norman Corwin, whose anthology series often involved fantasy elements.

7. Ayn Rand, "What is Romanticism?" originally published June 1969, reprinted in *The Romantic Manifesto, Revised Edition* (New York: Signet, 1975), p. 121.

8. I use these terms as follows. A Realist is someone who aims for a certain aesthetic effect: namely, the impression of reality as it actually exists, non-idealized. A Naturalist is a Realist whose work conveys a belief in Fatalism, the notion that human choice counts for little because people are ruled by natural, historical, or economic forces that are beyond their control. John dos Passos was a Realist and Emile Zola was a Naturalist. Since Serling was

never a fatalist, I regard his early work as Realist in my sense, and not as Naturalist.

9. This at any rate is what Joel Engel says in his biography, *Rod Serling: The Dreams and Nightmares of Life in the Twilight Zone* (Chicago: Contemporary Books, 1989), pp. 84–6. Engel does not cite any source for this account, but it is certainly consistent with the style and content of Serling's early writing. In general, Engel's book is unfortunately not very reliable. See notes 10 and 16, below.

10. Rod Serling, in the CBS interview with Mike Wallace, September 22, 1959. The interview is presented entire in *The Twilight Zone Definitive Edition* DVD set, Season 2.

11. Joel Engel repeats as factual Serling's claim, misleading at best, that the Senate debates in "The Arena" are, in Engel's wording, "an incoherent mishmash, and cryptographic jumble," in *Rod Serling: The Dreams and Nightmares of Life in the Twilight Zone*, p. 125.

12. "The Arena," script marked "Second Revised Script," p. 46. Throughout the present essay, all the Serling correspondence and unpublished screenplays I quote or paraphrase are in the Serling papers in the Wisconsin Historical Society in Madison, Wisconsin.

13. *Patterns*, p. 20.

14. *Patterns*, ibid. Except where indicated, my account of the evolution of the "Noon" teleplay follows Serling's in the *Patterns* book.

15. This is how Serling later told the story in a panel discussion at Santa Barbara's Center for the Study of Democratic Institutions. *The Relation of the Writer to Television: A Center Occasional Paper*, Introduction by Marya Mannes (New York: Fund for the Republic, 1960), p. 11.

16. Letter from Serling to Kaufman, dated April 8.

17. Joel Engel erroneously reports that Serling did make that change. *Rod Serling*, p. 125.

18. Max Youngstein of United wrote back that "while I think it has many wonderful ideas in it, there is just too much talk, talk, talk in it as it stands to make it a full length feature picture." Letter to Serling dated April 16, 1956.

19. This at any rate is how Serling describes the critical reaction to the show in a letter to Junes Eddy, an Ohio friend of his, dated May 11, 1956.

20. Postcard dated April 26, 1956.

21. Letter of May 12, 1956.

22. *Patterns*, p. 22.

23. "Noon on Doomsday," draft marked "REHEARSAL SCRIPT 4/4/56," Act III, p. 15.

24. Letter of June 12, 1956.

25. "Noon on Doomsday," theatrical version, revised draft, Act II, p. 5.

26. "A Town Has Turned to Dust," script marked "revise as of 5/26/58," p. 112.

27. "A Town Has Turned to Dust," p. 117.

28. Jack Gould, review of June 20, 1958. Text available on the website of the Rod Serling Memorial Foundation, http://www.rodserling.com/NYTtowndust.htm.

29. *Cincinnati Post*, May 23, 1958. This is the date that Gordon F. Sander gives for this article in his *Serling: The Rise and Twilight of Television's Last Angry Man* (New York: Penguin USA, 1992), p. 261 n. 9, but it must be erroneous, since it would put this comment before the show's air time, an event to which it refers in the past tense.

30. "A Town Has Turned to Dust," p. 114.

31. This draft is marked "First draft as of 4–21–58" and is the only other draft of this script in the Serling papers at the Wisconsin Historical Society.

32. "Rod Serling: Submitted for Your Approval," *American Masters* series, produced for WNET, 1995.

33. See note 6 above.

34. Interview presented in "Rod Serling: Submitted for Your Approval," *American Masters* series, produced for WNET, 1995.

35. Letter of June 1, 1956.

36. J. M. Coetzee, *Giving Offense: Essays on Censorship* (Chicago: University of Chicago Press, 1996), p. 123. Actually, Coetzee is at this point quoting, but with approval, the words of a certain Sidney Monas.

2

Tales of Dread in The Twilight Zone

A Contribution to Narratology

NOËL CARROLL

INTRODUCTION

There are several different sorts of story-types among the episodes of
The Twilight Zone. Although most are dramas, there are also a number of
comedies, including "Mr. Dingle the Strong," "Mr. Bevis," "The Whole
Truth," "Once Upon a Time," "Showdown with Rance McGrew," "Hocus-
Pocus and Frisby," "Cavender is Coming," "I Dream of Genie," and "The
Bard," among others. Likewise political allegories appear with regularity
in the series; some examples are "The Monsters Are Due on Maple Street,"
"The Obsolete Man," "The Shelter," "The Quality of Mercy," "The Mirror,"
"The Gift," "He's Alive!," "Number Twelve Looks Just like You," and
"I am the Night – Color Me Black." Nevertheless, the story-type that seems
to appear most often is that which we may call the Tale of Dread.

As will emerge in what follows, I define a Tale of Dread as: 1. a narrative fantasy; 2. about an event in which a character is punished; 3. in
a manner that is appropriate (the punishment fits the crime); and 4. mordantly humorous (for example, often ironic). I call these stories Tales of
Dread because they mandate that audiences entertain paranoid or anxious

imaginings – specifically that the universe is governed by an all knowing and controlling intelligence that metes out justice with diabolical wit.

Although the Tale of Dread recurs frequently in *The Twilight Zone*, the Tale of Dread is not unique to *The Twilight Zone*. It appeared as soon as popular authors began to mine supernatural themes for inspiration. For instance, "The Black Cat," by Edgar Allen Poe, is a Tale of Dread. After hanging one black cat, the narrator acquires another almost identical-looking one, which develops strange white markings around its neck that gradually take the shape of a scar as caused by a noose. Later, the second cat preternaturally divulges the place where the narrator has hidden the body of his wife whom he had axed to death only days earlier. Though it is never said outright that the second cat is the first cat reincarnated or a ghost thereof, it is difficult to resist the thought that the action of the second cat is connected to the violence done to the first cat as a sort of cosmic revenge.

Tales of Dread, of course, predate pulp fiction. For example, Aristotle tells the story of the statue of Mitys in Argos, which falls upon the murderer of Mitys who traveled to Argos to evade apprehension and punishment for his crime only to be crushed by an image of his victim. Although this tale makes no explicit reference to a causal relation between the murder and the death of the murderer, readers have a strong feeling that there is a kind of magical linkage between the two events. Again, the universe itself appears to be enacting its own species of retribution.

Tales of Dread often appear next to horror stories in periodicals, short-story compilations, and anthology-type TV series, such as *Tales from the Darkside*.[1] Like horror stories, Tales of Dread may use either supernatural fancies or science-fiction inventions to induce the anxiety in which they specialize. That is certainly the case with respect to *The Twilight Zone*.

In this chapter, while making reference to episodes of *The Twilight Zone*, I will attempt to elucidate Tales of Dread. I will try to explain not only what they are but the way in which they elicit the sensation of dread that it is their function to engender, while also indicating the ways in which they both resemble and contrast with horror stories.

TALES OF DREAD: SOME EXAMPLES FROM *THE TWILIGHT ZONE*

Tales of Dread, it seems to me, are the most frequently recurring kind of story in *The Twilight Zone*. Here are few examples. There are many more where these came from.

"Judgment Night": Carl Lanser, a German, does not know how it has come about that he is on ship called the *S.S. Queen of Glasgow*. But he is sure that the boat is going to be attacked by a Nazi submarine. And low and behold, a U-boat does crest through the waves at 1:15 a.m., and Lanser, through a pair of binoculars, sees himself on the deck of the warship. He is the captain of the submersible and he orders that the *Glasgow* be torpedoed and that the survivors, including Lanser-the-passenger, be gunned down.

The episode concludes: "The *S.S. Queen of Glasgow*, heading for New York, and the time is 1942. For one man, it is always 1942 – and this man will ride the ghost of that ship every night for eternity. This is what is meant by paying the fiddler. This is the comeuppance awaiting every man when the ledger of his life is opened and examined, the tally made, and then the reward or the penalty paid. And in the case of Carl Lanser, the former Kapitan Lieutenant, Navy of the Third Reich, this is the penalty. This is the *justice* meted out [emphasis added]. This is judgment night in the Twilight Zone."[2]

Another example from the first season is "The Four of Us Are Dying." Arch Hammer has the ability to reconfigure himself, including his face, at will. A rather seedy lowlife, Hammer uses this talent for ill, seducing a woman and then inveigling money from a gangster. But when the gangster catches on, Hammer evades him by assuming the look of a boxer whose picture he sees on a poster. However, the father of the boxer runs into Hammer and, mistaking Hammer for his son, shoots him for the disgrace the boxer caused his family. Just deserts? Karma? We have the strong impression that Arch Hammer is being punished by the universe for the misuse of the gift it had bequeathed him.

Tales of Dread not only occur regularly in the first season of *The Twilight Zone*. For instance, in the third season, there is an installment entitled "Four O'Clock." Oliver Crangle is a McCarthyite type, engrossed in tracking down and unmasking mercilessly those whom he takes to be suspect. He is presented as an altogether vile and despicable human being. Although it is never explained how he intends to pull this off, we learn that he plans to shrink all those he deems evil to a height of no more than two feet tall. This way, he reasons, they will be readily detectable. The mass reduction is scheduled for four o'clock. But when four o'clock rolls around, only Oliver Crangle has been downsized.[3]

As the voice-over narration observes: "At four o'clock, an evil man made his bed and lay in it, a pot called the kettle black, a stone thrower broke the windows of his own glass house. You look for this one under 'F' for fanatic and 'J' for *justice* – in the Twilight Zone." [emphasis added][4]

Thus as is often the case in Tales of Dread, Crangle, like Arch Hammer, is undone, ironically enough, by his own design, or, as Shakespeare puts it in *Hamlet*: "For 'tis the sport to have the engineer/Hoist with his own petard."[5]

THE NATURE AND FUNCTION OF TALES OF DREAD

Tales of Dread obviously fall under the broad category of poetic justice – a phrase introduced by Thomas Rymer in 1678 in his *The Tragedies of the Last Age Considered*. Basically, poetic justice is the notion that, when it comes to literary works, evil doers must be punished for their misdeeds. That is, virtue and vice must both receive their due. What goes around, comes around.

Of course, the notion captured by the phrase "poetic justice" predates Rymer. It is perhaps first suggested by Aristotle who points out in his *Poetics* that if a virtuous person is destroyed, tragedy will misfire, for rather than eliciting pity from the audience-members, they will respond with outrage at this cosmic miscarriage of justice. Poetic justice is also a concept beloved by censors, such as the Hays Office, which scrutinized Hollywood scripts in order to make sure that no transgression – from sexual promiscuity to murder – went un-penalized by the last reel of the film.

We may think of the structural requirement that no wrong go un-chastised as the basic or ground-level version of the idea of poetic justice. It is the demand that there be justice-*in*-poetry (in literature, in fictions), especially in terms of evil being castigated. But there is a related, yet more complex and richer, notion of poetic justice as well. It is that of *poetic* justice, by which I mean that the punishment have a symbolic dimension – that it almost allegorically *fits* the crime. Evil is not only punished, but there is something appropriate or symbolic about it. The punishment, in a manner of speaking, *says* something about the crime.

So many of the penalties in Dante's work belong in this category. In the *Inferno*, for example, as its translator John Ciardi points out, the Opportunists have to "race round and round pursuing a wavering banner that runs forever before them in the dirty air. . . . As they sinned, so are they punished."[6] Likewise, in *Purgtory*, the wrathful are enfolded in a foul-smelling cloud of smoke. Ciardi notes "As wrath is a corrosive state of the spirit, so smoke stings and smarts. As wrath obscures the true light of God, so the smoke plunges all into darkness."[7]

The word often used to describe these images of punishment in Dante is "contrappasso" which simply means "retribution" or a "return punishment," an idea that can be traced to Aristotle's *Nicomachean Ethics*. However, in Dante's usage, the punishments are more than that. They also amount to poetic reflections upon the offenses of the damned.

Of course, this variety of poetic justice is not restricted to the Renaissance. A classic twentieth-century example of it occurs in Proust's letters where the garrulous Madame Strauss is said to eventually suffer cancer of the jaw. Here, the coincidence between Madame Strauss's characterological flaw and her affliction appears so arrestingly fitting that one entertains the thought that Fate had a hand in it, albeit Fate with a somewhat diabolical, if not perverse and mocking, sense of humor. Indeed, often with respect to Tales of Dread, poetic justice takes the form of an ironic twist of fate, in which a character's actions lead precisely to the opposite outcome that he or she intended. The narrative trajectory of the Tale of Dread, that is, resembles what Hegel would catalogue under the rubric of the Cunning of Reason.

In *The Twilight Zone*, poetic justice can be the result of overt supernatural agency, as in "The Chaser" (which involves a love potion), or by explicitly elaborated, science-fiction means as in "Execution" (which employs a time machine). But even where fantasy elements like these are not overtly incorporated into the plot, a supernatural agency always seems *covertly* at large.

In "I Shot an Arrow in the Air," for example, the character, Corey, thinking his rocket ship has landed on an asteroid, kills a fellow astronaut in order to increase his own share of food and water; but soon after the murder, Corey discovers that his space ship has actually fallen back to Earth – near Reno, Nevada – where he will have to pay for his cowardly crimes. The commentary calls it a *"Practical joke* played by Mother Nature and a combination of *improbable* events" [emphasis added].[8] That is, even though, on the face of it, this set of events might be explicable naturalistically, it strikes the viewer as if the universe – here identified as Mother Nature – has set Corey up, in order to reveal his true and corrupt inner nature, and then has taken him down. Ironically, the actions he undertakes to save himself damn him.

Whether or not Tales of Dread explicitly invoke magical or science fiction elements, they nevertheless impress us – as they weave their web of poetic justice – as trafficking in the supernatural at their deepest structural level of organization. For they involve coincidences and vastly improbable events that defy – or, at least, virtually defy – explanation in terms of mundane causal regularities and nomological principles. Moreover, these events are invested with so much apparent significance – they are so replete with *poetic* justice – that the forces governing the fictional world would appear to have no counterparts in ordinary experience. And this, in turn, prompts us to hypothesize that they are the product of some mysterious, controlling agency. The universe appears as if authored, and events seem to manifest a powerful, diabolical intelligence in operation, guiding the way in which circumstances unfold.

Of course, most narratives, in fact, yield the impression of an organizing intelligence; most involve some unlikely events and coincidences. If there weren't something unusual about them, most stories might not be worth telling. Gregory Currie and Jon Jureidini call this feature of narrative hyper-connectedness "overcoherent thinking."[9] However, naturalistic or realistic narratives generally attempt to downplay or, at least, draw attention away from their artifactuality.

Tales of Dread, on the other hand, revel in their "overcoherence" and they use it as a means to encourage the audience to abandon reliance upon the regularities that we depend upon to make sense of the world in which we live and, instead, invite us to infer the operation of a different order of causation – a kind of moral causation rather than physical causation.[10]

Whereas the authors of many realistic or naturalistic narratives strive to deflect attention away from themselves, the creator of the Tale of Dread aspires to elicit the uncanny feeling or apprehension that the world represented in the fiction is itself authored – that is, governed ontologically by a presiding intelligence. With its blatant, even shameless, emphasis upon the improbability of its events and its coincidences – not to mention the way in which these occurrences are charged with poetico-moral and often ironic significance – the Tale of Dread is a hypotrophic narrative, a narrative, in other words, of an extremely high degree of overt narrativity.

The Tale of Dread resembles nothing so much as a schizophrenic or paranoid delusion with its presumption of a mysterious and powerful agency that has special knowledge and control over the character or characters upon whom the story is focused. If characters in the Tales of Dread in *The Twilight Zone* often seem on the verge of madness, then that may be because the situations in which they find themselves are structured after the fashion of a schizophrenic worldview. Tales of Dread are expressive of paranoid thinking – expressive of a paranoid frame of mind.[11] Perhaps part of the attraction/fascination of Tales of Dread and of series like *The Twilight Zone* has to do with the way in which they acknowledge the paranoid – or the paranoid tendencies – in each of us.

Of course, the primary function of the Tale of Dread is to provoke a shudder of fear, apprehension, or anxiety. The Tale of Dread succeeds in this by inducing us to entertain the thought of or to imagine a world governed by a mysterious and powerful but *diabolical* intelligence. That intelligence is diabolical in two senses. Just as the devil in the Old Testament was an agent of Yahweh's justice, so the agency that rules the Twilight Zone is dedicated to righting wrongs. Of course, it rights these wrongs in a poetical fashion, which is to say that it frequently punishes the wicked by means of tellingly appropriate, darkly humorous, or ironic twists of fate, as when the U-boat commander torpedoes himself for eternity. Just as the devil is often a trickster, turning into nightmares by means of punning interpretations the wishes of those who broker their souls to him,[12] so the Twilight Zone itself, as an agent, tempts or seduces and entraps wicked humans like Corey and then, in jest-like fashion, hoists them upon their own petards.[13]

Here I want to stress that I take the analogy between Tales of Dread and stories of demonic tricksters (including genies) quite seriously. Consider two of the episodes of *The Twilight Zone* that involve devils: "A Nice Place to Visit" and "Of Late I Think of Cliffordville." In the first, a hood named Rocky Valentine dies. He thinks he has gone to heaven. An angelic-looking figure (he's dressed in white), Mr. Pip, indulges Rocky's every sordid appetite. When eventually and predictably Rocky is sated, he wants to check out the "Other Place," to which Pip replies with, shall we say, diabolical pleasure that "This is the other place." In the Tale of Dread, on the other hand, the devil as an explicit character in the fiction is subtracted out and the Twilight Zone itself, animistically construed, takes on his function.

In "Of Late I Think of Cliffordville," the demon – one Miss Devlin – offers Mr. Feathersmith, an unscrupulous millionaire, the opportunity to return into the past to his home town, Cliffordville, on condition that he turns over all his fortune, save $1,400, to Satan. Miss Devlin does not bargain for Feathersmith's soul, since he's already lost it. Feathersmith jumps at the opportunity, since he believes that he can parlay this $1,400 into an even greater fortune than his present one by purchasing land in Cliffordville that he knows contains oil. Unfortunately for Feathersmith, the land is not yet accessible to drilling at the time he buys it and, flat-broke, Feathersmith finds himself marooned in 1910.

However, Miss Devlin reappears and offers Feathersmith a chance to take a magical train back to the present for a price; but in order to secure the train ticket, the now penniless Feathersmith has to sell the land he has just purchased. Thus, he returns to the present a poor man, his greediness facilitating his seduction by the devil in a manner that results in Feathersmith destroying himself in a cruelly ironic way, but a way that warrants a devilish chuckle.[14] Here, the devil is meting out justice in this life and is rubbing Featherstone's face in it in a particularly taunting fashion.

In most of the installments in *The Twilight Zone*, there is no devil figure.[15] For in those episodes involving Tales of Dread, the Twilight Zone itself performs the function of Miss Devlin.[16]

The correlation between the Twilight Zone and the devil suggests the way in which the Tale of Dread is able to discharge its central purpose – to engender dread, anxiety, or fear. In his *Poetics*, Aristotle notes that tragedies are able to stir fear in the breasts of viewers because the viewers recognize that insofar as the tragic hero is like them – that is to say, not a saint – the kind of unforeseeable calamity that befalls an Oedipus might befall them too. Tragedy, according to Aristotle, instills fear because it brings viewers face to face with the fact that they are fortune's pawns. At any moment, disaster may overwhelm one. Thus, realizing that they are like the tragic victim, tragedy strikes fear in the hearts of the audience – fear for themselves.

The Tale of Dread also provokes fear in audiences, for in entertaining the thought that the universe is governed by forces that have complete knowledge of and complete power over us, we surmise that there is, or, at least, there may sometime be – especially if the temptation is great – some wickedness on our part that will rouse these forces against us.

Perhaps needless to say, the Tale of Dread is different from Greek tragedy, as theorized by Aristotle. In a way, it is less profound. What Aristotle took to be central to tragedy and crucial to the fear that it arouses is that tragic occurrences can lay low people who have done nothing to deserve their own destruction. In other words, tragedy reminds us that bad things can happen to good people (or, at least, non-bad people). That is, it makes us aware of what Martha Nussbaum has called the *fragility of goodness*. The Tale of Dread, on the other hand, reassures us that bad things will happen to bad people. But since almost all of us feel guilty about something or recognize that we are capable of being led into temptation, the thought that the universe is being policed so effectively can evoke a premonition or palpable tremor of apprehension in us.

However, fear and anxiety are forms of distress. Thus, as with the case of horror stories, Tales of Dread raise the question of why we would subject ourselves to something like *The Twilight Zone*, if it is designed to cause unease in us. That is, there is a paradox in the offing here, namely: unease is something that we avoid, but *The Twilight Zone* has done nicely over time. It enjoyed five seasons on air, is often re-run, is available on DVD, and it has won a cult following substantial enough to warrant an anthology like the one you presently hold in your hands. Clearly, people are not avoiding *The Twilight Zone*; rather they seek it out, because it gives them pleasure. But dread, fear, and anxiety are not pleasurable; they are unpleasant states of mind and body. So, if a characteristic aim of Tales of Dread is to induce dread, then how can folks derive pleasure from them?

The answer, I think, lies in the fact that, even if Tales of Dread exact some quotient of displeasure in terms of apprehension, that is more than compensated for by the pleasure we derive from such stories. And that pleasure is connected to the diabolical character of the universe in Tales of Dread. In the case of *The Twilight Zone*, the Twilight Zone itself is demonic, an agent of justice with a sense of ironic wit. To the extent that we realize that all flesh, including our own, is weak, that stimulates a palpitation of fear in us.

But, on the other hand, most of us realize that we are not *that* bad – not bad enough for the universe itself to pay much attention us – and, anyway, even really bad people underestimate or rationalize away their wickedness. Thus, most of us are glad to entertain the thought that it is in the nature of things – in this case, the Twilight Zone – that wrongs will be righted.[17] That is, poetic justice appeals to our sense of justice, even though it does not match up with the implementation of justice in the world that we inhabit.

The Tale of Dread is gratifying because it mandates us to imagine a state of affairs where Ideal Justice prevails – not in the world as we know it, but in a Twilight Zone. And the satisfaction that that thought occasions outweighs the displeasure that comes with the passing fear that we might be on the Twilight Zone's hit-list.[18]

HORROR FICTIONS AND TALES OF DREAD:
A BRIEF NOTE

Earlier I noted that Tales of Dread are often featured alongside of horror stories in anthologies with titles like *Great Tales of Terror and the Supernatural*.[19] Likewise, there are horror stories, like "To Serve Man," next to the Tales of Dread in *The Twilight Zone*. An interesting question is why we find these stories seem to belong together. One factor, perhaps the most obvious, is that both rely upon imagining story-worlds that go beyond what is recognized as natural by contemporary science. Both horror stories and Tales of Dread deploy either magic or science fiction to concoct possibilities that exceed the boundaries accepted by the hard sciences.

However, horror stories have a feature that Tales of Dread lack, namely monsters including supernatural ones like vampires, aliens from outer space, spiders larger than houses due to their exposure to radiation, and so on.[20] And yet Tales of Dread seem to belong to the same family as the horror story. Why?

One suggestion, based upon the previous section of this chapter, might be that Tales of Dread invite an almost animistic way of regarding the universe. The Twilight Zone itself is a sort of being, a diabolical agency enforcing cosmic justice with a mordant sense of humor. Although there is no monster in evidence in the Tale of Dread, properly so-called, there is something like a monster, specifically the universe as a kind of controlling, retributive intelligence. Since this being is not physically manifest, as most of the monsters in horror fictions are, the Tale of Dread does not elicit the feelings of disgust that horror stories do on the basis of the anomalous biologies of the creatures that populate them.

Nor is the fear that the Tale of Dread invites precisely like that of horror stories. With horror stories, we fear for the characters beset by monsters. But in Tales of Dread, we momentarily fear for ourselves as the thought occurs to us that the imagined, vengeful universe in such fictions might have cause to get on our case. Thus, we feel apprehension. The Tale of Dread is premonitory, whereas the horror story confronts us with a clear and present danger. The Tale of Dread leaves a lingering feeling of uncanniness, while the horror most often attacks us frontally.

Nevertheless, the Tale of Dread is kin to the horror story, for like horror fictions, it contains a fantastic being – a cosmic force for poetic justice – which, in the case before us, goes by the name of The Twilight Zone.[21]

NOTES

1. TV shows of this sort appeared very early in the history of the medium, including series like *Tales of Tomorrow* and *Lights Out*.
2. Quoted from *The Twilight Zone Companion*, Second Edition, edited by Marc Scott Zicree (Los Angeles: Silman-James Press, 1992), p. 51.

3. "Last Night of a Jockey" is the inverse of this. Prompted by the spirit of evil in him, a jockey who thinks he has just been cashiered, wishes to be big – literally big. But once his wish is granted, it turns out that the decision against him has been reversed. The relation between stories like "Four O'Clock" and "Last Night of a Jockey" is an interesting one. In "Last Night of a Jockey," there is a demonic figure in the form of an internal voice that lays the trap for the jockey's downfall, whereas, in "Four O'Clock," it is the Twilight Zone itself that does the devil's work. We will have more to say about this parallel relation between Tales of Dread and stories with demons in them later in this chapter.

4. Quoted from *The Twilight Zone Companion*, pp. 275–6. Often the commentaries at the beginning and ending of *The Twilight Zone* recall those of programs like *One Step Beyond* and *The Inner Sanctum* where hosts like John Nuland prefigure the role Rod Serling plays in his series.

5. The episode "The Little People" is also a Tale of Dread. See Aaron Smuts's discussion of it in this volume. Smuts's piece is entitled "'The Little People': Power and the Worshippable."

6. John Ciardi, Headnote, *The Inferno* by Dante, trans. Ciardi (New York: Mentor Classic – The New American Library, 1954), p. 91.

7. John Ciardi, Headnote, *Purgatorio* (New York: a Mentor Classic – New American Library, 1961), p. 170.

8. Quoted from *The Twilight Zone Companion*, p. 98.

9. Gregory Currie and Jon Jureidini, "Narrative and Coherence," *Mind and Language*, volume 19, number 4 (September, 2004), pp. 407–27. Throughout this chapter, I have benefited from their article as well as from Currie and Jureidini's earlier article "Art and Delusion," in *The Monist*, volume 86, number 4 (October, 2003), pp. 556–78.

10. In this, the conclusion of a Tale of Dread resembles the punchline of a joke. It encourages the audience to hypothesize an explanation for what has just been recounted, albeit a hypothesis that goes against good sense. On punchlines, see Noël Carroll, "On Jokes," in *Beyond Aesthetics* (Cambridge: Cambridge University Press, 2000).

11. See David Shapiro, *Neurotic Styles* (New York: Harper Torchbooks, 1965), especially Chapter 3.

12. Stories like this give meaning to the expression "the devil's in the details." For, when the contract for the soul of the human character is drawn up, there is virtually always a loophole in the details through which the devil turns the victim's wishes against himself.

13. Often, in stories that have demonic figures in them the devils appear to be practical jokers, especially in terms of the way in which the devils manage willfully to misinterpret or mislead the humans who traffic with them. In this regard, it is particularly interesting that the Twilight Zone itself is portrayed as a practical joker in "I Shot an Arrow in the Air." Again, as in

"Four O'Clock," it is the Twilight Zone that performs a function parallel to that of demonic figures in meting out poetic justice.

14. Tales of Dread involve reversals of fortune on the part of the pertinent characters. However, this should not be confused with stories that involve reversals of the audience's expectations, even though these too involve an ironic punch. In *The Twilight Zone*, episodes that involve the subversion of the audience's expectations include "Third Planet from the Sun," "Eye of the Beholder," "Invaders," "Midnight Sun," and "Probe 7 – Over and Out." These contrast with Tales of Dread, since Tales of Dread usually fulfill our expectations. These exercises in ironic reversals of the viewers' expectation in *The Twilight Zone* seem undertaken thematically, in the main, in order to defamiliarize our earthly condition.

   The episodes I've just listed all belong to the kind of story said to have snapper or surprise endings or to conclude with O. Henry twists. In his article in this volume, Carl calls these endings *frame shifters*. See Carl Plantinga, "Frame Shifters: Surprise Endings, and Spectator Imagination in *The Twilight Zone*."

15. One episode that lies halfway between Tales of Dread and stories with the devil in them is "Nick of Time." For here the audience is not sure whether the fortune-telling machine (with the bobble-headed devil on top) is itself a demonic agency or whether it is merely a snare set for unwary humans by the diabolical Twilight Zone. This episode is discussed in this volume by Carl Plantinga, "Frame Shifters: Surprise Endings and the Spectator Imagination in *The Twilight Zone*," and by Aeon Skoble, "Rationality and Choice in 'Nick of Time'."

16. It should be noted that, in addition to Tales of Dread, there are also what might be called Tales of Redemption in *The Twilight Zone*. These are cases – like "The Last Flight" and "Night of the Meek," where the universe gives the protagonist a second chance. Interestingly, Tales of Redemption are paralleled by stories with angelic intermediaries – like "Mr. Denton on Doomsday" and "A Passage for a Trumpet" – just as Tales of Dread are paralleled by stories with diabolical figures.

17. Moreover, perhaps the fear that the Tale of Dread instills may be required in part to deliver the pleasure we take in imagining such a justice-driven universe insofar as the fear we feel may phenomenologically reinforce our transitory feeling that a vigilant universe is on the lookout for evil-doing everywhere, including in our very own hearts.

18. Also, the fear component in our response to the Tale of Dread may not be altogether displeasurable. For an account of the satisfaction that may accompany the fear that supernatural stories engender, see Noël Carroll, "The Fear of Fear Itself: The Philosophy of Halloween," in *The Undead and Philosophy*, edited by Richard Greene and K. Silem Mohammad (La Salle, Illinois: Open Court, 2006), pp. 223–36.

19. Herbert E. Wise and Phyllis Fraser (eds.), *Great Tales of Terror and the Supernatural* (New York: The Modern Library, 1944, 1972).
20. This view is defended in Noël Carroll, *The Philosophy of Horror: Or, Paradoxes of the Heart* (New York: Routledge, 1990).
21. I would like to thank Joan Acocella and Lester H. Hunt for their comments and suggestions regarding this article. However, they are not responsible for the flaws herein. The Twilight Zone is.

3

FRAME SHIFTERS

SURPRISE ENDINGS AND SPECTATOR IMAGINATION IN *THE TWILIGHT ZONE*

CARL PLANTINGA

In many regards, *The Twilight Zone* is about the human imagination. Rod Serling's narrated introduction to the series, in one of its manifestations at least (it changed over the years), refers to the series as a journey "of mind . . . whose boundaries are that of the imagination." Many of the series' episodes serve as cautionary tales, warning the viewer about the liabilities of mental complacency and the mindless acceptance of received opinion and conventional attitudes. This also makes the series an implicit celebration of a form of critical thinking we might call "perspective taking." I say more about perspective taking below, but for now it could be thought of as the imagination of alternatives to habitual patterns of thinking and conventional ways of viewing the world.

Did *The Twilight Zone* actually encourage critical thinking of this sort? The answer to this question would finally need to take into account the nature of the audience for the series. Audiences are self-selecting, and those averse to perspective-taking (and who ironically may be most in need of its benefits), could well find *The Twilight Zone* to be threatening or irrelevant. We can approach the issue from another angle, however (there will be no eschewing of perspective taking here!). Setting aside the question of the historical audience, we might ask, all things being equal, what narrative strategies used by *The Twilight Zone* encourage critical thinking generally, and perspective-taking in particular? This is the question I attempt to answer in this chapter. In doing so, I will concentrate on the "snapper endings" with "O. Henry twists" for which *The Twilight Zone* is justifiably famous. My argument will be that a particular sort of surprise ending, which I call a "Frame Shifter," is particularly suited to the elicitation of perspective-taking and to the exercise of the human imagination.

NARRATIVE, COGNITION, AND EMOTION

Before a discussion of surprise endings, we must examine the functions of endings in narratives generally, and before that, we must briefly consider what approach to take in the study of narrative. I don't mean to define narrative here, but rather to insist on recognizing the relationship between narrative and human response. In the theoretical movement known as structuralism, narrative was explored separately from the mental activities and responses it generated. Structuralists aimed to discover the deep structure of narrative, those components that characterize all narratives. The focus of the study of narrative was not in the direction of the viewer or reader, but in the other direction, toward the deep structural grammar, the system of signs and functions that were thought to underlie all narrative.[1] It was as though the narrative were a kind of machine, the chief interest in which is the identification of its component parts and their architecture, rather than the functions of the machine for the individuals who use it. In part this approach resulted from the anti-realist bent of the time, which conceived of literary characters, for example, as "actants" or even "functions," and which successfully excised from the study of narrative the actual way in which people experience fictional characters, as worthy of pity and compassion, for example. To make an analogy, we might consider the exploration and naming of the parts and architecture of the automobile without reference to gas mileage, speed, relative safety, comfort, or the function of the automobile in transportation.

Recent cognitive approaches put more emphasis on narrative form in relation to spectator cognition and response. For David Bordwell, the viewer is mentally active while viewing a narrative film, making assumptions and inferences and also anticipating and drawing hypotheses about possible narrative developments.[2] Noël Carroll's "erotetic" theory of narrative, similarly, posits a question–answer progression in the narrative form of movies, suggesting that the erotetic narrative proceeds by stringing narrative events one after the other according to this principle: succeeding events answer questions posed by earlier events (either partially or in whole), and raise further questions that the spectator desires to have answered. Thus the process of erotetic narrative is one of constant question raising, the receiving of answers, and subsequent further question raising.[3]

Cognitive film theory and philosophy have considered not only the viewer's cognitive activity, but also how visual narratives produce other kinds of responses in viewers, ranging from paradigmatic emotions to affects such as moods and affective mimicry.[4] If the narrative forms the backbone of visual storytelling, then much of the inference-making, question answering and asking, and in general, appraisals of the narrative situation will lead to a progression of emotional responses. Moreover, the visual media incorporate the sensual elements of image and sound to facilitate affective responses in diverse bodily registers. Cognitive film theory is very much interested in narrative form and style, but with an eye to the means by which formal elements elicit cognitive activity and affective response in the viewer.

OPEN AND CLOSED ENDINGS

I will characterize the functions of endings in narratives, then, by identifying the means by which they initiate particular cognitive activities and affective responses. The conventional narrative has a closed ending. Putting this first in cognitive terms, this means that by the film's end, all of the macro-questions and most of the micro-questions generated by the narrative will have been answered. The conventional narrative moves toward complete knowledge on the part of the spectator. The process of anticipation and inference-making draws to a close as future outcomes become less pressing, past problems are solved, and the narrative "present" suggests no further problems with regard to the main narrative line. In dramatic and affective terms, the ending of the conventional narrative is a kind of conventional emotional experience; it is subsequent to the rising tension, climactic confrontation, and resolution that are the hallmarks of the conventional dramatic arc. The traditional closed ending brings a sense of calm with the resolution of problems and perhaps a coda that draws lessons from, or in some other way makes sense of, the preceding narrative events. One of the hallmarks of an "involving" narrative is that it generates strong spectator desires for various outcomes in relation to character goals or well-being, or in relation to the curiosity and anticipation elicited by the story as such. The end of an involving and closed narrative releases audiences from their desires about the contours of future narrative outcomes and from their desire to know what will come next.

The *Twilight Zone* episode "The Nick of Time"[5] provides an example of an episode that is closed in some regards, yet open in others. It tells the story of a couple, Don and Pat (William Shatner and Patricia Breslin), who decide to have a meal at a local diner while their car is being repaired. In a booth at the diner, they find a fortune-telling machine in the form of the head of Satan. Superstitious by nature, Don imagines that the slips of paper he obtains from the machine provide useful information and advice about the future. He becomes obsessed with the machine, continually leading the couple back to the diner for more sessions of question-asking and answer-getting in the form of the dispensed little fortunes on small cards. It is only by the persistent and patient appeals of Pat that Don is able to break free of the machine's spell. Their car finally repaired, the couple leave town, free to determine their own destinies. At the end, we see another couple enter the dinner, similarly obsessed with the fortune-telling machine; their fate is yet to be determined.

This ending is closed in that the main narrative plot is resolved. The macro-question – Will Don be able to resist the insidious fortune-telling machine? – has been answered in the affirmative. The major problem – Don's superstitious obsession with getting his fortune told – is resolved as the couple drive away. The spectator's suspense is likewise dissipated. Yet this ending is only partially closed, for it leaves open the question of whether the other couple will be able to rescue themselves in similar fashion. In a larger context, the trouble and worry introduced by the machine still exists, both for this other couple and for the world in general. The narrative also raises thematic questions it does not answer, such as whether this infernal device is actually some kind of demonic presence or whether its hold on humans is the result of superstition and human weakness. Such is the nature of *The Twilight Zone*, that even when the dramatic arc comes to a resolution, basic questions remain about the nature of the world represented. Indeed, the purpose of many of the episodes seems designed precisely to foster such questions.

Unlike their counterparts, open endings fail to resolve the narrative in either a cognitive or dramatic sense. They leave important macro-questions unanswered (the cognitive), or else fail to resolve problems or conflicts (the dramatic), representing such problems as ongoing. Open endings may also feature ambiguity, such that the relevant macro-questions cannot be clearly identified. In this case, the spectator attempts to understand the narrative or its characters, and the nature of dramatic problems and conflicts is itself unclear. Or the spectator may give up the drive to understand altogether, and instead enjoy the making of associations or various more free-ranging sorts of mental activity. Thus open endings are often features of narratives that are alternative in their construction throughout, and not merely at the story's end. In dramatic terms, open endings often withhold the sense of calm that accompanies complete knowledge and the satisfactory resolution of all dramatic conflict. Using the language of desire, we might say that, assuming spectator involvement, open endings sometimes leave audiences with a continuing desire to know and understand.

A clear example of such an open ending in *The Twilight Zone* is "The Odyssey of Flight 33,"[6] in which a modern airliner on a flight from London to New York begins to accelerate for some unexplained reason, finding itself in a mysterious jet stream. Trying to land, the pilots discover that the jet and its inhabitants have traveled backwards in time to prehistory, to a world with wandering dinosaurs and no sign of human habitation. The pilots bring the jet back into the jet stream in an attempt to escape this time frame, but as they descend for a second landing the plane's 1961 occupants discover themselves flying above 1939 New York. The narrative ends as the pilots return to the time-warping jet stream once more, in the hope that eventually they will reach the right time period. The episode offers little by way of a causal explanation of what has happened; there are some references to an inordinately strong tail wind and increased speed of travel, but these are only hints. And there is no resolution of the chief dramatic problem.

SURPRISE ENDINGS

The concept of the surprise ending assumes that as a narrative progresses, certain means of ending the narrative are probable because they fit conventional narrative patterns or other schemas. The answers to the questions the narrative raises, solutions to problems it poses, and in general, the direction of future narrative outcomes, are typically somewhat predictable in genre films and television series. If all endings were equally likely, then there could be no surprise ending. A surprise ending, then, diverges from what is expected, offers an unpredicted solution to a problem, or answers the narrative question in a way that would not normally be anticipated. It generally will countermand expectations rooted in narrative or genre conventions or general rules of thumb about "how the world works."[7] Surprise endings may well elicit the emotion of surprise in relation to violations of expected outcomes or in response to discoveries about the nature of the (fictional) world.

To better understand the nature of a surprising ending, let us briefly consider an episode with an ending that is *not* particularly surprising, but rather emerges as the "logical" or "appropriate" result of a narrative trajectory. In "I Sing the Body Electric"[8] a widower purchases a robotic surrogate mother, or "an electronic data processing system in the form of a nanny," to care for his three children. "Grandma" wins over two of the children almost immediately, but Anne still resents her birth mother's death, and grants Grandma her trust only gradually. Grandma provides loving support for these children throughout their formative years, playing her role well. When the children are about to go away to college, she tells the children that her job is finished, and that she will return to her manufacturer, Facsimile Limited. There Grandma will be recycled and/or work for another family.

The ending is not unexpected because Grandma's departure is presented as fitting both in her role as grandmother and as household appliance. The cycle of life dictates that since as the children age and mature, so must grandparents eventually age and die (or in this case, depart). As an appliance, Grandma's function diminishes as the children age and she (it?) may be discarded. Although the ending raises philosophical issues about the possibility of love and nurture by machine (or perhaps whether humans are merely elaborate machines, or machines are persons), the ending fits with general patterns of expectation, schemas as to what happens both to aging grandmothers and to appliances that have outlived their usefulness.[9] A surprise ending, for example would suddenly reveal that the children, like Grandma, are also machines, for example, or that Grandma's intentions were actually malevolent, and that she raised the children so carefully in order that they might make better slaves to her kind, or that the entire episode is a nightmare in someone's mind. The existent ending is unsurprising because it logically follows the development of a causal narrative, and because it results in no rapid shift in the spectator's framework of understanding.

TYPES OF SURPRISE ENDINGS

SPECTATOR OR CHARACTER SURPRISE

Surprise endings come in several varieties. We can ask, first, for whom the ending is surprising – the spectator and/or a character or characters. Three possibilities suggest themselves; the ending may be surprising for a character and not the spectator (the spectator knows less than the character), for the spectator and not the character (the spectator knows more than the character), or for both spectator and character together. The latter two possibilities are the most common in *The Twilight Zone*. In the famous episode "Time Enough at Last,"[10] Burgess Meredith plays Henry Bemis, an unhappy husband who secrets himself in a bank vault at every opportunity to engage in his chief love in life, reading. In the vault he also escapes the demands of his wife and boss, neither of whom will allow him to read. While in the vault, a nuclear bomb strike destroys his city (and perhaps the world), but leaves him alive and alone. He nearly commits suicide, but then discovers the remains of the public library and thousands of books. He becomes jubilant. It is the reading misanthrope's dream – no interruptions and plenty of time to read. In a cruel twist of fate, however, his spectacles fall from his nose and break, making reading impossible. He shouts that it isn't fair, and we leave him in despair. "Time Enough at Last" is a clear example of an episode with an ending that surprises both audience and character.

Many of the endings in *The Twilight Zone* give the audience more information than the characters, however, such that the ending is surprising only for the audience. The examples are many. In "The Invaders,"[11] a UFO lands in the attic of an isolated house inhabited by an impoverished old woman. She soon becomes panic-stricken as tiny spacemen begin to stalk her, apparently attacking her. She seems to be getting the upper hand against these diminutive space attackers. After an epic battle, we then hear a radio transmission that completely alters the spectator's frame of reference. The small spacemen are Americans who have apparently landed on a planet of behemoths, and are about to meet their demise at the hands of a tremendous old lady alien. The ending surprises not the spacemen or the giant woman, but only the audience.

SURPRISE OF PROSPECTS VERSUS SURPRISE
OF UNDERSTANDING

A surprise ending may feature surprising prospects for the character or characters or a surprise in the way the spectator and/or character understands the narrative world, the latter typically brought on by a change in reference. "Time Enough at Last," then, is an ending that signals a change of prospects. Henry Bemis revels in his imagination of a future of uninterrupted reading. He even makes stacks of books corresponding to the month in which he plans to read them. When his spectacles break, he is unable to read; his sole remaining joy in life is removed from him, and he is now alone in a cruel and uncaring universe. His prospects suddenly change from ideal to miserable.

In "The Invaders," on the other hand, the surprise comes not from any alteration in the prospects of either the large alien lady or the spacemen from Earth. Rather, this is a surprise of understanding for the spectator. The narration suddenly reveals new information; the spacemen are not aliens and by Earth's standards are normally sized. It is the old woman who is an alien and a giant. The ending alters the framework of assumptions (the schemas) which the spectators had heretofore used to form allegiances with the old lady and to make inferences about the nature of the battle between her and the tiny beings that attack her. The ending leads to a sudden and dramatic change in understanding.

RESOLUTION OF AMBIGUITY OR ALTERED FRAME
OF REFERENCE

Surprise endings can work to resolve narrative ambiguity in somewhat unpredictable ways or they can completely alter the spectator's frame of reference. "Nightmare at 20,000 Feet"[12] is an example of the former. In this episode we meet Robert Wilson (William Shatner) and his wife on a plane. We learn that Wilson has spent the past six months in a mental asylum and is on his way home, apparently cured. His original mental breakdown that resulted in his stay at the asylum occurred on a plane. Thus when he sees some sort of monster or gremlin on the plane's wing, trying to rip the plane apart, the audience assumes that Wilson is probably having another mental breakdown. Failing to convince the other passengers and the plane's crew that this gremlin exists, Wilson steals a gun, cracks open the emergency window, and shoots the gremlin dead. The passengers and crew restrain him, thinking him insane. At the episode's end, we see him strapped to a gurney, a calm look on his face. His wife tells him, "It's all right now, darling." The camera tilts up to the plane's wing and fuselage, revealing significant damage at the spot where Wilson had seen the gremlin. The ambiguity here is between two hypotheses. Either Wilson is crazy or this gremlin actually exists. The narration does much to cause the audience to strongly suspect that Wilson is insane. His previous insanity, his wide and crazed eyes, the fact that even his wife does not believe him, the fact that no one else sees the gremlin – all of this leads spectators to expect one ending, when another more surprising ending is in store. The gremlin actually existed, and the narrative ambiguity is resolved in a surprising way.

Other episodes do not resolve ambiguity, but rather lead to completely unexpected developments. In "Probe 7 – Over and Out,"[13] a space probe crashes on an alien planet, and a spaceman finds himself apparently alone there. He contacts home base, where he learns that not only will he not be rescued, but that the world he left is about to be destroyed in a war. He speaks with mission control a few times, but the communication soon stops completely. In his last transmission, his contact expresses good wishes for his friend, and tells him that wherever he is, if he does get a chance to start over, he should do it differently than humans have on his planet. In an event of surprising good fortune, the spaceman comes across an alien woman with whom he forms a bond. The spaceman and woman try to communicate with each other. They decide to call their new planet Earth, and reveal that their names are Adam and Eve. That the lonely spaceman meets a woman on an alien planet is certainly a surprise, but the ending is best characterized as a wholesale change of reference. Rather than the future, we have been viewing the distant past. Rather than an alien planet, we have been watching events on Earth. The ending not only alters the frame of reference, but suggests that Adam and Eve's progeny may also be doomed to experience the same failures as their distant ancestors. Thus instead of a story of the future, this is a story of the past and a cautionary tale for the present.

ELEVATING AND DEFLATING SURPRISES

Surprise endings of elevation improve the prospects of characters and suggest understandings of the world or of humanity that imply improved prospects. Endings of deflation do the opposite, offering endings that suggest bad prospects and pessimistic interpretations of the world. Some of the ending of episodes of The Twilight Zone are elevating, such as "Nothing in the Dark" (1962), in which an old woman who has long feared death learns to accept it (albeit in the person of a policeman played by Robert Redford!).[14] In an era in which the mass media are primarily designed to please, placate, and comfort audiences, however, a hallmark of *The Twilight Zone* is its use of sometimes disturbing endings that suggest failure, death, loneliness, and a cruel universe governed by uncaring fate. In "Time Enough at Last," Henry Bemis faces a dismal and lonely future, devoid of his spectacles and unable to read. In "The Invaders," the American spacemen are about to be obliterated by a giant alien. The crew and passengers of "The Odyssey of Flight 33" seem doomed to repeat their attempts to return to Earth at the right time, but their plane is rapidly running out of fuel and their chances are uncertain.

Even the relative "happy endings" of some episodes usually suggest some element designed to encourage anxiety and the sense that all is not well. Although Pat enables Don to escape the attraction of the infernal fortune-telling machine in "Nick of Time," the other couple seems trapped by its allure. Merely knowing that such an evil device (or being) may exist is enough to set one on edge. In "I Sing the Body Electric," Grandma carefully orchestrates her departure from the family such that the children will not be unduly traumatized, yet the episode deals squarely not only with the possibility of loss, but also with troubling issues about the nature of love. Can a machine fill the role of a mother or grandmother? And if so, what does this imply about humanity?

NARRATIVE AND CRITICAL THINKING

With some of the contours of surprise endings in mind, we can now ask how such endings relate to critical thinking and the imagination. Media scholars have long been interested in the degree to which films and other media have the capacity to initiate changes in thinking, to shake up audience preconceptions, to cause self-reflection and perhaps even self-criticism, and to lead to social critique. Recent trends in film and media studies call for an emphasis on the uses to which various audiences put the various media, and downplay the role of the text itself in such processes.[15] Nevertheless, the question of how media texts themselves influence the spectator is still vitally important. In qualitative (as opposed to quantitative) research, most of the serious thinking on the issue of how the text itself can encourage or discourage critical thought has been neo-Brechtian, and emphasizes "estrangement" or the alienation effect.

The underlying assumption here is that spectators who are absorbed or whose focus is solely on the fictional world of the text and its story are rendered unable to engage in critical analysis. Thus various techniques can be used to alienate or estrange the spectator from the fictional world, interrupt the suspension of disbelief and thereby allow for acknowledgement of the text as text and for critical thinking. One such technique, reflexivity, is thought not only to remind the spectator of the constructed nature of the text, but to acknowledge that every communication is constructed and ideological.[16] Reflexivity is initiated when the media-maker reveals him or herself within the body of the text through voice-over narration or appearing on-screen, perhaps talking about the genesis of the project or the assumptions behind its approach. Edgar Morin and Jean Rouch employed such techniques, for example, in their famous documentary *Chronicle of a Summer* (*Chronique d'une été*, 1960). Another method of reflexivity is to short-circuit viewer absorption through disruptive editing and sound, for example, or by having a character talk directly to the camera. These are the favored techniques of filmmaker Jean Luc Godard.

Elsewhere I have argued that although the question about how texts might be structured to initiate critical thinking is an important one, the role of alienation and reflexivity in such processes have been exaggerated.[17] The neo-Brechtian view falsely assumes that viewer absorption and passivity are coextensive, as though the fictional world and the narrational presentation of fictional events cannot themselves engage the viewer in critical thinking. In my view, they can and do. The estrangement view also assumes that the most important critical thinking on the spectator's part must occur while the spectator views the play or film or television program, while I claim, alternatively, that the most important such thinking occurs after the viewing. If this is so, then a strongly absorbing and moving narrative may elicit more such critical thinking than one that alienates and estranges its audience.

The term "critical thinking" is broad, and so here I wish to delimit my discussion to one aspect of such mentation. Humans have a way of allowing their thinking to become sedimented, habitual, and rigid. We develop background assumptions or schemas, procedures of thought, or habits of mind that sometimes interfere with suppleness of thought and stifle the imagination. Once we develop a set of beliefs, a way of self-understanding, or a template for looking at the world or at others, it becomes very difficult to change.[18] One element of critical thinking, then, might be the ability to consider an issue, event, problem, or person from varied and alternative perspectives or frameworks. We might consider how another person would view an issue or problem. We might consider the significance of an issue or problem in another context. We might take on the persona of someone diametrically opposed to our way of thinking, or consider an issue using background assumptions that we had never before considered. Instead of a blinkered myopia, the critical thinker is able to examine an issue with imagination. I referred to this at the beginning of the chapter as "perspective taking."

FRAME SHIFTERS

To determine the possibility that a given narrative might lead to critical thinking, we must consider the spectator's response both during and after the viewing of a work. A surprise ending functions to generate at least one strong emotion at the film's end: surprise. The emotion of surprise will not necessarily generate much thought after the fact, however. When Henry Bemis breaks his spectacles at the end of "Time Enough at Last," this deflating surprise won't necessarily cause the spectator to think much about the nature of the world Bemis inhabits or about Bemis's fate. This world has already been shown to be cruel, and the surprise ending merely extends this cruelty to him. It is a particular sort of surprise ending, I will argue, that has the greatest chance of generating critical thinking.

Many episodes of *The Twilight Zone* have endings with a particular combination of the elements listed above; they feature spectator surprise (as opposed to character surprise), surprises of understanding (rather than surprises of prospects exclusively), and lead to a rapid and decisive shift in an epistemic frame of reference. These episodes are also deflating rather than elevating. A sample and by no means complete list would include "The Invaders," "Third from the Sun," "Eye of the Beholder," "Monsters are Due on Maple Street," "A Game of Pool," and "Probe 7 – Over and Out." I call narratives of this sort, and with the above characteristics, "Frame Shifters."

For purposes of illustration, I will make my argument using "Eye of the Beholder"[19] as an example of a Frame Shifter. This episode tells the story of Janet Tyler, who we first meet with her head swathed in bandages, the result of a medical procedure designed to refashion her hideously deformed face. In a culture in which "The Leader" preaches the virtues of "glorious conformity," Janet's abnormal face has made her a life-long social outcast. This is her eleventh visit to the hospital, and her last chance at a cure because the state has decreed a maximum of 11 attempts before banishment to a community of similar unfortunates. The kindly doctors and nurses do their best, but when the bandages are removed, the doctors and nurses recoil in horror. The treatment has failed again. The spectator is shown Janet's face, which is, surprisingly, extremely beautiful. The doctors' and nurses' faces are then revealed for the first time, previously having been blocked from view by careful shot compositions, the blocking of actors, shadows and darkness, and visual obstructions. Their faces are hideously grotesque, with misshapen contours and pig-like snouts. Crying hysterically in response to her fate, Janet Tyler meets Walter Smith, a strikingly-handsome man and an "abnormal," as she is. He comforts her, telling her that she will be loved in her new community and he reminds her that "beauty is in the eye of the beholder."

Frame Shifters may have open endings, or may feature partially closed endings. Notice that the Frame Shifters I mentioned above have endings that are closed only in the sense that a central dramatic problem is resolved, or a specific narrative question answered. They cannot be completely closed because they must raise philosophical questions that cannot be answered within the bounds of the narrative or its viewing. In "Eye of the Beholder," the ending answers a central dramatic question. Will Janet Tyler be cured and will her face become normal? At the level of dramatic events, the spectator understands that Janet will be sent off to a segregated community of abnormally-faced people, but her prospects there are uncertain. The narrative closes one major dramatic line, although it leaves some questions about Janet's future unanswered. At the level of thematic implication, which initiates the possibility of significant philosophical thought, this dramatic ending, through its surprise, initiates a level of questioning and thought that, for those with any philosophical curiosity whatsoever, extends far beyond the ending. (Having seen it as a small child, this episode made a strong impression on me that has lasted over 40 years). Is beauty really in the eye of the beholder? Are judgments of beauty, taste, or morality learned and/or genetically programmed? Frame Shifters may be closed at the level of the story (although they often are not) but they do not close off thematic or philosophical questions.

Frame Shifters dramatically and decisively alter the spectator's frame of reference. This isn't a gradual process, which is why the element of surprise is central. When Janet Tyler's bandages are removed, the spectator sees that despite the repulsion reactions of those around her, her face is beautiful by (actual) conventional standards. This is the first surprise. Expecting to see some hideous deformity, we instead see a beautiful face. The question is raised: why, given her beauty, do the doctors and nurses react with shock and disgust? Hasn't Janet been cured? Next we see the second surprise, that the doctors and nurses have deformed, pig-like faces, and it soon becomes clear that the spectator's frame of reference must be altered in one important respect. The spectator had heretofore regarded herself/himself as an insider, but now becomes an outsider. Prior to the surprise, and indeed throughout the episode, the doctors and nurses treat Janet Tyler with sensitivity and sympathy, also eliciting sympathy on the spectator's part for Janet's "condition." The spectator is encouraged to develop allegiances with the kindly doctors and nurses, and pity for poor Janet. After the surprises, however, the spectator questions not only the doctors' and nurses' revulsion and pity, and not only Janet's reaction to her own face, but *their own* responses of pity to Janet's plight. If Janet is to be pitied for a face that the spectator finds to be beautiful, then is the spectator to be pitied as well? Where the episode had previously elicited spectator responses rooted in social conformity, the surprise developments suddenly throw the spectator's responses out of kilter with this imagined society, and thus wholly alter a conformist frame of reference.

Frame Shifters do not involve a surprise of prospects but rather a surprise of knowledge or understanding. The audience is led to suspect all along that the medical procedure performed on Janet might not work. This is the eleventh try, and the first ten attempts have all failed. Thus when the bandages are removed, it is not the failure of the procedure that surprises the spectator, but rather that Janet's face is beautiful, and that the faces of those around her hideous. A work of media that might be thought to engage critical thinking, I would argue, cannot simply offer a surprise of prospects, but also a surprise of understanding that itself raises philosophical issues.

Frame Shifters generate a surprise for the spectator, but not necessarily for the characters. In "Eye of the Beholder" the change in frame of reference occurs for the spectator, not the characters. The characters' frame of reference, sympathies, and general orientation toward Janet and their society remains the same from beginning to end. Janet learns that she must be banished, but this isn't so much a surprise as the confirmation of her worst fears. It is the spectator who is given the most significant surprise. Thus Frame Shifters give the spectator superior knowledge. If the spectator changes her or his frame of reference, the characters do not.

If the spectator is led to understand the fictional world from an altered perspective, the characters continue in their ignorance. This sense of epistemic superiority is essential in the workings of Frame Shifters on spectators because it not only generates a sense of satisfaction (pride) at being the sort of person who can "see through" conventional epistemic and social frameworks, but it also celebrates the very possibility of such changes in frame of reference. This is where the chief pleasure in viewing such Frame Shifters lies.

Frame Shifters tend to be deflationary, as is "Eye of the Beholder." The episode's ending leaves Janet inconsolable, and the society from which she is banished remains conformist and totalitarian. Conventional media endings often reassure the spectator that all is now well. The end of the romantic comedy, for example, sees the happy couple embrace in a sign of apparent eternal bliss. The spectator is not encouraged to consider the future life of the couple, but rather to leave them behind in thought. The end of the romantic comedy is reassuring, optimistic, and idealized – designed to lead to repose.

After the end of the romantic comedy has done its psychological work in reassuring the spectator of the possibility, beauty, and redeeming power of romantic love, its next function is to enable the spectator to forget all of the prior questions, worries, and problems that occupied the mind during the course of the narrative.

The endings of Frame Shifters, on the other hand, are troubling, anxiety provoking, worrisome, and unsettling. Notice that all of these words signify affective states that lead to additional cognitive processing, ranging from a mild consideration to an obsessive mulling over in the mind, depending on the degree of upset. When one considers that such affective responses occur as the result of a sudden alteration in frame of reference, and when one considers that this alteration occurs toward the end of the episode, then it becomes clearer why the ability of a narrative to elicit critical thought must consider the spectator's continued mental activity after the viewing has been completed. Frame Shifters are designed to linger on the mental palate after the initial "tasting," with a somewhat bitter aftertaste.

This raises an issue that might be termed the *paradox of negative affect*. Why would audiences subject themselves to this worry, to narratives that generate anxieties? A convincing solution to this paradox is clearly beyond the scope of this chapter. For now, I will be content to conjecture that such anxieties are the price spectators pay for other affective pleasures that outweigh the worries and anxieties. Chief among these are various pleasurable emotions such as curiosity and fascination.[20] I have also mentioned the sense of superiority that Frame Shifters afford the spectator, perhaps resulting in positive emotions such as pride and self-satisfaction. That the world might be fundamentally different than we think is sure to generate anxiety; it also would generate fascination and curiosity, perhaps even exhilaration. It may elicit pride in that the spectator has perceived the altered frame of reference that is suddenly revealed, unlike the characters that inhabit the fictional world. These various emotions may linger in the spectator long after the viewing is finished.

To summarize, both the affective responses and mental activities elicited by Frame Shifters are designed to prompt critical thinking in the spectator. The jarring nature of the framework shift generates an emotional response of surprise that initiates further cognitive activity because it is intended to foster curiosity and fascination in its wake. If it works, it also causes a kind of cognitive dissonance in the spectator whereby previous epistemic frameworks must be discarded for new ones generated by the text. This is an exercise in perspective-taking that is beneficial in its own right, since it might legitimately be thought of as a useful mental exercise of the imagination, and since it clearly implies that the accepted moral or ideological frameworks of a given culture are relative and quite possibly seriously flawed.

Yet this is not all that need be said about the matter. The "pleasure" that films and other media offer have often been a source of suspicion among those interested in the means by which narratives generate critical thinking. "Screen Theory," for example, a mode of thought rooted in psychoanalysis and Marxist political thought, held that the pleasures of the text were inherently regressive, and like lures or snares led to "subject positioning" and regressive psychological states rooted in early childhood development.[21] But it is not only the psychoanalytic Marxists who have distrusted pleasure. Brecht, as we have seen, also distrusted the pleasures of the text in his call for alienation effects and estrangement to counteract what many audiences find to be pleasurable about interactions with fiction: "identification" and the spectator's absorption in the fictional world of a play. Victor Perkins notes, in the harsh reactions of some critics to the pleasures of movies, that he knows of no "more succinct reassertion, in terms of cinema, of the old notion that virtue consists in hardship, and that what's pleasant must be regarded with suspicion." The experience of the movies, he goes on, may "become so diverting that the possibility of an underlying profundity is too easily dismissed."[22]

Note that one of the chief pleasures of the Frame Shifting text is the experience of the shift itself, together with the subsequent mental re-orientation that must occur when epistemic frames of reference are suddenly altered. The shift in framework results not only in pleasurable emotions such as surprise, fascination, and exhilaration, but also in vigorous critical thinking of the sort I have called perspective taking. If I am right in my claims about the cognitive and affective experience of certain surprise endings in *The Twilight Zone*, then it will be the case that the critical thinking elicited by Frame Shifters is not only compatible with spectator pleasure in this regard, but fundamentally depends on it.

Repeated viewings of certain narratives and narrative types, a repetition in part encouraged by the pleasures such narratives offer, encourages various mental activities and tendencies. *The Twilight Zone* is a remarkable television series in part because its episodes consistently question social conformity and conventional thought. The series also poses philosophical questions or offers its narratives as illustrations, counter-examples, and thought experiments in relation to implicit philosophical ideas.[23] As I have argued, it is through the narrative structure of many of the series' episodes that *The Twilight Zone* encourages critical thinking, in that the surprise endings I have called Frame Shifters make perspective taking and the exercise of the imagination a somewhat troubling, yet also a pleasurable activity.

NOTES

1. As a goal on the horizon, structuralists hoped to shed light on the place of narrative in human life, but in practice they were systematizers who arguably did not connect the narrative systems they described with the human functions of narrative, or emphasize the means by which narratives generate thought and response. For more on structuralism, see, for example, Jonathan Culler, *Structuralist Poetics: Structuralism, Poetics, and the Study of Literature* (Ithaca: Cornell University Press, 1975).

2. David Bordwell, *Narration in the Fiction Film* (Madison: University of Wisconsin Press, 1985).

3. See Noël Carroll, *Theorizing the Moving Image* (Cambridge: Cambridge University Press, 1996), pp. 86–90.

4. See, for example, Carl Plantinga and Greg M. Smith (eds.), *Passionate Views: Film, Cognition, and Emotion* (Baltimore: Johns Hopkins University Press, 1999); Murray Smith, *Engaging Characters: Fiction, Emotion, and the Cinema* (Oxford: Clarendon Press, 1995); Noël Carroll, *The Philosophy of Horror*

(New York and London: Routledge, 1990); Torben Grodal, *Moving Pictures* (Oxford: Clarendon Press, 1997).

5. Written by Richard Matheson, directed by Richard L. Bare, originally aired on November 18, 1960.

6. Written by Rod Serling, directed by Justus Addiss, originally aired on February 24, 1961.

7. For a description of mental schemas and their function in narrative comprehension, see David Bordwell, *Narration in the Fiction Film*, 30–40.

8. Written by Ray Bradbury, directed by James Sheldon and William Claxton, originally aired on May 18, 1962.

9. An interesting variation on this theme is explored in *Artificial Intelligence: A.I.* (2001), in which David (Haley Joel Osment) is a robotic boy designed as a surrogate child for a grieving mother. Unlike Grandma in "I Sing the Body Electric," who apparently expects no love in return for what she offers, David longs for love himself.

10. Written by Rod Serling, directed by John Brahm, originally aired November 20, 1959.

11. Written by Richard Matheson, directed by Douglas Heyes, originally aired on January 27, 1961.

12. Written by Richard Matheson, directed by Richard Donner, originally aired on October 11, 1963.

13. Written by Rod Serling, directed by Ted Post, originally aired on November 29, 1963.

14. Written by George Clayton Johnson, directed by Lamont Johnson, originally aired on January 5, 1962. Even in this case, it should be noted, this episode deals with a subject usually off limits to television – the fear of an inevitable death.

15. See, for example, Henry Jenkins, *Textual Poachers* (New York: Routledge, 1992); Janet Staiger, *Perverse Audiences: The Practices of Film Reception* (New York: New York University Press, 2000); Melvyn Stokes and Richard Maltby (eds.), *Hollywood Spectatorship: Changing Perceptions of Film Audiences* (London: British Film Institute, 2001).

16. See John Willett (ed. and trans.), *Brecht on Theatre* (New York: Hill and Wang, 1974).

17. See my "Notes on Spectator Emotion and Ideological Film Criticism," in Richard Allen and Murray Smith (eds.), *Film Theory and Philosophy* (Oxford: Clarendon Press, 1997), 372–93. See also Murray Smith, "The Logic and Legacy of Brechtianism," in David Bordwell and Noël Carroll (eds.), *Post-Theory: Reconstructing Film Studies* (Madison: University of Wisconsin Press, 1996), 113–27. For a critique of reflexive techniques in documentary, see my *Rhetoric and Representation in Nonfiction Film* (Cambridge: Cambridge University Press, 1997), 214–18.

18. The documentary filmmaker Errol Morris has dedicated his career to exploring the "mental landscapes" of people, and is especially fascinated by their belief systems, which seem intransigent. See my "The Philosophy of Errol Morris," in William Rothman (ed.), *Contemporary Documentary Filmmakers: McElwee, Morris, Rouch* (SUNY University Press, forthcoming).

19. Written by Rod Serling, directed by Douglas Heyes, originally aired on November 11, 1960.

20. This solution to the paradox of negative affect is similar to Noël Carroll's solution to the paradox of horror in *The Philosophy of Horror* (New York: Routledge, 1990). There Carroll argues that the horror film spectator is willing to experience fear and revulsion as the price for the pleasures of a narrative of continuous revelation of the unknown and seemingly impossible. See pp. 158–95.

21. For a sympathetic account of Screen Theory, see Robert Stam, *Film Theory: An Introduction* (Blackwell, 2000), 130–79. Noël Carroll's *Mystifying Movies: Fads and Fallacies in Contemporary Film Theory* (New York: Columbia University Press, 1988) is a philosophical critique of Screen Theory.

22. V. F. Perkins, *Film as Film: Understanding and Judging Movies* (Da Capo, 1993).

23. On the relationship of narrative media and philosophizing, see Murray Smith and Thomas E. Wartenberg (eds.), *Thinking Through Cinema: Film as Philosophy* (Malden, MA and Oxford: Blackwell, 2006).

4

THE TREACHERY OF THE COMMONPLACE

MARY SIRRIDGE

I remember that one where they take the bandages off, and she's, like, beautiful, and the doctor and nurses look like pigs!

Teenage Library Worker

The teenage library worker was describing the revelation scene in *The Twilight Zone* episode, "The Eye of the Beholder."[1] At this point the viewer has been shocked into making the same kind of mistake the characters have been making – into the snap judgment that Janet Tyler, who fits *our* ideas of beauty, is the *really* beautiful one, and if the other characters could only see themselves as we see them, they would know how ugly they *really* are!

It does not occur to any of the characters to question the absoluteness of judgments about personal beauty and ugliness. Probably they should have known better, and it will turn out in the end that their aesthetic tunnel vision is matched by a much more reprehensible failure of moral vision. But the viewer should surely have known better, for the viewer knows that he or she is in the Twilight Zone.

In the Twilight Zone, there is no assumption so basic, and no reaction so natural, that its reliability cannot reasonably be called into question.

The *Twilight Zone* approach to evidence and knowledge has the effect of forcing questions that the normal context of thought and action allows us to dismiss because – in the normal context – it would be unreasonable to ask questions like: What if I am really dead already, and just do not know it?[2] What if the person next to me is not really my spouse of 23 years, but a cleverly disguised alien? As I will argue, the shock-strategy of *The Twilight Zone* is based on invalidating particular assumptions that normally do not get questioned – precisely because they are so commonplace a part of the normal context of thought and action that neither they nor the warrants for them are normally made explicit. To steal a description from David Lewis, the Twilight Zone presents us with "a context with an enormously rich domain of counter-examples to ascriptions of knowledge."[3]

The situation of *The Twilight Zone* viewer is partly participative, partly reflective. As the episode unfolds, the viewer is ordinarily identified with the protagonists and shares the problem or puzzle with which they are confronted and their limitations with respect to evidence, misleading cues, and the urgency of the situation. In retrospect, i.e., reflecting on the events of the episode, the viewer is in the position of judging whether the characters' and his or her own judgments were warranted.[4] Usually not, since these meta-judgments are made from the Twilight Zone context, where the epistemological standards are very high. But even during the episode the viewer is often not in exactly the same epistemological position as the characters; the viewer has been warned, sometimes explicitly in Serling's opening remarks, that the standards that apply here are those of the Twilight Zone, which is not a context in which accepting commonplace assumptions and ignoring improbable alternatives is epistemically efficacious.[5]

I will examine three episodes that illustrate the Twilight Zone approach to knowledge and justification particularly clearly, though in different ways. These episodes also illustrate a second point about the Twilight Zone approach to knowledge and belief; like many other episodes, they enforce an ethic of belief. It is not just that *Twilight Zone* characters frequently meet with poetic justice for attitudes and beliefs that are morally unacceptable, at least in the broad sense that they make for unworthy human lives. In addition, *Twilight Zone* characters are held accountable for reasoning that does not meet the standards of the Twilight Zone, whether or not they know they are in the Twilight Zone. In the Twilight Zone, it is the characters' success in knowing, not how well they tried, that counts.[6]

"TO SERVE MAN"[7]

In this episode, the earth has been visited by the Kanamits, nine-feet-tall, humanoid and apparently limitlessly benevolent; they bring with them a manual entitled *To Serve Man*. Ultimately Michael Chambers, a cryptographer engaged in decoding the book, learns only after he can no longer escape his flight to the home planet of the Kanamits that the book they have worked so hard to decode is a cookbook. We last see him in his compartment on the spaceship, being urged by the Kanamit caretaker to eat heartily: "Eat hearty – we wouldn't want you to lose weight."

Chambers and his associate have had two questions before them. Their official assignment was to determine the meaning of the book the Kanamits have left at the UN; they have gotten as far as the title, *To Serve Man*. Some people, at least, see decoding the book as essential to determining the Kanamits' motives and intentions; somebody in the White House, the general tells Chambers, thinks there is a connection between figuring out what the book says and determining "what the Kanamits are up to." From the start, Chambers himself fairly uncritically accepts the view that the Kanamits' intentions are "charitable"; the evidence is the good they do: barren land turned arable overnight, impenetrable barriers that put an end to international conflict, and practically cost-free energy. In the face of this sort of evidence, decoding the book is unnecessary, he thinks, although once translated, the title of the book, *To Serve Man*, confirms his optimistic view of what the Kanamits are up to; in a world of peace and prosperity, he thinks, decoding and interpretation become completely unimportant. Chambers is intelligent; and even if he is not doing so with the appropriate energy and curiosity, he is asking the right questions: What does *To Serve Man* mean? And why are the Kanamits so interested in serving man? Nonetheless he fails in both cases; and his punishment, in the words of Serling's epilogue, is that he is in the process of going "from being the ruler of the planet to an ingredient in someone's soup."

Chambers' two epistemological failures are of a similar sort, and they are connected. In both cases, he is faced with a problem of interpretation; and he does not draw the range of interpretive possibilities widely enough to include the right answer. And, as we see in the moment of revelation, had he found the correct interpretation of *To Serve Man*, he would immediately have had a timely answer to his question about the Kanamits' motives. Had he gotten the right answer to the motivational question, he would have spotted the double meaning of "to serve man" and adjusted his field of interpretation for the manual accordingly.

Why does Chambers fail? In the case of the manual, he, of course, does not consider the possibility that it might be a cookbook. He also does not consider the possibility that the title might be a deliberate double-entendre. Neither of these possibilities is very prominent on the normal field of interpretive possibilities for everyday conversation, still less for a commonplace piece of institutional prose or a manifesto. In speculating about the Kanamits' motives, Chambers himself accepts the easiest and most comfortable answer; even observers who are more careful appear to consider only the commonplace range of ulterior motives, colonial exploitation and the like.

By accepting these limitations of the range of possibilities, Chambers and the others are operating on assumptions that are so commonplace that they are not ordinarily made explicit. None of the decoders ever says: Let's rule out the possibility of intentionally misleading double meanings from the start. More importantly, nobody ever says: Let's assume that these beings see us more or less as we see ourselves, as their intelligent near-equals, and thus as the sorts of beings who cannot rightly be used solely as means. Or: Let us assume that these beings would regard eating human beings with the kind of horror the prospect has for us. Or: Let us assume that we can treat the decoding question and the question about the Kanamits' motives independently. Neither does the viewer. Of course, making assumptions explicit does not guarantee that they will be questioned when they need to be; but in the Twilight Zone not making such assumptions explicit is a sure recipe for being blind-sided by the treachery of the commonplace.

Everybody has taken far too many things for granted. Everybody – most particularly the viewer – should have known better. In retrospect, it is easy for Chambers – and the viewer – to see what has been missed. As a decoder, Chambers ought to have looked more critically at common-place assumptions about the interpretation of language, thought, and behavior that we do not ordinarily make explicit. In addition to being alert to the possibility of straightforward double meanings, Chambers should have wondered, at least, whether in speculating about the mot-ives of the Kanamits he should ignore alternatives outside the ordinary. He might very well have realized that human beings could not rely on the Kanamits' seeing human beings as we see ourselves; the reason the decoding project is stalled, he says, is that the Kanamits are "five hun-dred times more intelligent and a thousand times more complex" than human beings. Perhaps more importantly, their use of speech, and perhaps of writing, is an accommodation to dealing with human beings, since their own communication is "mental rather than verbal." The capacity for language is a time-honored criterion for having the moral status of a person among humans; a little further thought might have led to the suspicion that the capacity to communicate in a way that supersedes language could have the same weight for the Kanamits. Even on the highly questionable assumption that the Kanamits are moral in some sense, and even that they are some sort of eerie Kantians, it is surely possible that they do not ascribe much more moral significance to human beings than human beings ascribe to cows.[8]

As *Twilight Zone* episodes go, "To Serve Man" is quintessentially epistemological. There may be some hint of a moral point in Serling's description of the Kanamit as "a Christopher Columbus from another Galaxy and another time," a hint of a reproach for human colonizers. But probably not. The dominant ethic here is an ethic of belief; what leads to a fall is the complacent acceptance of the commonplace contextual margins for investigation, evidence, and belief – in the Twilight Zone. And in the Twilight Zone people are answerable for not getting things right. The silly, complacent people boarding the Kanamit ship are completely blind to the unhappy implications of the fact that nobody ever comes back from the Kanamit home planet; they are empty-headedly making a life and death decision in the Twilight Zone. In the Twilight Zone, it serves them right to be served up as "tonight's bill of fare."

Few viewers, in fact, do much better than Chambers and his fellow citizens.[9] Nearly everyone is surprised by the ending, even though the viewer has somewhat more evidence than the characters do. The viewer sees, for example, that the Kanamits are *repeatedly* interested only in the weight of the human passengers taking off for their home planet. The viewer first encounters Chambers involved in a stream of self-castigation; the rest of the tale is told in flashback. It is clear from the start that he has made some serious mistake. The viewer is thus very effectively dislodged from complete participation in the universe of the story; he or she knows that this is the Twilight Zone, and thus that there is likely to be some blind-siding twist at the end of the episode.

Chambers and the participant viewer have been set up. Like the manual, much of what the Kanamits do has an ordinary, innocuous interpretation – it would be perfectly natural, for example, to consider the weight of the passengers when getting ready to lift off in a spaceship. Moreover, though Chambers is presented to the viewer as complacent and careless in his reasoning, it is not clear until it is too late that this is a life or death situation, and thus that much higher epistemological standards should be in use. Finally, the characters who express the greatest suspicion of the Kanamits' "charity" are the ones that have the most to lose in the face of global peace and prosperity: politicians and the military establishment. We know these types; neither the main characters nor the viewers are inclined to trust these people or to think that they are very smart; almost inevitably what these characters say is rejected because of who they are, which turns out to be a fatal *ad hominem*.

Chambers is not a very satisfactory tragic hero – he is more complacent and lethargic than tragic, with a tendency to whine. Still Chambers makes a fairly serviceable Everyman, and so the episode successfully makes its point about typically human complacency and lack of imagination and reluctance to rock the boat. Chambers is in the Twilight Zone. His own retrospective judgment of what he did wrong, "We ought to have been prepared for every eventuality," goes too far. Not for *every* eventuality. The lesson to be learned in the Twilight Zone is almost never that everything ought to be questioned, or even that very many assumptions ought to be questioned very often. The trick is to spot the right commonplace, to hit upon the extraordinary alternative that should not be ignored. And in the Twilight Zone there is no mercy for those who get the wrong answer.

"WILL THE REAL MARTIAN PLEASE STAND UP?"[10]

Most of the characters have gotten off a bus for a rest stop at a diner; the driver fears that the winter storm may have rendered a bridge ahead of them unsafe. The police arrive with the unwelcome news that some sort of UFO has landed in a nearby pond, and that footprints lead to the diner. It is quickly discovered that there is one more "passenger" in the diner than boarded the bus to start with. The atmosphere of menace and distrust deepens, as the juke box turns on and off on its own and the lights flicker; and everyone is relieved when the phone rings with the information that the bridge ahead is safe. They leave escorted by the police car. Shortly thereafter, one passenger returns. The bridge was not safe; and he is the sole survivor. The phone call, like the behavior of the juke box, was "illusion." Lighting his cigarette over coffee with all three of his hands, he reveals to the counterman that he is the Martian, on earth to scout for a Martian invasion, only to have the counterman lift his hat to reveal a third eye; he is a Venusian, and the Martian invasion forces will not be arriving after all.

In this episode, the viewer is blind-sided, and so is every character except the Venusian. But unlike the characters in "To Serve Man," the people in the diner know that they are in a Twilight Zone situation.[11] Given the crazy behavior of the lights and juke box, the tracks leading from the pond to the diner, and the mysterious addition to the number of passengers, they could hardly fail to understand that they are outside the ordinary. As the wacky old passenger with the rolling eyes puts it, "She's just like a science fiction, that's what she is! A regular Ray Bradbury!"

Again, unlike the characters of "To Serve Man," these people start by examining assumptions that we normally do not make explicit. Of the fussy businessman, the old wacky old passenger says, "This lemon-sucker here . . . he's the most suspicious of the lot!" The two married couples are beyond suspicion, the "professional dancer" says, because it is only one additional "passenger" they are looking for; both wives immediately take a closer look at their husbands. One sees a mole that she does not remember seeing before, and the other suddenly views her husband of 23 years with suspicion. The attractive lady with no identification, who hesitantly has described herself as "a professional dancer," is the next to fall under suspicion; but the bus driver says that she is the only one of the passengers he is sure of having seen board the bus. He is himself then accused of being the alien by the wild-eyed old man: "But who noticed *him*! How do we know *you* are the same one who got on the bus?"

In trying to find out who among them is "the Martian in a diner," the people in the diner reason fairly well to a point. They are aware that they are in a situation in which normal assumptions need to be questioned, and they know that the stakes may well be high. They are right to think that the couples ought to be eliminated, though not just because "twenty-three years is long enough for a woman to know who she is mar-ried to," as one indignant husband says; these couples are not meeting each other over the breakfast table, but trapped in a diner with an alien among them. But in fact, the original reason for eliminating the couples was correct. An increase of two passengers would leave the couples sus-pect. But barring collusion with one of the wives, the only way an alien could have joined the passengers by way of a couple would have been to substitute itself for the erstwhile spouse; thus by way of the couples, there would either be no increase in the number of passengers, or an increase of two – but not the one additional "passenger" they are looking for. Similarly, no one ultimately takes seriously the hypothesis that the driver is the alien, and they should not, even though he would normally be under suspicion precisely by virtue of being one of the ordinary human "fixtures" no one ever pays any attention to. In this case, the driver is in fact placed *above* suspicion by his role. A driver drove the bus to this place. The driver in the diner could be the alien only if the alien had substituted itself for their driver; but a substitution for the driver would not increase the number of people on the bus. And if the driver is above suspicion, the dancer is probably eliminated as well; it seems likely that the driver – this driver anyhow – *would* notice so pretty a girl as the "professional dancer" boarding his bus. Again, then, if the lady is the alien, the alien has to have taken the real dancer's place; and there would be no extra person on the bus.

Still these people do not get the right answer. As a group they are at fault for several reasons. Most obviously, they do not finish the elimination; the choice is down to the crazy old man and the fussy businessman when they are distracted first by the odd behavior of the electrical system, and then by the reassuring phone call from the county engineer. And the old fellow has already given them both the right answer; and more or less the right criterion: "Check 'em for wings! Look under their coats! How many legs?" Counting the remaining suspects' limbs would have gotten them the right answer and counting everyone's eyes as well – also suggested by the old passenger – would have worked still better. All the right suggestions come from the wrong person, and so they fall victim to a fatal *ad hominem*. In the Twilight Zone, people are answerable for not getting the right answer. All the earthlings in the diner die when the bridge goes out.

In retrospect, it is easy for the viewer to see what the characters – and the participant viewer – have missed. In addition to being distracted from the process of elimination and failing to consider a suggestion on its merits, the characters fail to get the right answer because they become so focused on the process of elimination and on the importance of getting out of their dangerous situation in the diner that they are no longer appropriately critical of other assumptions. When the Martian who returns to the diner as sole survivor of the collapse of the bridge, the stunned counterman asks him about the phone call from the county engineer assuring them that the bridge was safe. "Illusion," says the Martian; he promptly causes the juke box to behave as it did before. The Martian is making the proper epistemological point: in a situation in which someone may be manipulating the electric equipment it is foolish to trust the telephone without a second thought. But an anonymous call on the ever-reliable telephone comes in from an anonymous "county engineer"

– another human "fixture"; and no one asks, "What if the call is of a piece with the crazy behavior of other electric things?" All the human beings, at least, take its reliability for granted. They do so in part because they uncritically assume that the danger lies in being cooped up in a diner in a storm with the alien.

Like "To Serve Man," "Will the Real Martian Please Stand Up?" is essentially an epistemological exercise. The people come to grief because they make mistakes. It looks like the Martian will come to grief too. Not because he has just sent nine people to a watery grave, but because he has uncritically assumed that the Martians are the only aliens with an interest in earth – and that the "fixture" at the counter can safely be told the whole plan before (we assume) being easily disposed of. There is no subtle and well developed epistemology here; the aim is to leave the viewer saying, "Ah, so *that's* what I missed! . . . and also *that!*" The lesson to be learned here is that it is very easy to be blind-sided by the treachery of the commonplace, even when forewarned.

"THE EYE OF THE BEHOLDER"

Suspended in time and space for a moment, your introduction to Miss Janet Tyler, who lives in a very private world of darkness, a universe whose dimensions are the size, thickness, length of a swath of bandages that cover her face.

Serling's prologue

We first meet Janet Tyler as she is getting toward the end of her wait to see whether this eleventh medical attempt to change her hideous face has succeeded – or whether she will live out her days exiled to a village for deformed persons. Janet Tyler is not hoping for beauty, she says, just to be acceptable enough that people do not scream when they look at her. The nurses are sympathetic to a point; behind her back they are more frank about her deformed face: "If it were mine I'd bury myself in a grave someplace . . . *some* people want to live, no matter what." On television in the background as nurses and doctor discuss Janet Tyler's case is "Leader" haranguing his viewers about the importance of "glorious conformity."

The doctor in charge of Janet Tyler's case in fact has his doubts about whether people's fate should hang upon whether they look sufficiently like others:

I've looked underneath those bandages, deeper than that pitiful lump of flesh. I've seen that woman's real face, the face of her real self. It's a good face. It's a human face. . . .

In response to a nurse's comment that it is a lot easier to think of Janet Tyler as a human being when her face is bandaged, he says:

Why must we feel that way, Nurse? What is the dimensional difference between beauty and something repellant? Is it skin deep? Why, Nurse. . . . Why shouldn't people be allowed to be different?

He is quickly reminded that this sort of nonconforming idea is dangerous . . . "treason," in fact. Janet Tyler's bandages are slowly unwound and the light grows steadily stronger. The doctor and nurses cringe at her appearance; the procedure has failed. The camera settles on Janet Tyler's face; she is stunningly beautiful. Slowly, the camera reveals the faces of the medical personnel one after the other; they look like deformed pigs. Janet Tyler flees down a nightmarish hospital corridor, where screens with Leader on them denounce all forms of difference as a "cancer that will destroy us." She flees into the waiting arms of the handsome Walter Smith, who will lead her off to a village reserved for her kind; he assures her that there she will be loved, that it does not matter why people like the two of them end up incurably ugly because "Beauty is in the eye of the beholder," an idea that is repeated in Serling's voice-over epilogue:

Now the questions that come to mind. Where is this place and when is it? What kind of world, where ugliness is the norm and beauty the deviation from that norm? You want an answer? The answer is, it doesn't make any difference. Because the old saying happens to be true. Beauty is in the eye of the beholder . . . in this year or a hundred years hence, on this planet or wherever there is human life, perhaps out among the stars. Beauty is in the eye of the beholder. Lesson to be learned . . . in the Twilight Zone.

Here, as in "To Serve Man," the viewer is drawn into the Twilight Zone by identifying with the protagonist, whose assumptions and attitudes get adopted fairly uncritically. As in "Will the Real Martian Please Stand Up?" an elaborate trap is still being set in the revelation scene, when the viewer thinks the trap has closed. To the viewer, who has discovered that his or her sympathies and access to the evidence have been manipulated in ways unlikely to be noticed, it seems clear which cues have been missed or misinterpreted and which treacherous assumptions accepted uncritically. Then the real trap springs shut with Serling's epilogue – the viewer has been shocked into making an absolute judgment about beauty and deformity, into the trap of making exactly the same kind of mistake the doctor and nurses have been making.

"The Eye of the Beholder" has a much more calculated artistic technique than we find in the first two episodes. This is in part because Serling's objective here is more complex than in the other two episodes. Here blindsiding the viewer is not an end in itself; instead the lesson about faulty reasoning is in the service of a further moral agenda. The result is that in dealing with this episode we find not just a springboard to philosophical reflection, but the sort of philosophical content that can be confronted critically.

Though it is not Serling's main objective, the idea is clearly on the table that judgments of personal beauty are not so absolute as they seem. But "Beauty is in the eye of the beholder" would hardly be an "old saying" if everybody did not more or less already know that personal preference, custom, and the vicissitudes of taste and fashion heavily influence judgments of personal beauty and repulsiveness. So what is Serling's point in prodding the viewer into saying: "Perhaps *I'm* making the same sort of mistake they made – I suppose that using their standards they look just fine, and Miss Tyler and I are horribly deformed?"

One clue to what Serling, the director, and the make-up artist were up to lies in the design of the revelation scene. The girl who emerged from the bandages had to be "incredibly beautiful by our standards," and the "uglies" had to be "monsters"[12]; the uglies' judgments had to be – from our point of view – incomprehensible. The beautiful Janet Tyler and the "uglies" had to be, that is, outside of the ordinarily accepted range of alternatives for what counts, in the words of the doctor, as "beauty and something repellant." Thus what the viewer is in fact shocked into saying is: "I suppose that by their standards, *which have no less objective validity than mine*, some of them are as gorgeous as Miss Tyler looks to me, and Miss Tyler and I are freaks." This sort of radical relativity with respect to judgments of personal beauty and deformity, the view that such judgments amount to nothing more than unthinking reliance on responses that are completely determined by the currently and locally prevailing standard, is *not* a widely accepted home truth, even among people who are aware that there are a lot of different standards of personal beauty. Pulling the rug out from under the reader in this way is, of course, not an argument for the radical relativity of standards of personal beauty, which would require at the least a theory about what judgments of personal beauty are about and what they express and how they are arrived at, and an argument to the effect that the relevant beautiful-making feature is culture- or context-relative. It is probably not necessary to show that with respect to personal beauty there is no fact of the matter and no universally determining human basis for the judgment. It could be, for example, that judgments of personal beauty, though largely arising from the vicissitudes of cultural taste, have some universal relationship to species survival and social stratification. For Serling's objectives in this episode, no such grounded philosophical reflection is really needed; the dramatic revelation scene and Serling's epilogue suffice to undercut the viewer's unthinking assumption that judgments about personal beauty and ugliness are no less objective than other complex perceptual judgments.

In the context of "The Eye of the Beholder," the relativity of judgments about personal beauty is obviously connected to a further, moral point. Miss Tyler, the doctors and nurses, and the viewer are, of course, in the Twilight Zone, where people's faces can apparently be very radically trans-formed by means of surgery, and where the penalty for looking different is exile. Even in the Twilight Zone some people object to using people's appearance to determine their worth as people and how they are treated. Miss Tyler herself, despite the fact that she spends most of her time long-ing to look like everyone else, greets the prospect of being "congregated" with others of her kind with an angry outburst: "Congregated? You mean segregated . . . a ghetto designed for freaks! The state is not god!" The doctor, too, has expressed reservations about enforced homogeneity of appearance and about ostracizing the ugly; this view; the nurse's hushed and frightened response reminds him, is "treason."

The doctor and Miss Tyler are obviously right. The application of this "lesson learned in the Twilight Zone" to the real world is obvious: It is all too common – and wrong – to decide what people are worth and how they should be treated on the basis of their appearance. Still this lesson, though important, is again not Serling's main objective. Maxine Stuart, who played the bandaged Janet Tyler, quite correctly described "The Eye of the Beholder" as "a script about conformity"[13]. The episode is most centrally aimed, not at cosmetic homogeneity, but at enforced conformity of a much more important kind, enforced orthodoxy with respect to thought and ideas. It is important to this central objective that the doctor's ideas be obviously correct and place him at odds with the mainstream ideo-logy of his society. (That it is conformity itself about which he has non-conforming ideas is a clever additional twist, but it is not essential to Serling's point.) Because the doctor is obviously right, the nurse's response gives

the viewer a very pointed sense of the consequence of living in an atmosphere of enforced conformity with respect to thought and ideas. The immediate result of thought-control enforced by threats is that potentially useful
discussion is stifled; the doctor and the nurse speak no more about the
dubious moral character of the enterprise they are involved in.

The other results of this enforced conformity with respect to ideas
are quite a bit worse. Most people, like the nurses, do not give a second
thought to the State's policy exiling the failures, once 11 attempts to
make people like them look like everyone else have failed. And no matter
what reservations he or she may have about the policy, everyone, the
doctor and Janet Tyler included, ends up going along with it completely.
When Janet Tyler asks about the possibility of just being killed instead
of "segregated in a ghetto for freaks," the doctor tells her that her
"only alternative" is to be "congregated" with other people of her kind;
"extermination of undesirables" is sometimes allowed, he says, but not
in cases like this. It is the doctor who explains to Janet Tyler that she has
had as much opportunity as she has a right to expect. There is a reason
why these rules are in effect, he tells her; "Each of us is afforded as much
opportunity as possible to fit in with society . . . to look normal . . . the
way you'd like to look." In this situation having a little more moral vision
than other people is no protection against falling in completely with the
fundamental ideology of the society. Neither is being a victim.

The ranting of Leader on the ubiquitous television screens is the
ultimate expression of the demand for "glorious conformity." As the
speech progresses, delivered with more and more yelling and arm-
waving, it is at the same time progressively more difficult to make the
speech hang together linguistically; toward the end, background noise
drowns out all but important phrases. Still it is absolutely clear what
the central idea is:

> A single purpose, a single law, a single approach, a single entity of people, a
> single virtue, a single morality, a single frame of reference! A single philo-
> sophy of government. . . . We must cut out all that is different like a cancerous
> growth . . . it must not destroy us!

Serling's ultimate point is political. Enforced conformity with respect to
thought and ideas breeds the intellectual passivity and cowardice and
bad faith that pave the way for falling victim to the evils of totalitarian
regimes, in this case a regime that is transparently modeled on Hitler's
Germany.

It is tempting to relegate the facial homogenization of "The Eye of the Beholder" to the crazy machinery of the Twilight Zone, a wacky and exaggerated backdrop for presenting Serling's moral and political agenda. This may indeed be all Serling intended. But whether or not it is a conscious part of Serling's agenda, in this case the "machinery of the Twilight Zone" itself raises a further question, i.e., whether there may not be more than an accidental connection between aesthetic conformity, enforced or not, and conformity with respect to thought and ideas, so that they lead in separate, but interconnected, ways to submission to repressive and totalitarian political regimes. Certainly Serling's historical touch point is one clear case in which the constellation was present; in Hitler's Germany regulation of the arts, a prescribed aesthetic, and ideals of personal beauty went hand in hand with "the elimination of undesirables," widespread moral complicity, and a totalitarian state. As a student of mine observed – correctly, I think – we have only *their* word for it that Janet Tyler will end up in "a ghetto for freaks," and not be transported from that ghetto to an oven! Walter Smith could as easily be a Judas goat as not.

The characters of "The Eye of the Beholder" are punished for their lack of moral vision. The hospital staff live in a world of fear, repression, and stupidity; our only regret is that they do not know how awful their lives are. Miss Tyler is punished as well. Her life has been miserable, and her future may not be so bright either. Should we really expect that being accepted by others because she is no worse deformed than they are will reconcile Janet Tyler to living out her life surrounded by people no less deformed than she is? Maybe, and maybe not.

Could they have avoided their mistakes? In one sense it does not matter, since being subjectively justified does not make people in the Twilight Zone less answerable for getting things wrong. Still, on Serling's view, the hospital staff pretty clearly are at fault; they have sacrificed independent thinking and truth for the comfort of conforming. The doctor is really little better; he is in the end so complicit with the whole arrangement that his reservations shrink to the level of self-indulgence compounded by admiration for his own depth. Such mistakes can be explained, but not excused. And even if we cannot reasonably expect Janet Tyler to think beyond her physical appearance and give up the beliefs and dreams of a lifetime, we could at least expect her to look at her face in a mirror for herself – which she refuses to do in the revelation scene, and apparently has never done.

Surprise is essential to Serling's plan, and pulling off this surprise demanded more sophisticated technique than was required to bring home the comparatively simple lessons in how to assess evidence that we find in "To Serve Man" and "Will the Real Martian Please Stand Up?" Both Janet Tyler's physical beauty and the deformity of the medical staff have to be a complete surprise for the viewer, but not in a way that makes the viewer feel cheated or tricked. In fact, for Janet Tyler Serling used two actresses. The eloquent voice and gestures of Maxine Stuart, "a great actress," were to lure the viewer into uncritical acceptance of the bandaged Janet Tyler's understanding of her situation; the beautiful Donna Douglas was used to pull off the revelation scene. The faces of the medical staff, who are supposed be "monsters," but "of the same species,"[14] were achieved by affixing a small number of deformed features to the actors' own faces, and thereby creating uniquely, but similarly deformed faces. The result is fairly horrifying – faces that are individual, but not significantly so, and that seem to have expressions, but are unreadable. None of the characters, of course, are ever seen full face until the moment of revelation. In retrospect, the viewer thinks, surely one ought to have noticed that the medical staff are seen in part, from behind, in shadow – from every angle but the one that would reveal what their faces look like.

For the medical personnel, blind-siding the viewer was worked in part by exploiting commonplace assumptions about perception. The director developed an intricate use of the camera "by which you were seeing these doctors and nurses all the time, but actually they would be passing one another at exactly the same moment that the camera would be, so that you wouldn't really see their faces, or they'd go behind a pillar just as they were turning toward the camera and so on."[15] This technique exploits the fact that with respect to much of the world much of the time we project complete objects, people's full faces, etc., from very scanty evidence (any of the people sitting in the coffee house with me *could* be missing the other side of his or her face, but I assume that the other sides of their faces are pretty much like the side I can see.) In commonplace situations, it does not pay to worry all that much about how little sensory evidence we ordinarily have for judgments about the way the physical world is.

The other important reason why the viewer is not suspicious has to do with the director's fairly heavy use of the visual techniques and familiar narrative types of film noir.[16] We hear voices, and do not see the speaker, or see only the speaker's hand, or only smoke from the speaker's cigarette. We see the room from distorted angles, from behind pillars. The camera lingers on a hand and a box of cigarettes obscured by smoke.

Most of the scenes are dark and shadowed. In the dramatic unveiling scene, the camera was operated from inside a swathed fish bowl that was gradually unwrapped, so that the viewer picks up more and more of "the various shadings of light" and outlines of objects that Janet Tyler sees. These are commonplaces of the style. The other factor is that the nurses, the doctor, and their scenes together appear to be so true to type. The viewer recognizes the very typical Late Night Scene between the very typical Nurse expressing very typical Concern about the very typical Questioning, Caring Doctor, who is overworking and getting too involved. Even Janet Tyler, alienated and suffering, more at home in shadows than in light, is a familiar *noir* presence. The viewer is thus blind-sided in large part by commonplace visual techniques and the familiar narrative types of a familiar artistic idiom. Even viewers unfamiliar with the idiom's particularities are very likely to write off the overall effect as "artistic."

Still, Serling and the director of this episode took some risks. The substitution of actresses might, for example, have been detected or have been seen in retrospect as a trick, instead of a genuinely successful trap. The greatest risk, however, lay precisely in the parallel Serling's script drew between the cosmetic level and the moral and political level. Serling, of course, wanted the viewer to take away from this episode the idea that freedom of expression, and the possibility of intelligent dissent from the views of the majority or the authorities are morally and politically valuable, and that to enforce orthodoxy by ostracism was to start down the road to totalitarianism. But he ran the risk of having the viewer take a further step and say, "Just as I made the uncritical assumption that my standards of personal beauty are absolute, so I have made the uncritical assumption that *my* values, which include freedom of expression and allowing ideological dissent, are absolute. From *their* point of view, my standards, *which have no more objective validity than theirs*, are no doubt as awful as I think their standards are. Like beauty, moral and political legitimacy are in the eye of the beholder." He ran the risk, in short, of undercutting the validity of his own message of toleration. Can the reflective viewer accept Serling's radical version of "beauty is in the eye of the beholder," while joining in Serling's rejection of the beauty of conformity?

"The Eye of the Beholder" is to some extent protected from this response by its historical touch point. In Nazi Germany the fatal constellation of standardization of aesthetic response, enforced orthodoxy, and a totalitarian state were all present, with an outcome whose badness no reasonable person could deny. But more importantly, to suppose that

Serling's message about personal beauty is that every perspective is authoritative in its own right, is to mistake his meaning on the aesthetic level; his real message is that there is no authoritative perspective on personal beauty and deformity. The parallel point about moral and political ideas is that any perspective that insists on its absolute authority is mistaken – about its authority. Whether Serling is entirely aware of it or not, this is essentially an epistemological stance with respect to moral and aesthetic judgments, even if it has practical consequences for thinking and acting. Serling's advocacy of toleration is thus not just one more moral perspective, no more authoritative than any other. It is a meta-moral perspective.

CONCLUSION

There is a continuity among these three episodes and a common focus: stupidity, uncritically accepting commonplaces on next to no evidence – because everybody says so or thinks so – is in itself bad. Even in normal-looking situations, Serling seems to be saying, there's always the possibility that we are really in the Twilight Zone. In the Twilight Zone payback for failures of imagination and constricted vision is swift and often fatal. But when such stupidity turns up in the value sphere, as it is prone to do, the results are far worse: parochialism, the tyranny of the ordinary, "elimination of undesirables." This sort of stupidity is downright dangerous; and again, there is always the possibility that we are in actuality in the Twilight Zone. Lesson to be learned . . . in the Twilight Zone.[17]

NOTES

1. "The Eye of the Beholder," written by Rod Serling, directed by Douglas Heyes, first aired on Nov. 11, 1960.

2. This question may not be worth worrying about, though several *Twilight Zone* episodes raise it, e.g., "The Hitch-Hiker" and "The Passerby." And at least one philosopher, St. Augustine, thinks it is possible that the souls of the dead do not realize that they do not have bodies, though they do know that they are the souls of the dead. Cf. M. Sirridge, "Dream Bodies and Dream Pains in Augustine's *De Natura et Origine Animae*," *Vivarium* XLII.2 (2005), 213–49.

3. David Lewis, "Elusive Knowledge," *Australasian Journal of Philosophy* 74, no. 4 (December, 1996), 549–67, 559. Like others, Lewis distinguishes between

the relationship between context and "the subject" S, who is confronting the evidence and making judgments and planning courses of action, and the relevance of context to "the ascriber," the epistemologist who is deciding whether and how S's judgments are justifiable or amount to knowledge. It is consistently the ascriber's context with which he is concerned. Still the terminology of "context" and "ignoring alternatives" is useful in describing the situation of the subject as well as the ascriber, and so I will use it for both. Ordinarily the context will make it clear what level of context is at issue.

4. Usually, the issue of knowledge ascriptions does not arise, since usually the primary level judgments are wrong because characters and involved viewers have been blind-sided. The issue will thus be whether their judgments were justifiable, albeit wrong.

5. Catherine Elgin, "The Epistemic Efficacy of Stupidity," *Synthese* 74 (1988), 297–311.

6. David Lewis, "Elusive Knowledge," 554, though Lewis is here discussing the relevance of actuality to the ascriber's judgment. For characters in *The Twilight Zone* the situation they are actually in is always a relevant alternative; even if they do not suspect what their actuality really is – the Twilight Zone penalizes them anyhow.

7. "To Serve Man," written by Rod Serling, directed by Buck Houghton, first aired on Jan. 26, 1961.

8. Suppose human beings have only middle status in some hierarchy of beings, asks Robert Nozick, in *Anarchy, State and Utopia* (Basic Books, Inc.: New York, 1974), 45–7. Might not beings that are higher up think that we ought to be sacrificed for their sakes? Indeed, perhaps we should sacrifice each other for their sakes.

9. Marc Scott Zicree, *The Twilight Zone Companion*, 2nd edition (Silman-James Press: Beverly Hills, CA, 1989), describes the punch line of this episode, "It's a cookbook!" as "one of the most shocking punch lines of any episode," 236.

10. "Will the Real Martian Please Stand Up?" written by Rod Serling, directed by Buck Houghton, first aired on May 26, 1961.

11. Serling's prologue makes the common denominator explicit: "Well, stay with us now, and you'll be part of an investigating team whose mission is not to find that proverbial needle, no their task is even harder. They've got to find a Martian in a diner, and in just a moment, you'll search with them, because you've landed in the Twilight Zone."

12. Douglas Heyes, director of the episode, quoted in Zicree (1989), 146.

13. Zicree (1989), 147.

14. Heyes, director of the episode, quoted in Zicree (1989), 146.

15. Heyes, director of the episode, quoted in Zicree (1989), 148.

16. Film noir adapts "old expressionist techniques to the new desire for realism": "Film noir demonstrates a style in its purest form, a style that

viewers then and now perceived without the need for any superimposed indicators." Silver & Ursini (2003), 2–4. Film noir "translates both character emotion and narrative concepts into a pattern of visual usage"; and the basic emotion of the noir character is alienation: "The assailant is not a person but an unseen force. The pain is more often mental than physical, the plunge into spiritual darkness," Alain Silverman & Elizabeth Ward, *Film Noir: An Encyclopedic Reference to the American Style* (Overlook Press: Woodstock, NY, 1992, orig. pub. 1979), 4, 5.

17. I would like to thank Jeff Roland for serving as a consultant in epistemology, Eric Mack, and Lester Hunt, without whose suggestions, this chapter would lack a conclusion.

5

WHERE IS THE TWILIGHT ZONE?

―――

RICHARD HANLEY

You're looking at a tableau of reality, things of substance, of physical material: a desk, a window, a light. These things exist and have dimension. Now, this is Arthur Curtis, age thirty-six, who is also real. He has flesh and blood, muscle and mind. But in just a moment we will see how thin a line separates that which we assume to be real with that manufactured inside of a mind.

Rod Serling, "A World of Difference"

As a metaphysician, one of my favorite boundaries is that between the real and the fictional, and *The Twilight Zone* seems rather fond of it, too. Surprising things happen, apparently, when the imagination is applied. Mannequins and dolls come to life. Fictional characters appear and interact with their authors. An actor becomes his character. In "The Sixteen Millimeter Shrine," a movie star disappears into the world of her own movies. Where do the fictional characters come from, and where does the movie star Barbara Jean Trenton, go to? The Twilight Zone!

"Zone" is a spatial term, but if you say a ballplayer is "in the zone," the expression is figurative, referring roughly to their state of mind. We regularly employ spatial metaphors for this purpose – "in a bad place," "down," "in the back of the mind," and so on. Likewise, if someone were to say you're in the Twilight Zone, the expression is figurative. Presumably, they would mean that you're off with the fairies, out to lunch.

So perhaps when Rod Serling speaks of the Twilight Zone in spatial terms like "area," and "plane," he's also speaking figuratively. But let's at least ask, what if someone were to claim that the Twilight Zone is literally a place, or at least that the Twilight Zone literally is somewhere? Must they be wrong? I'm going to present some different ways in which they can be right. This will take us on a journey to another dimension, a dimension not only of sight and sound but of mind; a journey into a wondrous land whose boundaries are that of the imagination, and in turn will shed light on how we should understand the *Twilight Zone* storylines mentioned above.

WAY 1: FICTIONAL TRUTH

A good start is to consider whether or not it's true according to the fiction that is the television series, *The Twilight Zone*, that the Twilight Zone is a place. Then much of the time, we can just omit the explicit "according to *The Twilight Zone*" prefix, as when we say that Sherlock Holmes is a detective, that Barbara Jean Trenton is an actress, or that hobbits have hairy feet.

Now some object to calling this *truth*. One objection is on ordinary language grounds. "Nah-ah . . . It's *fictional*, and *not* true, that Holmes is a detective." Fair enough. We do speak this way. But what we mean is that it's fictional, and not non-fictional, that (unprefixed) Holmes is a detective. (Whereas it's fictional, *and* non-fictional, that – unprefixed – London is in England.) If something is fictional, then it's true that it's fictional, and that's all I need. It's a matter of stating facts *about the story*.

(Compare it with saying Fred believes in fairies. Unprefixed, *fairies exist* is false, but that doesn't stop us saying truly that Fred believes in them. We might express this as "In the world of Fred's beliefs, fairies exist," or "It's true according to Fred that fairies exist.")

A second objection is on theoretical grounds. According to one philosophical view, if there is no such thing as Holmes or the Twilight Zone, then no proposition can be expressed using such empty names or titles.[1] Now this isn't a problem if you believe in Holmes and other fictional objects (see the other "Ways" below for details). But it isn't a problem anyway. If you think "Holmes" is an empty name you can either: hold that you can still use it in a proposition (by regarding the name as a disguised definite description – say, "London's greatest *fin-de-siècle* detective" – or by taking a more relaxed view about propositions, permitting them to contain empty names); or else state the propositions we intuitively accept by merely *mentioning*, rather than *using*, the name.[2]

With those objections out of the way, is it fictional that the Twilight Zone is somewhere? This question is pretty hard to answer without some theory. For one thing, although fiction appreciators do well on determining large numbers of fictional truths, intuitions are much less reliable when dealing with relatively unusual plotlines. I suggest we return to this question at the end, after we've considered ways in which the Twilight Zone might *really* be somewhere.

WAY 2: OTHER DIMENSIONS

Obscure metaphysical explanation to cover a phenomenon, reasons dredged out of the shadows to explain away that which cannot be explained. Call it parallel planes or just insanity. Whatever it is, you find it in the Twilight Zone.

Rod Serling, "Mirror Image"

Missing: one frightened little girl. Name: Bettina Miller. Description: six years of age, average height and build, light brown hair, quite pretty. Last seen being tucked in bed by her mother a few hours ago. Last heard – aye, there's the rub, as Hamlet put it. For Bettina Miller can be heard quite clearly, despite the rather curious fact that she can't be seen at all. Present location? Let's say for the moment – in the Twilight Zone . . . The other half where? The fourth dimension? The fifth? Perhaps. They never found the answer. Despite a battery of research physicists equipped with every device known to man, electronic and otherwise, no result was ever achieved, except perhaps a little more respect for and uncertainty about the mechanisms of the Twilight Zone.

Rod Serling, "Little Girl Lost"

This might seem too obvious to state. But if our world – the actual world – contains a Twilight Zone, then isn't it really somewhere? Well, maybe. Suppose that the main plot point of "The Parallel" – where astronaut Robert

Gaines goes into orbit and finds himself in a "parallel world," a lot like his own familiar one, but also different – is *actually* true. Then there's at least one other world *just as real* as our familiar one, with its own astronaut Robert Gaines who goes into orbit, and perhaps with its own version of *you*.

But how might there be an actual place like this, like another world? Presumably it's not in what we *normally* call the universe, so perhaps it's (at least partly) in another dimension, literally – after all, Serling uses the word "dimension" *a lot* in his references to the Twilight Zone. Suppose the world we occupy contains more than the familiar three spatial dimensions we call length, breadth, and height. Suppose, say, that there is a fourth spatial dimension at right angles to the other three.

Then we would be in a situation analogous to that of the inhabitants of Edwin Abbott's *Flatland*. They are two-dimensional and perceive only two dimensionally, so they can identify each other as circles, or squares, and so on. Their world is in fact three-dimensional, but if a sphere or a cube passed through Flatland, they wouldn't recognize it as anything other than two-dimensional. If they regard it as a continuing object at all, they would perceive it as a two-dimensional thing growing or shrinking, or otherwise changing size or shape, before disappearing altogether.

And if you said to the inhabitants of Flatland, "imagine a third spatial dimension at right angles to the other two," they doubtless would at first blush say that it was impossible, since there wasn't any*where* for it to be. But just because they don't perceive it, doesn't mean it isn't there. And just because *we* don't perceive a fourth, doesn't mean *it* isn't there, either. (Nor does it mean it is there, of course.)

What would a four-dimensional object look like to us, and how would this differ from how it really is?[3] Again, think how Flatlanders might conceptualize a three-dimensional object, such as a cube. There are two basic ways to represent a cube in two dimensions: *unfolded*, and *in perspective*. In the unfolded representation in Figure 5.1 below, the six squares have their proper size and shape, but much topological information (about how the squares are connected to each other) is lost. In a perspective representation such as that in Figure 5.2, topology is preserved, and all six squares appear, but at most two have their actual size and shape – the other four are skewed. The perspective in Figure 5.3 conveys more of what a cube-shaped object looks like to us, but a lot of information is missing, two-dimensionally speaking – notice that only three squares put in an appearance, and only one is true. (By the by, there is nothing privileged about perspectives that have *true* squares – imaginatively rotate one of the cubes outside the plane of the page, and you will soon get a perfectly good perspective with no true squares at all. The crucial difference between the two perspectives is hard for us 3-D perceivers to appreciate. Figure 5.2 is a genuine 2-D perspective, preserving all the topology of the cube (that's why it is a famous illusion – the Necker cube – it has no stable 3-D interpretation, since there are two equally good ways of "seeing" a cube in it), whereas Figure 5.3 is what we might call a 3-D perspective. Without the ability to perceive in 3-D, it's not a perspective of a *cube* at all. Flatlanders would perceive it as two different colored parallelograms abutting a square. So, in order to get a 3-D perspective, you have to eliminate much of the topological information in a genuine 2-D perspective.

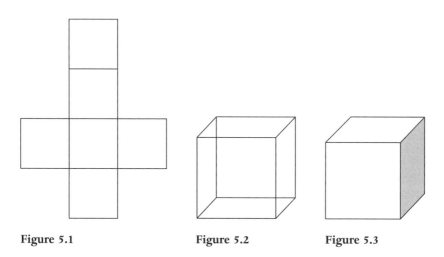

Figure 5.1   Figure 5.2   Figure 5.3

Now consider the four-dimensional object that is a *tesseract*, or *hypercube*. Let's build it conceptually first. Begin with a point, and "stretch" it into a spatial dimension a distance ℓ, forming a line segment. Then extend the line segment distance ℓ into a second spatial dimension at right angles to the first, forming a square. (Notice that this forms three other line segments of length ℓ.) Then extend the square distance ℓ into a third dimension to form a cube. (Forming five other squares of sides ℓ.) Then extend the cube distance ℓ into a fourth dimension to form a tesseract. To do this we form seven other cubes of ℓ–sided squares. Just as a cube is six squares folded together, a tesseract is eight cubes folded together. Below is a two-dimensional, solid perspective representation of a tesseract unfolded into three dimensions. It preserves neither the size and shape of the eight cubes (though it does accurately represent them as having the same size and shape), and most of the topology is lost. Consider the unfolded cube above again. One of the squares (the second from the bottom) has much of its topology preserved, and this makes it appear special. But this is just an artifact of the unfolding – in a cube, *every* square abuts another square on each of its four sides. Similarly, in the unfolded tesseract below, one cube is shown abutting six others, but it is not special. In a tesseract, each of the cubes abuts another cube on each of its six sides.

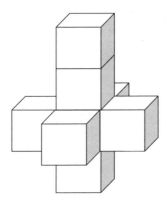

Figure 5.4

Can we do better than the above representation? You bet. We can represent in three dimensions rather than two. The proper "unfolded tesseract" analogue of the unfolded cube (Figure 5.2) is not Figure 5.4, but rather is the *three*-dimensional object Figure 5.4 is a mere representation of. I can't make one on the page, but you can easily build one by assembling eight cubes, stacking four on top of one another, and gluing the other four to the second cube from the bottom of the stack. (Remember, just as only one of the squares in Figure 5.1 has other squares on all four sides, only one of the cubes in your handiwork will have other cubes stuck to it on all six sides.) We could also construct three-dimensional perspectives analogous to Figure 5.2 above, which is "made" by taking two equal squares, offsetting them without rotation, and connecting the corresponding vertices, "filling in" the remaining four squares, but in skewed perspective. To make a similar perspective on a tesseract, build two equal cubes and offset them without rotation (so that two vertices – one from each cube – overlap), and connect the corresponding vertices. (Exercise: find the six skewed cubes that you thereby "fill in.") And analogous to Figure 5.2, this perspective will be a genuine 3-D perspective, with no privileged interpretation. Here's another fun 3-D one. Build a large cube, and a small cube, put the small one inside the large one without rotation, and connect the corresponding vertices with equidistant line segments. (Exercise: find the six skewed cubes – they will appear as square pyramids with their tops chopped off.) What's weird is that in this one, the two "true" cubes appear to be different sizes, but they are not! Finally, note that (not being 4-D perceivers), we cannot construct, in three dimensions, a recognizable 4-D perspective of a tesseract (the analogue of Figure 5.3).

Here's how a fourth spatial dimension can explain a plot like "Little Girl Lost." Return to Flatland for a moment, and suppose that some clever architect[4] has built a six-roomed house that looks like Figure 5.1. Unfortunately, the world is really 3-D, and an earthquake causes the house to *fold up* into a cube, so that now, only *one* face of the cube is *in* Flatland (picture the cube as resting on the plane that is Flatland, so that exactly one of the rooms is still in it). Our architect now enters the house. He will be visible to his neighbors as long as he remains in that particular room, but as soon as he enters another room, he will *disappear* from view! (He might re-enter from another room, in which case he will appear to have teletransported.) But perhaps, thanks to the greater refraction of sound waves, he might still be heard.

(Add to this the fact that the objects in our world are opaque, and you get weirder possibilities still. If there are four-dimensional *objects*, then all we see of them is the analogue of Figure 5.3. That is, we see what we *think* are complete 3-D objects, but in fact they are hopelessly skewed, *and* topologically incomplete, perspectives on something much bigger!)

Now, once you have conceptualized a tesseract, you can conceptualize a *hypertesseract*, the five-dimensional object you get by extending our tesseract distance 1 into a *fifth* spatial dimension at right angles to the other four. If you've noticed the arithmetic progression already, you'll see that a hypertesseract is ten tesseracts folded up into the fifth dimension, each abutting eight of the others. (You can keep going to six dimensions, and seven, and so on . . .)

So is Rod Serling speaking of *five* spatial dimensions in this opening narration?

There is a fifth dimension beyond that which is known to man. It is a dimension as vast as space and as timeless as infinity. It is the middle ground between light and shadow, between science and superstition, and it lies between the pit of man's fears, and the summit of his knowledge. This is the dimension of imagination. It is an area which we call . . . THE TWILIGHT ZONE.

Maybe not. We have been speaking of a *hypothetical* fourth dimension, but perhaps *time* is enough like space that it is an *actual* fourth dimension. (Perhaps *The Twilight Zone* endorses this view of our world, since it includes time travel stories, and arguably, time travel requires spatialized time.) Then our familiar world is already a four-dimensional one, and in imagining a tesseract we have been imagining a *fifth* dimension, by imagining four spatial dimensions and one temporal one.

Then again, if we're starting from three spatial dimensions and one temporal one, perhaps the extra, fifth dimension is not spatial but temporal. Then time (so to speak) sweeps through a plane rather than a line. Call the extra temporal dimension *hypertime*. Then each event is located in hypertime as well as time (just as location in a plane requires two spatial coordinates), and perhaps this accounts for the apparent "past-changing" storylines in *The Twilight Zone*, such as "Back There," "Of Late I Think of Cliffordville," and "Walking Distance."[5]

Hmmm. . . . You might think that adding another *temporal* dimension doesn't add a *place* where we might say the Twilight Zone is. But really it does. The point is the same whether or not the fifth dimension is spatial. Granting that we are 4-D perceivers (3 spatial + 1 temporal), then we have only a skewed 4-D perspective on the 5-D whole (which may contain a Twilight Zone, and a Barbara Trenton). Putting it bluntly, we perceive but one 4-D plenum amongst the many that actually exist, and this is true no matter what the nature of the fifth dimension. Perhaps in the hypertime case this is easier to understand if we say *world* instead of "4-D plenum." In "The Parallel," for instance, *our* world is one "3+1" plenum, and the one that Robert Gaines crosses over into is another. We benighted 4-D perceivers *think* that a world is a complete space-time, but of course we have only a hopelessly skewed and topologically incomplete perspective on the 5-D truth! Perhaps the Twilight Zone just is the fact of this extra temporal dimension, since our access to it (absent time travel, and other exotica) is, after all, imagination.

INTERLUDE: *COULD* THERE HAVE BEEN A TWILIGHT ZONE?

To the wishes that come true, to the strange, mystic strength of the human animal, who can take a wishful dream and give it a dimension of its own. To Barbara Jean Trenton, movie queen of another era, who has changed the blank tomb of an empty projection screen into a private world. It can happen – in the Twilight Zone.

Rod Serling, "The Sixteen Millimeter Shrine"

The modus operandi for the departure from life is usually a pine box of such and such dimensions, and this is the ultimate in reality. But there are other ways for a man to exit from life. Take the case of Arthur Curtis, age thirty-six. His departure was along a highway with an exit sign that reads: "This way to escape." Arthur Curtis, en route to . . . the Twilight Zone.

Rod Serling, "A World of Difference"

In "The Sixteen Millimeter Shrine," "A World of Difference," and "A World of His Own," characters interact with fictions in (to put it mildly) an unusual way. Barbara Trenton enters the world of her own movies, and Arthur Curtis enters the world of his own fantasy by apparently becoming the character he portrays. Playwright Gregory West brings persons into existence by describing them into a dictation machine, and eliminates them completely by burning the tape.

Imagine a somewhat analogous occurrence in our world. Suppose that, instead of somehow disappearing *into* the movie world, Barbara Trenton instead stepped *out of* the movie screen, into *our* world! Could this happen? Well, not on any respectable metaphysical view that I know of.

(In philosophy, you nearly always have to qualify what you say, and so it is here. I'm assuming that it's just a movie screen, and not an inter-dimensional-transporter or some such. But it isn't clear exactly how to interpret "The Sixteen Millimeter Shrine." The scene we see on the movie screen is not of one of Barbara Trenton's movies, but rather of the interior of her own house, as if she's having all her old movie co-actors, in character, over for a party. And her servant says, "She's here, but . . . she's not here like you and I are." So maybe she's slipped into another dimension, after all, and not into any mere fiction.)

What is merely fictional can't *become* real, it seems. And that rules out merely fictional characters coming to life, as in "A World of His Own." But could an otherwise coherent fictional story just *turn out* to have been true all along? Take a story like "The Silence," where Jamie Tennyson takes a bet from Archie Taylor that he can be silent for an entire year, for a reward of one million dollars. He has his vocal chords severed to ensure victory, but Taylor turns out to be broke. Bummer! Couldn't this have actually happened, names and the rest of the details unchanged? Saul Kripke has a famous argument to the surprising conclusion that, in fact, what is merely fictional and not true, *couldn't* have been true.[6]

Begin with some considerations about language. Whatever your name is, probably someone else has that name, too. So how does anyone manage to speak about *you* and no one else by using the name? Kripke (and most other philosophers) think that such reference succeeds by virtue of causal connections between utterances of the name and the individual named. Folks who know you have causally grounded your name in *you*, and so can refer to you even when you're not around. And folks who have never met you can also refer to you, if they've had appropriate encounters – involving namings of you – with folks who have met you. You get the picture. This ability to refer by name is like a contagious disease, spreading quickly on linguistic contact.

Now apply this to the name "Jamie Tennyson." If Rod Serling just made this name up, then it is not *grounded* in any actual person. So it doesn't refer to any of the actual Jamie Tennysons. Does it refer instead to a non-actual Jamie Tennyson? Not if there's no such thing! So although there are possibilities involving persons named "Jamie Tennyson" who have lives like that described in the story, "The Silence" is not *about* any one of those persons.

Does that mean there couldn't have been a Twilight Zone? This is a bit trickier. It depends, for Kripke, on whether "the Twilight Zone" is a proper name like "the United States," or a definite descriptive title like "the President of the United States in 2008." While George W. Bush was the one and only President in 2008, it was possible for someone else to have been the one and only. But it is not possible for some other nation, no matter what it is called, to be the United States. Now, some descriptive titles have no actual denotation – for instance, "the Prime Minister of the United States in 2008." But they *could have* had a denotation. So even if there is no actual Twilight Zone, if this is a descriptive title, there could have been one (given that it's at least a coherent notion).

What about the *kinds* of things that turn up in Twilight Zone episodes? For instance, in "To Serve Man," there is a malevolent alien race, the Kanamit. Serling tells us they are a little over nine feet tall, and weigh "in the neighborhood of three hundred and fifty pounds." They are also depicted visually, with oddly shaped skulls. Now suppose that tomorrow an alien race visits earth, whose members exactly fit the description and depiction of the Kanamit, who are called "the Kanamit," and so on. Is "To Serve Man" *about* tomorrow's visitors? Not if Serling just made the story up. According to Kripke, the way we fix reference to natural kinds such as species is by means of salient features which need not be essential features. So, for instance, we fix reference to tigers by descriptions including stripes. But there could be a tiger without stripes. When we fix reference to an actual species, we (somehow) are picking out the essence of the kind, even if we don't know what that essence is. Okay, back to the Kanamit. For Serling's uses of the name "Kanamit" to have referred to tomorrow's visitors, they must have been causally grounded in at least some members of the species. But they weren't – Serling just made the "species" up. So even in the astonishing coincidence we are imagining, Serling was *not* referring to the actual Kanamit.

Suppose there are no actual Kanamit at all (surely the truth). Then isn't it *possible* for them to have existed? Here Kripke again says No. There could have been a kind matching the depiction, all right – indeed, there are many such possible kinds, with different essences – but none of them are *named* by our term "Kanamit."

Kripke's view is tempting in this sort of case. But his own example, that of the *unicorn*, seems less convincing (indeed, *he* says it convinces no one). The basic argument is the same: given that someone just *made up* the fiction of unicorns, then no actual species, and no merely possible species, is named by "unicorn." Kripke says that even if we find the fossil bones of a horse-like creature with a single horn, we would not have discovered a unicorn. But I have my doubts about this argument. What would we have more reason to believe in such a case: on the one hand, that it is a mere coincidence, or on the other, that "unicorn" *wasn't* just made up, but was after all grounded in some now extinct species?

Even given Kripke's view, there is still a way to "get lucky," so to speak, and have an invented fictional name pick out a natural kind. All that is required is that one describes the *essence* of an actual natural kind that is unknown at the time of invention. Suppose I write a story that includes the scientific discovery of "Kripkenite," described only as the element with atomic number 111. If such an element exists, then it seems that my name "Kripkenite" indeed refers to it.

Such a strategy is more difficult in the case of an individual such as a human person. Common intuition regards genetic near-identity as necessary, for instance, and it seems unlikely that an author could describe an unknown actual person's genetic make-up in sufficient detail to pick them out from the crowd. And if the Twilight Zone is not described fully enough for Kripke's taste, then if the Twilight Zone is possible, Kripke must be wrong. I'll return to this issue in my conclusion.

WAY 3: REAL NON-EXISTENCE

The nineteenth-century German philosopher Alexius Meinong famously distinguished being from existence.[7] To cut a long story short, he postulated that there are non-existent things in addition to the existent ones. Barbara Trenton doesn't exist, all right, but for Meinong this means that she is to be found instead amongst the non-existents. And unlike existent persons she is *incomplete*. There are properties she neither has nor lacks, like the property of being a Republican, or having type O blood.

But she does have the property of being spatially located. And if she is in the Twilight Zone, then the Twilight Zone presumably also is incomplete, and also spatially located. This would be so even if the Twilight Zone is an impossible thing, because Meinongians think there are impossible non-existents in addition to the possible ones.

The problem of incompleteness delivers another reason why "A World of His Own" couldn't happen. Gregory West gives only the most superficial description of "Mrs. Mary West," yet a *complete* individual appears. (Maybe the dictation machine uses the *Jurassic Park* technique for reconstructing dinosaur DNA: filling in the gaps from some standard template?)

WAY 4: MODAL REALISM

There are more things in heaven and earth than is dreamt of in your philosophy, Horatio.

Hamlet, quoted in *"The Last Flight"*

If we gave the part of Horatio to Meinong, his reply might be "Wanna bet? I've got it all." But the eminent twentieth-century philosopher David Lewis goes much further, in one way at least. In order to account for the intuitive truth of *modal* statements (statements about possibility or necessity), Lewis postulates a plurality of worlds distinct from the actual world, and ontologically on a par with the actual world.[8] (That is, they are no less real than the actual world, and in any respect in which some other world is a lesser one than ours, others still will be greater than ours. Bottom line – there's nothing objectively *special* about the actual world.) Big as the actual world might be – a 5-D plenum, say – it is but a tiny part of all that exists. Indeed, the only thing that makes it *actual* is that it's the world we occupy. To occupants of another world, theirs is actual, and ours is not.

Lewis's view, known as *modal realism*, is analogous to the most common spatializing view of time, according to which all times exist, and the present time – now – is not objectively special. (And analogous in turn to how we ordinarily think that all spatial locations exist, and the present location – here – is not objectively special.) All the worlds are complete, and all their inhabitants are complete. So in one sense, Lewis has less in his ontology (his list of what there is) than Meinong. But in another way, he has more. Lewis thinks our world is not likely amongst the most abundant, so there must be "alien" properties and individuals present in other worlds. These things really aren't in heaven or earth, yet Lewis dreams of them.

So, if Lewis is correct, there really is a non-actual Barbara Trenton, and a non-actual Twilight Zone. (More precisely, there are lots of them, since there are many worlds of which it can truly be said that they contain a Barbara Trenton, or a Twilight Zone.) At least, this is so if the description of the Zone is coherent, since Lewis does not believe in impossible worlds where contradictions are true.

And every world, no matter how big, no matter how many dimensions it has, is a discrete space–time region. So given that the Twilight Zone is a coherent notion, there are plenty of places it is. And given that there is no actual Twilight Zone, our only access to it is through (coherent) imagination, since the many worlds are not causally related to each other. This has the consequence that a story like "A World of His Own," in which an author interacts with his own fictional creations, is incoherent. Gregory West can't have it both ways. Either he actually creates a flesh-and-blood Mary, in which case she *isn't* merely fictional, or else he actually "creates" (by describing) a merely fictional Mary, in which case she isn't *actual*.

The same goes for West himself, who is after all a fictional character, when he in turn interacts with Rod Serling, who is actual, making Serling disappear! Of course the mind-twister here is that if Serling himself is merely fictional, then perhaps we all are. But rest easy; your very existence in the actual world entails that you are not merely fictional.

WAY 5: ABSTRACT FICTIONAL REALISM

Let's distinguish fictional characters from the non-fictional characters who put in fictional appearances. Intuitively we think of the former as *created* by authors. But if Barbara Trenton is in some other 4-D part of a 5-D actuality, or is a Meinongian nonexistent, or is in one or more of Lewis's plurality of worlds, then she is not created by the author at all. The author's imaginative act seems more one of *discovery*. But there is a view of fictional characters according to which they are literally created by imaginative acts.

In this respect they are like the stories of fiction themselves. In writing a story the author creates something in the actual world, and so it is with fictional characters. There actually is a Barbara Trenton, which is just to say the actual world includes Barbara Trenton. But she (or more properly, *it*) is not a flesh and blood creature. She is an *abstract* thing, as is the Twilight Zone.

Amie Thomassen has the most worked out version of this view.[9] So let's put our question to her – is the Twilight Zone literally somewhere in the actual world? Her answer is an emphatic No:

> . . . fictional characters lack a spatiotemporal location and thus are abstract in that sense . . . .
>
> Apart from the locations they are ascribed [i.e. "in the story"], the only other obvious candidate for the spatiotemporal location of a fictional character is to say that it is "in" the literary work and so is wherever that work is. But where are literary works? Only a copy of the literary work, not the work itself, is in a particular location . . . although it may appear in various token copies, it cannot be identified with any of them because it may survive the destruction of any copy, provided there are more. Nor can it be classified as a scattered object present where all of its copies are, because the work itself does not undergo any change in size, weight, or location if some of its copies are destroyed or moved.
>
> It would thus be wrong to locate fictional characters where copies of the literary works in which they appear are located, recited, or performed.[10]

Perhaps it would be wrong, but this argument doesn't show it. There is an important possibility for locating literary works that Thomassen doesn't account for. I grant that the work can survive the destruction of any copy (provided there are more). I grant further that the work is not identical with any aggregate of its copies (though I can imagine a reasonable person simply denying the intuitions driving Thomassen's argument here).

The alternative view understands "abstract" as lacking specificity in some way, and is closely connected with the notion of mentally "abstracting away" from the concrete by leaving out certain details. Without defending it, I'll simply state the conception: an abstract individual lacks some of the properties of the space–time region it occupies. A concrete individual lacks none of them. On this conception, it is up for grabs what sort of an abstract entity a literary work is. For instance, Thomassen's intuitions may show that the work does not plausibly have size or weight. (Or color, or smell, and so on.)

On this alternative view, if fictional characters are actual abstract individuals, they can after all be where their containing stories are. And this provides a coherent way in which an author can actually interact with a character. Since Thomassen grants that causal relations are only possible in the presence of spatiotemporal relations, her view strictly rules out causal interaction between author and character (so it looks less like literal creation, after all). Of course, on neither view can one, merely by speaking into a dictation machine, bring a flesh and blood Mrs. Gregory West (Victoria *or* Mary) into existence!

CONCLUSION

Can we make sense of "A World of His Own"? If Gregory West's dictation machine (and for that matter, Barbara Trenton's movie screen) is in fact a portal to another dimension, then it is after all possible for his "creations" to be flesh and blood. So extra dimensions of the sort discussed in Way 2 seem the best hope. And extra dimensions overall probably give the best account of all that happens in *The Twilight Zone*, with its common theme of causal interaction between the everyday world of our experience and the Twilight Zone. On balance then, I judge that it is indeed fictional that the Twilight Zone really is somewhere – it is, or is in, another spatiotemporal dimension.

And the bonus is that if my diagnosis is correct, then a Kripke-style argument fails to show that the Twilight Zone isn't possible. Even if there is no actual Twilight Zone – if it is merely fictional – it is well enough described that we can identify merely possible situations in which it would have existed.

NOTES

1. One proponent of this view is Kendall Walton, *Mimesis as Make-Believe: On the Foundations of the Representational Arts* (Cambridge, MA: Harvard University Press, 1990).

2. This last is Walton's own solution. W. V. O Quine takes the first option in "On What There Is," *The Review of Metaphysics* 2, 21–8, 1948. The more relaxed view about propositions is taken by Fred Adams, Gary Fuller, and Robert Stecker in "The Semantics of Fictional Names," *Pacific Philosophical Quarterly* 78 (2), 128–48, 1997.

3. One of the interesting things about our world is that space isn't Euclidean – it's *curved*. I'll ignore this complication in what follows, and assume no curvature.

4. The Flatland counterpart of Robert Heinlein's architect in "And He Built a Crooked House," which would have made a *great Twilight Zone* episode.

5. Most time travel episodes of *The Twilight Zone* do not involve changing the past, and are coherent given a single time dimension – for instance, "The Last Flight," "No Time Like the Past," "Spur of the Moment," "The Odyssey of Flight 33," and "The 7th Is Made Up of Phantoms."

6. Saul Kripke, *Naming and Necessity* (Cambridge, MA: Harvard University Press, 1980).

7. Alexius Meinong, "On the Theory of Objects," in Roderick Chisholm (ed.), *Realism and the Background of Phenomenology* (Glencoe, Ill.: Free Press, 76–117, 1960).

8. David Lewis, *On the Plurality of Worlds* (Oxford: Blackwell, 1986).

9. *Fiction and Metaphysics* (Cambridge: Cambridge University Press, 1999).

10. Ibid., pp. 36–7.

6

EXISTENTIALISM AND
SEARCHING FOR AN EXIT

———

SUSAN L. FEAGIN

The title of "Five Characters in Search of an Exit" alludes to two of the most significant plays of the twentieth century, Luigi Pirandello's "Six Characters in Search of an Author," first produced in 1921, and Jean-Paul Sartre's best-known play, "No Exit," first produced in 1944.[1] "Five Characters" inherits at least two important themes from Pirandello: first, the idea that what is fictional from one point of view is real from another, and, second, the challenge to personhood and a sense of self that can arise when characters are identified in terms of roles rather than as individuals with proper names. "Five Characters" inherits additional themes from Sartre: that we are confined to circumstances we have not chosen and do not understand, that we are compelled to search for knowledge, both of ourselves and of the world, that necessarily eludes us, and that the need to act in the absence of sufficiently good reasons to believe our actions will be successful makes life absurd.

My ultimate aim in this chapter is to show that "Five Characters in Search of an Exit" expresses an existentialist philosophical sensibility, in particular, that of Jean-Paul Sartre's "No Exit" and of his major philosophical work, *Being and Nothingness: An Essay in Phenomenological Ontology*.

Sartre's existentialist views contrast with the rationalist confidence of René Descartes, who claimed centrally that one can know with absolute certainty that one exists. I begin with a summary of those components of the Cartesian position that are the target of philosophical concern in two episodes of *The Twilight Zone*, "Five Characters" and "In His Image."[2] I then describe various existentialist aspects of "Five Characters," beginning with its depiction of "the human condition," in Section II, and continuing in Section III with questions about personal identity and knowledge of oneself, bringing out their particular existential character by comparing their treatment with similar themes as they are developed in some other episodes, including "A Game of Pool"[3] and "The Shelter."[4]

It may appear that the fit between existentialism and "Five Characters" is not perfect, particularly with respect to the benign way that the characters relate to one another. In "No Exit," for example, Garcin famously remarks that "hell is – other people."[5] In Section IV, I argue that the benign and even helpful attitudes that the five characters have towards one another only reinforce, rather than undermine, the episode's existentialist sensibility. To help make the case, I contrast "Five Characters" with "In His Image," which deals with some of the same basic questions about personal identity, but in which the non-existential possibility of hope is real.

I. KNOWING ONESELF:
THE CARTESIAN PROJECT

Both Sartre and Descartes held that, in the very act of questioning whether one exists, one manifests something important about the nature of the being who is doing the questioning. Nevertheless, they reached very different conclusions about what that is. According to Descartes, if I question whether I exist, then I am thinking, and in order to think I must exist. Thus, he arrives at one of the most famous (though, ironically, often misunderstood) pronouncements in the entire history of philosophy: *Cogito ergo sum*, or, I think, therefore, I am. It is essential to the logic of the Cogito that one does not merely parrot the words. One must engage in the reasoning process oneself and understand its rationale: If I try to doubt I exist, I am thinking, and as long as I am thinking, I must exist. Descartes is mindful of exactly what it is that the Cogito (allegedly) proves: only one's own existence, and only at the time when one consciously engages in the reasoning process. Though the scope of the claim is small, extending only to one's own existence and only for the moment when one consciously comprehends the Cogito's logic, the knowledge it provides is allegedly absolute. And absolute certainty – something about which there is no conceivable possibility that one might be wrong, no matter how trivial the knowledge claim might be – is his goal. Even if nothing else is as I conceive or perceive it to be, and even if everything is just a dream, I still must exist in order to have that dream, and in order to conceive or perceive things the way I do.

Descartes reasoned further that if I know I exist simply through this process of thinking, then I must be a being whose essence or essential nature is to think. I am not identical with the series of thoughts, the stream of consciousness, or whatever goes through my mind; I am the one and only individual who *has* all those different thoughts at different points in time. Thus, he reasons, whatever it is that constitutes the individual must not change, even though the thoughts – the contents of consciousness – manifestly do. Something must remain the same that continues to be me, the same "me" who exists through a period of time. I am *the* thing that is conscious, *the* one and only thing that is thinking all those thoughts.

Descartes is important historically in large part for his method, especially as it is manifested in the Cogito, a systematic process of reasoning that, in principle, anyone can employ. Each of us has the power to reason without the mediation of *anyone* else, such as a religious figure, whether a pope or a Delphic oracle, and without being dependent on *anything* else, such as a sacred text or a sudden revelation.

Sartre takes the fact that one can question one's own existence as indicating something very different about the individual doing the questioning. I am a being who is able to question *endlessly* the nature and existence of myself and others.[6] My process of thinking yields results only in relation to the boundaries of my own context: my mental powers and my limitations, the character of my physical embodiment, my living in a particular cultural context and historical time, and my temporal finitude. Neither the questioning nor a logical process of reasoning can yield absolute knowledge, according to Sartre. My being-in-the-world and the limitations of my own "horizons," far from providing epistemic privilege, restrict my potential to know anything that is significant or meaningful in a broader sense. I cannot get outside of my own "world" to see what I am and what my situation is really like, to see if my own ideas match reality. "Five Characters," I propose, should be seen as a dramatic allegory of the Sartrean view of the human condition, one that simultaneously critiques Cartesian claims both to knowledge and about the nature of the self as an entity that exists, unchanged, through time.

II.   WHERE AM I? BEING IN THE WORLD

The oddity of the environment inhabited by the characters in "Five Characters" is striking from the beginning. The Major – as in Pirandello, the characters are identified by their social roles or professions, rather than by their names – is slumped against a wall. He wakes up and looks around, puzzled. As he begins to explore his surroundings, tapping on the metallic-sounding wall, squinting at a bright light above, he stumbles upon The Clown (portrayed incomparably by Murray Matheson, whose compelling performance makes the episode worth viewing all by itself). After some mildly amusing, upbeat banter initiated by The Clown, The Major begins to look distressed. "Problem?" The Clown inquires. "Problem, no; no, no problem," The Major replies, disingenuously, because we see clearly that he is vexed: "It's just that a couple of very important items seem to have eluded me, like *who I am*." As if he suspects he is the victim of some kind of hoax, The Major demands to know why The Clown is there: "Is there a circus around here somewhere?" The Clown laughs and with palpable irony agrees that there is, though clearly not thinking of a circus of the conventional kind. He repeats the key points of The Major's inference: "A clown, a circus; an officer, a war. That's logic, isn't it?" More stern than ironic, he adds, "But it doesn't figure a'tall, not at all." "Why not?" The Major inquires. "Because there is no circus. And there is no war. . . . You're just like the rest of us." On cue, the other three characters appear: The Dancer, The Tramp, and The Bagpipe Player.

The Major's anxiety escalates along with his questions: "Where are we? What are we? Who are we?" The others assure him that they have asked these questions many times before and that there are no answers. "One guess is as good as another," The Clown intones. But The Major is convinced that if he could get to the top of the container where that light is, he might get some answers; maybe then he could see where they are, and find a way for them all to get out. Following up on a suggestion by The Dancer, The Major convinces them all to help – even The Clown, who is at least temporarily willing to give up his pose of ironic detachment. Standing on each others' shoulders – a visual metaphor if ever there was one – The Major eventually reaches the top. But he uncontrollably topples over the edge, revealing to the audience – and notably not to himself or to the others – that he is not a person at all, but a toy. He *is* like the rest of them, in spite of the fact that only he is actively engaged in questioning the nature of his own existence: they are all toys. A child finds the doll lying face down in the snow and throws him back into the metal bin, where the four others are sprawled lifeless at the bottom, perhaps some day to wake up and carry out the entire anxiety-ridden but fruitless effort, over and over again.

M. Keith Booker, in his *Strange TV: Innovative Television Series from* The Twilight Zone *to* The X-Files, describes how several episodes of *The Twilight Zone*, including "Five Characters" and "In His Image," anticipate certain themes of postmodernism such as the ironic stance as a way of facing the impossibility of distinguishing fact from fiction, the absence of fixed values, and the endless possibilities for reinventing oneself.[7] The figure of The Clown is a particularly rich field for prefiguring these themes, with his mask-like make-up that flaunts his artificiality as a creature, his combination of seriousness and humor, and his malleability that enables him playfully to take on different roles. Nevertheless, his ironic detachment does not represent the stance of the episode as a whole, which is instead driven by The Major's unquenchable desire to keep searching despite the manifest futility of doing so. The characters are thrust into the world, not knowing where they came from, beset by chance and contingency, and required to make decisions without knowing enough about the context or probable effects to make logic and reason even relevant to the process of making a decision about what to do. Each of these themes – alienation from the world and one's environment, the poverty of logic and reason, and the limitations of one's own horizons – is a major component of the episode.

ALIENATION FROM THE WORLD

The characters move around at the bottom of a cylindrical container, devoid of furnishings, with a small bright disk overhead. As Booker observes, it could well be the setting for a Beckett play.[8] The stark lighting and camera placement throughout the episode accentuate the absurdity of the characters' situation; indeed, the apparent light source and the characters' shadows do not always cohere. What sounds like a large bell or gong rings occasionally, unpredictably, deafeningly, and shakes the container violently. The Dancer, with a sweetness that contrasts with the utter hopelessness of what she says, sums up the important features of their situation: "Each of us woke up one moment. Here we were in the darkness, nameless things with no memory – no knowledge of what went before, no understanding of what is now, no knowledge of what will be."

The five characters speculate about where they might be, producing a familiar range of Cartesian possibilities and others as well: they are characters in a dream, characters in each others' dreams, on another planet, on a spaceship to another planet, and, courtesy of The Major and with obvious reference to Sartre, in Hell itself. The Tramp proposes that this *is* the universe, at least for them, which echoes the conclusion reached by the characters in "No Exit." Though the other four characters appear to be resigned to this fact, having gone through all this questioning before, it is clearly not acceptable to The Major, whose conviction that there has to be a rational explanation for where they are and why they are there never wavers. And there is such an explanation, but it is not one that they are able to understand.[9]

THE INADEQUACY OF REASON

As the characters speculate about where they might be, we become aware of the fact that the power of human reason is no match for the power of human imagination. We are able to think beyond the superficial aspects of appearances, to imagine a wide range of possibilities, and are yet unable to determine whether even the farthest fetched speculations are true or false. Though there is simply no way to choose, rationally, from among the myriad possibilities, The Major persists with his questions. "You're wasting your time. You know that, don't you? You're an idiot," The Clown tells him. Even though he grants that The Major has asked "the best question of all" – How long will we be here? – "You're still an idiot," he intones, rolling onto his back and raising his leg to balance a silly-looking, useless little umbrella on his toes. After all, he's a clown, and clowns do silly things, at the same time, as in this case, accusing someone *else* of being an idiot. The character of The Clown draws on long literary and theatrical traditions that present the jester, the blind, and the insane – embodiments of what is not rational – as having more insight and wisdom than so-called rational persons. The difference is that The Clown knows he is being silly, whereas The Major cannot see that his questions are unanswerable.

The Major thinks the problem is that he simply doesn't have enough evidence, and so he persists in his efforts to reach the top of their "container."[10] The view from the top will provide a new perspective on things, but it is still a perspective, and hence no more valid for determining where they "really" are than the view from the bottom. When The Major finally reaches the top and moves to a new "horizon," so do we: we see that they are all toys. But this is revealed to the audience alone, not to them. It is simply a new predicament, one that was notably not among the possibilities they considered. The very idea is absurd, for toys cannot think or reason – though of course they do, just as do characters in a play, one of the strategic borrowings from Pirandello. The Major thinks, questions, reasons, chooses, and strives – but all for naught. The effort, the urgency, all the plans and hopes and schemes are pointless, except perhaps as a temporary diversion – the value of which depends on one's point of view as well. The Clown begrudgingly agrees to participate in the efforts to help The Major get to the top, clearly steering clear of any ultimate judgment on the point: "Observation: Things were far more simple before you arrived."

THE DOWNSIDE OF SUBJECTIVITY

After reaching the top, The Major is summarily and casually *thrown* back into that alien world, by a child no less, a visual pun on the existentialist view that we human beings are thrown into a world not of our choosing. A similar pun occurs elsewhere, for example, in "The Little People," which also employs a familiar *Twilight Zone* theme, i.e., that a shift in perspective can radically alter our sense of place in the universe, our value judgments and priorities, and our sense of what control we have over our lives. The fact that it is a child who does the throwing, a child who knows better who and what The Major is than The Major himself, deepens the critique of the Cartesian conviction that the first person perspective – the fact that *I* am doing the thinking – provides privileged access to the nature of one's own being. The first-person perspective, thought by Descartes to have such great potential – able to leap, in a single Cogito, over illusions produced by evil geniuses and dreams so vivid you would swear they are real – turns out to be an existential nightmare.

Each person has to find his or her own answers, so the questions and deliberations and anxieties that anyone goes through are of no benefit to anyone else. Simply to accept someone else's conclusions would show that one merely toyed with asking the questions without taking them seriously. That they should be taken seriously is endorsed by both Descartes and Sartre, a fact that creates a bond between them that contrasts with a postmodern sensibility. The bond is their shared view of the inappropriateness of making light of one's situation, which contrasts with the inability, according to the postmodernist, to do anything else. Descartes was not bothered by the need to rehearse the Cogito over and over again, as long as his goal of certainty would be achieved; he acknowledges the temporary, highly constricted claim that the Cogito makes. Sartre, in contrast, emphasizes the absurdity and futility of repeating the unending cycle that each person and others have undergone before. Thus, the renewed hope for an escape that The Major inspires among three of the other four characters (minus The Clown, who plays along, but has no hope) may seem like a good thing, but it just drives them to attempt the impossible, over and over again, which makes nonsense of whatever they might think is gained in the process.[11]

III.   WHO AM I? EXISTENCE PRECEDES ESSENCE

In Descartes' schema, an inference is required to move from *cogito ergo sum*, I think therefore I am, to *sum res cogitans*, I am the thing that thinks. Descartes sanctions the inference to the existence of a temporally extended being or entity that does the thinking and whose essence remains the same through time, but Sartre does not. According to Sartre, when one is conscious, one is always conscious *of* something; there is always a content to one's consciousness, but the content of one's consciousness is not and cannot ever be one's essential self.[12] As hard as one tries to get a glimpse of one's true nature or essence, one will always become conscious of some momentary or fleeting object of consciousness, not a temporally extended being that is conscious of whatever sensations, ideas, feelings, or desires that one feels at the moment. Where Descartes has "*I* think, therefore *I* am," Sartre has "existence precedes essence." I have no pre-ordained, unchanging essence to be discovered; I become who I am through what I do. Yet, I am never, not ever, identical with what I have already done, at least not as long as I am alive. As Sartre puts it, with a deliberate infringement of grammaticality: "I exist my freedom." I create myself in the choices I make, choices that can always be different from my previous choices and from any pattern of behavior that I have displayed in the past. As long as one is alive, one is always in the process of becoming, like it or not, not simply being who one is. With characteristic negativity, Sartre says that we are *condemned* to be free.

The six characters in Pirandello's play – The Father, The Daughter, and so on – are in search of an author. They have been thrown away by their previous author and are looking around for another, so they can appear in another play: they are searching for an entrance, one might say, rather than for an exit. They come upon several other characters in an actual play, whose identity is also established by their roles rather than by proper names, and who are decidedly inhospitable to these interlopers, whose existence threatens to usurp their own if they are taken into the fold. Much of "Six Characters" concerns how what from one perspective is a real, lived experience, from another is merely fictitious, and Booker's observations about Pirandello's anticipating the postmodern idea that the factual and the fictional are interchangeable are apt. In the postmodern comic strip "Calvin and Hobbes," for example, the child Calvin's stuffed tiger, Hobbes, converses and plays with Calvin when no one else is looking, but is a mere stuffed animal in the presence of adults. Something similar occurs in "Five Characters." The fact that the characters are toys does not prevent them from having a life when not observed by human beings, but when they are observed, they are incapable of engaging in any conscious activity at all.

As an allegory of the human condition, the existential problems faced by the five characters are more urgent, in a psychological sense, than the general metaphysical questions about whether the real is distinguishable from the fictional. "We're people," The Major protests, "We must have names." But they are *not* people – they just *think* they are. They are toys, whose identity is established not as individuals but as types. Like characters in plays, they have an essence, a fixed identity; people do not. People may take on various roles, such as that of teacher, or patriotic citizen, or father or mother, but to be a person is not simply to take on a role, or to find an identity and stick with it. Despite The Clown's attempts to defuse The Major's rising anxiety over his identity by reminding him that "you said you were a major," The Major knows at least that being "a major" does not provide a satisfactory answer to the question, "Who am I?"

The Major is a "very active chap," The Clown observes, with a little smile. The Major is impatient with the others' passivity and keeps telling them "I want to get out of here," as if that makes him more of a person, more authentic, than they are. There is a compulsiveness about him, as if he has to act the way he does – which, of course, he does: that is his role in the episode. But again, one's role does not constitute one's identity as a person. He is no more authentic than the others; he just thinks he is because they are not running around banging on walls, too.

Having a fixed role to play might be thought to alleviate one's existential anxieties about how to behave, but the choice to *be*, essentially and through time, a given sort of person arrives with its own burdens. In "A Game of Pool," Jesse Cardiff (Jack Klugman) claims to be the best pool player ever. He has dedicated his entire life to the game; he even sleeps in the pool room so he can practice at night when everyone else has gone. But it appears as though Cardiff can never actually prove that he is the best, because James Howard "Fats" Brown (Jonathan Winters) – acclaimed as the best pool player ever – is no longer alive. Despite his monomania, Cardiff, who has the rough edges of someone who grew up in impoverished circumstances, is somewhat sympathetic. When he discovered (notably, by chance) that he had a talent for pool, he realized that if he dedicated his life to it, he could conceivably end up being the best. It is not a life that many would choose – even Fats made time for other things. Cardiff, however, is given his chance: Fats returns from the dead to take up his challenge. When Cardiff wins, however, we discover where he went wrong. One can *become* the best pool player up to a given point in time, but one can never *be* the best pool player ever. There will always be another challenger, as there was for Fats, who had reached the point where he was frankly ready to give it up. "A Game of Pool" out-anguishes existentialism itself by denying that even when dead one has an essence.

There is also significance in the fact that the main character in "Five Characters" is a military man. Existentialism reached the peak of its influence as a philosophical theory in the 1950s and *The Twilight Zone* appeared when World War II and the Korean War were relatively recent memories. The Vietnam War also was heating up contemporaneously with the appearance of the series and provided the context for one of its episodes, "In Praise of Pip." Wartime provides an especially rich context for exploring whether there is such a thing as one "true character," since in war, the role of chance and quirks of fate are writ large and the stakes are high. The events in virtue of which one lives or dies defy reason, and hence undermine any sense that there is an ultimate meaning or significance to one's life or to the decisions we make, even when those decisions are made with great deliberation, anguish, and care.[13] War plunges people into situations where they are faced, in the most immediate way, with their own mortality, and survival typically has a lot less to do with reasoned choices than with luck. It is an environment where the answer to what The Clown describes as "the best question of all" – How long will we be here? – is dictated by happenstance, and even the illusion that one is able to control the meaning or significance of one's life is drained away.[14]

As a series, *The Twilight Zone* is replete with characters who break down under horrific stress and with those who rise to the occasion. We are continually asked to consider whether the normally kind and considerate person would revert to egotistical savagery under apocalyptic conditions, or whether one would succumb to the temptations of extraordinarily promising opportunities involving money or fame, at the risk of family and friends, relationships that are truly valuable: All of us might naturally wonder how we would act in extraordinary or extreme circumstances, and sometimes the "characters" whose questionable behavior is revealed turn out to be us, the viewers, whose erroneous assumptions about what we are viewing reveal the limitations of our own horizons.

The Cold War also makes notable appearances in *The Twilight Zone*. Hot wars have spatial locations and relatively recognizable boundaries; the Cold War represented a more pervasive and insidious threat, due to the capacity of "the bomb" to produce virtually total annihilation. If the explosion didn't kill you outright, the radiation would get you soon enough. Invasion from outer space, a much less plausible scenario, perhaps served to displace fears of deliberate thermonuclear obliteration at the hands of Cold War enemies, or accidentally by one's own. In any case, in the twentieth century and beyond, the multiple ways that one can imagine wholesale destruction of human life constitute contexts in which one lives with "extraordinary" circumstances every day, foregrounding the fact that we all live under sentence of death and must choose how to act without knowing when it will be carried out.

In "The Shelter," Dr. Stockton (Larry Gates) has built a bomb shelter and assembled the necessary provisions for himself and his family. His friends, who have kidded and chided him for what they view as misplaced industriousness, turn out to be "fair weather friends," opportunists who demand that he allows them into his shelter when it is announced over the television that a nuclear missile is headed their way. The neighbors know that the shelter contains only enough provisions to accommodate the members of Stockton's immediate family for a relatively short period of time, but in their panic they demand admittance anyway. When the bomb scare is revealed to be a false alarm, they are contrite and apologetic, but their *true* character has been revealed. Stockton explicitly refuses to accept the abnormality of the circumstances, a nuclear bomb scare, as an excuse for their irrational and bellicose behavior. "Fair weather friends" are not *real* friends at all, *whatever* the circumstances.

In many episodes of *The Twilight Zone*, the characters act according to type. Some are basically good people who are supposed to evoke our sympathies, and others are unsympathetic because deeply flawed. As has often been noted, characters that have desirable character traits, sometimes contrary to initial appearances, tend to be treated more generously than those that are selfish and malicious, who consequently suffer a variety of less enviable fates. On the face of it, this seems inconsistent with the existentialist position that one's identity is *not* fixed and that one "becomes" who one is through one's free choices, and I do think the non-existentialist reading is generally the intended one. However, it is interesting to note how often the virtuous characters are engaged in struggles to be better people and to do the right thing.[15] In these cases, they are characters of a sort who do struggle, who create their own opportunities, or at least recognize opportunities when they present themselves, and as such they often receive a second chance. Yet, though the "fighters" are, in general, rewarded, there are also numerous episodes where their struggles are clearly all for naught. In such cases, a cycle of events goes round and round along the lines of a Nietzschean eternal return, and the individual is powerless to change it. The fatalism implicit in such a world view is antithetical to a Sartrean existentialism, but it does not interfere with the "radical freedom" he claims is constitutive of human consciousness, the freedom *not* to be what one previously was. Nevertheless, it is not a part of the Sartrean view that, in exercising one's freedom, one will necessarily be able to change the course of events in the world in a fundamental way.

The Major at least thinks that he and the others are free to refuse to accept their current condition. He struggles, but it gets him nowhere. And even though the four other characters are benign, it is not enough to remove the existential character of their predicament: they remain alienated from their environment, not knowing who they are, how they got there, why they are there, what they are supposed to do, or how to escape. There is no exit. The existentialist credentials of "Five Characters" remain intact. It thus contrasts with "In His Image," which expresses a kind of existentialist sensibility in the way it depicts the contingency of life and the role of chance, but it also presents a decidedly non-existentialist basis for hope – a possible exit – for human beings who strive to overcome their loneliness and feelings of meaninglessness and alienation from the world and from other people.

IV. WHAT AM I?

At the beginning of "In His Image," Alan Talbot (George Grizzard) is waiting for the subway to take him to meet his fiancé, Jessica Connelly (Gail Kobe), when a strange mechanical noise drives him to recoil in pain. An old woman suddenly appears and tells him he doesn't look well, and that her husband looked just like that right before he died. He realizes she is a bit of a crank, and tries to be polite until the train arrives. But she won't give up. With a wild look in her eye, she pesters him about whether he reads The Good Book. Claiming that she has been "revelated," she gives him a pamphlet entitled "The Way to Salvation," after which the noise and excruciating pain begin again. He becomes enraged, throws her under the oncoming train, and then flees through a turnstile marked by two highly conspicuous "EXIT" signs. Arriving later at Jess's door, he playfully pretends to be a member of the Junior Woodchucks, asking for donations for some fanciful worthy cause. Jess enjoys his humor and has a quick wit herself. There is an unsettling problem, however: he is 45 minutes late and he has no idea why.

Since they have known each other for only four days, Alan is concerned that Jess does not know him well enough to agree to marry him. So they have decided to visit the small town of Coeurville, where he grew up and has lived all his life, but where his world now begins to unravel. He has been away in New York for only two weeks, but Coeurville has changed so much, it is as if 20 years have gone by. They head for the cemetery to look for his family plot, where "Talbots have been buried . . . for over fifty years," and find instead the graves of a Walter Ryder and his wife where those of his parents should be. As they drive off, the noise and pain return with a greater intensity than in the subway station; Alan barks at Jess to stop the car and he runs off, pleading with her to help him but then commanding her to go away because (wisely not disclosing this to her) he realizes he is again about to be overcome by a compulsion to violence, just as when he threw the Old Woman under the subway train. There are indeed things about Alan that Jess doesn't know (and that, at this point, Alan doesn't know) that would and should make her reluctant to marry him.

Jess drives off and as Alan stumbles to the street, a passing car grazes him, knocking him to the ground. He peels back the "skin" on his wounded wrist to find no blood but instead a bunch of wires and flashing lights. Back at his hotel, he looks up Walter Ryder's address in the phone book and finally meets his maker – literally, as well as metaphorically. Alan and Walter could be identical twins, but when Alan asks Walter, "Who am I?" Walter responds, "You're no one, Alan. No one at all." Walter created Alan "in his (own) image": not only do they look the same, but Walter installed chunks of his own memories, some of his talents and knowledge, "bits and pieces of myself," as he puts it, into his creation. "So now you're telling me that I'm you?" Alan asks incredulously. But something has gone wrong with Alan's inner workings. "Can I be treated?" he asks Walter. "'Repaired' you mean? I don't know." "But why not?" Alan inquires. Walter explains that chance played a large role in Alan's creation, so much so that he doesn't really know what made this effort as successful as it was, much less why there has been this malfunction.

Alan sees the writing on the wall. Knowing that he is doomed, he fishes a piece of paper out of his pocket and writes down Jess's name and address, urging Walter to go to her and pretend to be Alan, "so that, for the first time in [your] miserable life, [you can] be happy." Alan feels another murderous rage coming on (prompted by his discovery of "The Path to Salvation" in his pocket while searching for the paper), so he tells Walter to get out. Walter does not leave soon enough, and they end up fighting. The next thing we know, one of them is knocking on Jess's door, making another joke about being a member of the Junior Woodchucks, as in Alan's first scene with her. Jess, with unfailing patience and good humor, returns his playfulness and suggests that, if he is hungry, "Mother Connelly" could whip up a couple of eggs for him, "guaranteed to make a new man out of you."

There are existential aspects to this episode, most notably in the role of chance and the ineffectualness of questioning one's own existence, which has a distinctly anti-Cartesian air. Descartes called the types of things that think "mental substances," and distinguished them from things that don't think, such as dolls and robots, which he called "physical substances." But in the Twilight Zone, the lines are not clear. Dolls and robots – and, in other episodes, ventriloquists' dummies and wax figures – appear to be in various ways more lifelike, more human, than humans themselves. Alan questions his own existence, and asks about his own essence or nature, even though he is not human, not flesh and blood, but a mechanical device. That is, he is not the sort of thing Descartes would have thought of as being a mental substance, or that we would normally think of as having a mind or soul. But it really doesn't matter who is doing the questioning – man or machine – for no satisfactory answer is forthcoming in either case. The dialogue brims with anti-Cartesian irony and paradoxes about personal identity, as when Alan protests, "You expect me to believe I'm a machine when I know I'm not? That's ridiculous."

Through the first half of the episode (except for the scene with the Old Woman), Alan Talbot seems like a perfectly honest, friendly, and considerate person, in contrast with our first encounter with Walter Ryder, who appears mean-spirited and menacing. Walter, like Jesse Cardiff, is something of a hard-luck case: tough childhood, generally disliked and unloved. Yet, it is the machine, Alan, who is responsible for the most poignant moment in the episode, where, knowing he is doomed, he races against time to give Walter the chance to experience the happiness that Alan was looking forward to himself.[16] When he and Alan fight it out at the end, one might well find oneself rooting for Alan, the machine, over Walter, the human being – even though the clear moral choice is the reverse.

If there is a way out, a way to avoid existential angst, "Image" is pretty adamant that it will not be through religion, or at least not through religion that promises something miraculous. The wild-eyed Old Woman with her talk of being "revelated" and the pamphlet promising salvation may plausibly be read as an indictment of religion's claim to objective truth and its certainty about the nature of moral values. The obvious biblical allusion in the title of "In His Image" turns out to have a human rather than a theological referent: Walter Ryder creates Alan Talbot "in his image," and Walter's salvation depends not on God but, in part, on the mechanical device that he labored to create, against all probabilities, for the greater part of his adult life. It also depends, in part, on another person. As Garcin says in "No Exit," "If there's someone, just one person, to say quite positively that I did not run away, . . . that one person's faith would save me."[17] The "other person" here is Jess, whose name bears a striking similarity to "Jesus," and who is remarkable for her intelligence, wit, patience, love, and trust. The message is that one can live a life that is worth living through a meaningful relationship with another person, who has faith in you and who will stand by you, but not by being bullied by some crazy stranger into being "revelated."

In contrast, religion is treated gently in "Five Characters." The Major insists that "someone must know we're here," but no one pursues the theological option. Another subtle allusion occurs at the end, when The Dancer takes solace in The Major's promise to come back and get them. The Clown, of course, knows better: The Major will return, but he will not be their savior. He is simply thrown back into their world. The biggest sign of hope is in Serling's concluding remarks, that maybe someday they will be given life through the love of a child.

Walter understands that we need other people, for practical purposes and for deeper reasons. When he first shows Alan the well-equipped laboratory "where he was born," including the string of Alan's "brothers," botched attempts to produce a better version of himself, Alan asks if Walter did all this himself. He did not: his task, to create a genuinely intelligent being, was far too complex for one person. Interestingly, however, Walter notes that the computer experts who assisted him misunderstood his project. They thought it was to create an entity that simulated intelligent behavior, whereas Walter's ambition was to create real intelligence, a goal that he saw as superior to theirs. But Walter's ability to deceive is not limited to other people; he also deceived himself. He acknowledges that, for a long time, he convinced himself that his goal was scientific when it was personal and moral, that is, to create a better version of himself, someone who wasn't so mean and callous, but friendly and likeable, someone who could enjoy and appreciate others and relate meaningfully to them. By the time he shows Alan his laboratory, he acknowledges that the world might be better off if Alan survived rather than himself, since Alan is inherently good (despite his occasional psychotic episodes), even though he is not a person. Perhaps this is, ultimately, the symptom that Walter is a better person than he thinks, having acknowledged his shortcomings and gone all the way to the Twilight Zone to try to remedy them. As with characters in other episodes who are basically good but only belatedly enlightened, Walter is blessed with a second chance, for he escapes from Alan's final, murderous assault and knocks on Jess's door at the end, with the hope that he can sustain the relationship that he could not have initiated himself.

In sum, I have argued that the themes in "Five Characters in Search of an Exit" combine to provide it with an overall existentialist sensibility. Visually and sonically, the environment is alien, inhospitable, and incomprehensible to the characters. Reason does not help them to be more effective in pursuit of their goal to escape, or even to know the nature of their own existence. In Descartes, the power to reason and ask questions about oneself is taken to culminate in epistemic certainty about one's existence and one's nature as a thinking thing. In "Five Characters," this power to question is a curse, a compulsion to ask without being able to benefit from the fact that innumerable others have asked the same questions before, when there are no final answers, and in spite of the fact that even if there were answers, the questioner would not be able to understand them. The sole possibility of hope comes with a cautious speculation at the end about the love of a child: the possibility of redemptive faith and trust lies, if anywhere, with innocents who are ignorant of the bigger picture of life, and whose potential benefit is notably outside the possibility of control by any of the characters themselves. Numerous episodes of The Twilight Zone contain existentialist themes without their adding up to providing an overall existentialist sensibility. "In His Image," for example, examines Alan's (and later Walter's) efforts to know who he is and his efforts to live both a good and a happy life. Reason and hard work have a constructive role to play and the outlook, though still laced with contingency, is not nearly as bleak. The burden is still clearly on each individual to make what one will of his or her own life, but the desire to go it alone is depicted as pernicious and the attempt to act alone as futile. An "exit" from some of the nightmarish aspects of the human condition is presented in "Image" and numerous other episodes as a possibility, one that is dependent on having the right kind of relationships with another person. This real possibility, firmly denied in "No Exit," and highly speculative in "Five Characters" at best, prevents the overall sensibility of most episodes from being existentialist, even when other existentialist themes are pursued along the way.

NOTES

1. "Five Characters in Search of an Author" was first aired on 22 Dec. 1961; season 3, episode 14, Dir. Lamont Johnson, Prod. Buck Houghton, teleplay by Rod Serling adapted from a short story by Marvin Petal.
2. "In His Image" was first aired on 3 Jan. 1963; season 4, episode 1, Dir. Perry Lafferty, written by Charles Beaumont. The locus of Descartes' views described here is his *Discourse on the Method of Rightly Conducting Reason* and *Meditations on First Philosophy*.
3. First aired 13 Oct. 1961; season 3, episode 5; Dir. Buzz Kulik, written by George Clayton Johnson.
4. First aired 29 Sept. 1961; season 3, episode 3; Dir. Lamont Johnson, written by Rod Serling.
5. Jean-Paul Sartre, "No Exit," in *"No Exit" and Three Other Plays*, trans. Lionel Abel (New York: Vintage Books, 1946), p. 47.
6. *Being and Nothingness: A Essay on Phenomenological Ontology*, trans. Hazel E. Barnes (New York: Philosophical Library, 1956), p. 74. See Part Two in general for Sartre's views on the nature of consciousness and the self.
7. M. Keith Booker, *Strange TV: Innovative Television Series from* The Twilight Zone *to* The X-Files (Westport, CN: Greenwood Press, 2002), pp. 65–6. Booker does not follow up on his own suggestion that the title of "Five Characters" "perhaps" (p. 65) also contains an allusion to Sartre.
8. Booker, *Strange TV*, p. 65.
9. In this respect, they are like Alan Talbot in "In His Image," who finds it literally incredible that he is a machine. See Section IV. As Serling says in his voice-over early in the episode, these characters are living a nightmare, and even if we can explain it, we cannot end it. It is arguable that the existence of explanations one cannot understand makes life more, rather than less, absurd, but to explore the point goes beyond the scope of this paper.
10. The irrationality of compulsive behavior in many forms is a recurring theme in *The Twilight Zone*, including addictions (such as gambling in "The

Fever"), panic ("The Shelter"), obsessive devotion to an ill-conceived cause ("The New Exhibit," "Alone at Last"), or, as here, simply the drive to do something. The Major is to a degree reminiscent of "the man of action," reviled by the Underground Man in Fyodor Dostoyevsky's "Notes from Underground." See *Notes from Underground and The Double*, trans. Jessie Coulson (New York: Penguin, 1972).

11. "Death Ship" is one of several episodes that contain military figures who are men of action and who have sublime faith in their own judgment, even though later judgments contradict earlier ones, and even though sometimes they shift back again. This "eternal return," dramatized especially clearly in "Death Ship," is more reminiscent of Nietzsche than anticipatory of postmodernism.

12. Contrast Sartre's view that consciousness "must necessarily be what it is not and not be what it is," *Being and Nothingness*, p. 74.

13. "The Purple Testament" is one episode where knowing the future does make it possible to do something meaningful.

14. In the television special on Rod Serling's life, his wife said that, more than a decade after the war, he was still having nightmares about it, and that "the War was always with him."

15. There are cases, however, where characters are good and do not have to struggle, as with Jimbo Cobb (Buddy Ebsen) in "The Prime Mover." In Serling's voice-over, he describes him as "a man who thinks, and thereby gets things done."

16. Walter Ryder describes his situation as "sort of a reverse Jekyll and Hyde." A comparison with Mary Shelley's *Frankenstein* is also appropriate, where it is Frankenstein's monster, rather than the scientist, which (or is it "who"?) seeks, unsuccessfully, to establish contact with other people.

17. Sartre, "No Exit," p. 40.

7

THROUGH THE TWILIGHT ZONE OF NONBEING

TWO EXEMPLARS OF RACE IN SERLING'S CLASSIC SERIES

———

LEWIS R. GORDON

The classic television series *The Twilight Zone* had the unusual feature of addressing pressing social issues, often with existential reflections reminiscent of Jean-Paul Sartre's "The Wall," where irony always awaited the at times shocking climax of each episode. Among those pressing concerns are race and racism, in ways that are not often explicit. Unlike many series of the day, which required the appearance of blacks (if they appear at all) *as the blacks*, the series examined themes in ways that brought contingency to the lives of its black characters. This is particularly evident in episode 27, "The Big Tall Wish" (1960), of the first season. It features a little boy who transforms reality through the Promethean energy and faith he puts into his wishes. His efforts come to bear on the outcome of a fight by his best friend and hero, Bolie Jackson, a boxer who was supposed to have lost a fight because of his injured hand. Jackson was knocked down. The referee began to count. The boy, Henry, listening to the fight, wished, with the intensity of prayer, for Jackson to win the fight. The referee held up Jackson's hand, declaring him the winner. Jackson's opponent was on the floor, knocked out, and Jackson's injured hand was fine, as if it were never damaged. All was good. Later on, while celebrating Jackson's victory, Henry confessed his wish. Jackson became indignant and insisted that it was he who secured his own victory (although the memory of having injured his hand while preparing for the fight still lingers). He urged Henry to stop relying on the power of wishes. Henry repeatedly refused, until Jackson gave him a speech about the dangers of believing in wishing and of how foolish he was being. As Henry takes in and begins to accept Jackson's argument, he grows solemn as his faith in wishes disappears, and both return from that other, possible world of their ideal, the world in which Jackson won the fight, to the actual one, with Jackson unable to rise from the canvas after being knocked down, in which it was not only wishes that were lost. In this, actual world, Henry tried but witnessed the "failure" of his wish, ceased to believe in wishes, and began proverbially to grow up. Rod Serling's closing narration to this episode is rich with many levels of reflection:

> Mr. Bolie Jackson, a hundred and eighty-three pounds, who left a second chance lying in a heap on a rosin-splattered canvas at St. Nick's Arena. Mr. Bolie Jackson, who shares the most common ailment of all men, the strange and perverse disinclination to believe in a miracle, the kind of miracle to come from the mind of a little boy, perhaps only to be found in the Twilight Zone.

Serling here speaks to the audience at multiple levels. The cast from that episode was black. Although no signifier save the color of the actors' skin and the inflections of their speech pointed to race as the main point of the episode, it was an unmistakable feature for audiences of 1960, who were living through the immediate, painful efforts at integration where black children were accompanied by the National Guard to formerly all-white schools after *Brown v. Board of Education of Topeka, Kansas*. Serling, however, did more than hire a cast of black actors. The episode exemplified several considerations that were ahead of their time. Why did he use a black cast for all but the boxing scene (where white actors played Jackson's trainer and the boxer who knocked him down) when progressive politics favored mixed settings or were at least exploring such questions as attested to by the later *Guess Who's Coming to Dinner* (1967), which examined interracial marriage with Sidney Poitier as the black man proposing to marry the hypocritical liberal's white daughter. Serling's episode posed a challenge to the question of audience. On the one hand, he brought black people into the lives of television viewers as something unfamiliar to visual popular culture: black human beings. On the other, he seemed to have realized that the presumption of a white-only audience, or of whites *as audience,* limited the humanity of blacks through closing off their perspectival possibilities. The closing narrative, I suggest, addressed the twoness of American society by speaking to blacks directly both through the intratextual theme of the consequence of no longer believing in wishes and the extratextual reality of social justice in America as what Drucilla Cornell (2004) has characterized as an ideal to be defended. The episode offered an intergenerational question between the adult fighters of the civil rights struggle and the generation for whom they fought. Serling portended the danger of lost ideals, where, like Daedalus' admonition to Icarus, a generation of blacks whose expectations flew too high fell to despair as dreams, wishes, and hopes melted away. That Cornel West wrote about "Nihilism in the Black Community" three decades after "The Big Tall Wish" reveals the prescience of Serling's political-aesthetic critique. Moving to 2008, the Barack Obama campaign's rhetoric of "Yes, we can!" and the many boxing metaphors in the Democratic Primary competition between him and Hilary Clinton exemplify an almost eerie return of these themes that suggest a teleological grammar to intergenerational challenges of racial upliftment.

Portraying black people as people is not an easy task. W. E. B. Du Bois (1898a and b, 1903) reflected on this matter at the dawn of the twentieth century through a series of essays on problem people. Such people, he observed, are treated by American society and those who study it as the *cause* of their afflictions instead of as people upon whom suffering and injustice fall. This tendency affects how such people see themselves as well. They become the Groucho Marx joke of rejecting the conditions of their acceptance – that is, preferring not to be members of a club that would accept people like them. For such blacks, the role of the anonymous television viewer, who is often presumed to be white, is also theirs. Returning to the 1960 broadcast of "The Big Tall Wish," the image of black human beings on the screen must have been, for many black people, although at first a source of celebration and pride, surreal.

It is not always the case that race is examined through blacks. A logical consequence of racial differentiation is the notion that, if pushed to its extreme, it leads to species difference. Pushed further, the difference could become extraterrestrial. A poignant episode in the third season, "To Serve Man" (1962), which Serling adapted from Damon Knight's 1951 short story bearing the same title, presented a set of aliens, the Kanamits, who, after solving problems of famine and disease on earth, offered to take cargos of human beings to their world among the stars. Thought by the humans to be god-sent servants because of the aliens' book *To Serve Man,* many earthlings eagerly boarded the space ships. The climax of the episode was the realization that "cargo" is the right word since *To Serve Man* was a cookbook and the passengers were being harvested for food. From a race theoretical perspective, what was striking was how the aliens exhibited European models of civility and old eugenicist presuppositions about intelligence (e.g., they had big crania). This sense of the alien as familiar, which is a contradiction of terms, raises questions of the conditions of appearance. One cannot be seen without appearing, but one cannot appear without standing out, without existing (*ex sistant*). But there are criteria to be met that enable such emergence. These criteria are an unfolding chain of things that depend on other things. The result is one of being seen-*as*, to be seen is to be seen as something or another. Serling's screenplay explored these dynamics through the power of visual media. Because the extraterrestrials could be seen as civilized, in ways that dominate the imagination of civilization, such as being more like very tall and slightly odd Europeans, they were sufficiently familiar to become trusted. The episode revealed the danger of an expanded "we" of consumption versus communication.

The connection between the two episodes, as stories of race, is manifold. From the presumption of white viewers, both brought aliens into their living rooms on the nights they were aired. But the process of bringing the viewer closer to the lives of the characters also part company here, for whereas "The Big Tall Wish" revealed an underlying humanity, and hence affinity, "To Serve Man" reveals the genuinely alien *beneath the alien*. "The Big Tall Wish" dissolves a false alienness; "To Serve Man" reveals what true alienness might be. Yet there is a link here within the framework of racial grammatology. After all, in the process of *making blacks alien*, especially in aetiological terms of a distorted African past, the popular cultural iconography is the dark cauldron in which simmers white flesh. A continued analysis reveals, however, that company continues to part here as well, for the ascription of "cannibalism" to Africans offers contradictions within a racist schema because in order to be cannibals, Africans must also be human beings. The aliens in "To Serve Man," the Kanamits were originally called *Kanama* in the plural and *Kanamit* in the singular in Knight's short story. As well, their appearance was pig-like in Knight's story, whereas Serling's screenplay made them humanoid in form. The connection between *cannibal* and *Kanama* is suggestive, but only such since, in strict terms, an extraterrestrial species could only be cannibals if they ate each other. In this story, they are anthropovores or "man eaters." It is, however, the presumed shared world by virtue of communication and literacy that promised intersubjective relations that makes the cannibalistic theme return. In meeting such aliens, the understanding of the "we" and the "us" in the universe is supposed to be expanded. In Kantian terms, as co-rational beings, there is an imperative, indeed a *categorical one*, not to eat each other. The Kanamits, being rational, should understand that argument, which means their failure to be compelled by the categorical imperative raises some important challenges to ethical life on earth. The first is that the scope of ethical life, as human beings understand it, may be relative to human beings or at least the earth, which would mean that Kant's categorical imperative is in fact, what would be to Kant's chagrin, a moral anthropology. This would not be so, of course, if the Kanamits actually did understand the categorical imperative but *refused* to be moved by it; in which case they may just be evil, or at least very bad. There could, however, be an intergalactic version of something like cultural relativism, where the Kanamits fully understand the categorical imperative *as an earth value* but not part of their rituals and customs in their home planet, or it could be that they fully agree with its logic but add that its domain is relative: universally so for human beings in relation to other human beings; universally so for Kanamits in relation to other Kanamits. Each, in other words, would never eat its own kind, and both could dispute the range of what counts as *kind*. That ultimately this is a story created by human beings, however, suggests that it is in human terms that it should be understood, and here the consideration of audience returns. Serling, as we saw, was aware of the double world of segregation and racism lived by his audiences. If the earlier consideration of split meaning holds, Serling may have been aware that black audiences would see "To Serve Man" differently than white audiences. Here are some possibilities: Make the human beings black and the Kanamits whites, and the story could also be a retelling of the slave trade. Modern capitalism, with the slave trade and its concomitant racism, did, in a way, eat Africans. Another interpretation is for the black viewer to see the white human characters as now being placed in the situation of blacks in the modern world. It becomes a version of trying to show white viewers what it feels like to be in the place of those who have been crushed or consumed by the hunger of white supremacy and anti-black racism.

"The Big Tall Wish" and "To Serve Man" also offer considerations that are not welcomed in a society that seeks "feel good" responses to its racial challenges. In both episodes, the moment of discovery is also a moment of loss. Henry, no longer believing in the power of wishes, takes away his childhood (i.e., ends the child in the boy) and brings both to the world in which Jackson has lost the fight. Jackson, who did not believe in wishes, simply remains on the floor, defeated; but there is, at least for the viewer, the Jackson of the alternative world, who had encouraged Henry to become a man through giving up his childhood power, but the kind of man Henry appears to be becoming is a profoundly unhappy one. "Defeat" is doubly posed in the plot; one, of wishes in the alternative world; the other, in Jackson lying on the floor, in this one. In "To Serve Man," when the character Pat deciphers the book's true purpose and reveals it to Mr. Chambers while he is boarding the ship, the result is terror. Although the genre is a mixture of science fiction, fantasy, and horror, its allegorical dimensions, as with every *Twilight Zone* episode, suggest, always, the matter, for the viewer, of what lies beneath. Although tragedy and horror are the intratextual announcement, Serling's doubled understanding of the audience suggests, as well, the resources of Arthur Schopenhauer and Friedrich Nietzsche. The former, we should be reminded, argued, in *The World as Will and Representation*, that reality is blind will covered by illusions of individuation that enable us to take ourselves too seriously. Art manages to achieve a momentary pause in the movement of this blind will by forcing it, for an instant, to see itself through our seeing the futility of our efforts. Beneath all we do and all we wish for, everything ultimately will amount to nothing as blind, uncaring reality moves on in a stream of things that reveal the folly of individual notions of importance. Nietzsche, in *The Birth of Tragedy from the Spirit of Music*, argued from this realization that the genius of ancient Greek drama was its ability to present, in the suffering of innocence before the Greek public, the secret of life, which, apparently, was that life cannot be lived without suffering. The complete avoidance of suffering requires never having been born, which option is not available to someone who is alive. Even suicide is futile, given the precondition of having lived. The task, then, is to affirm life without hiding suffering as one of its dimensions. By these criteria, *The Twilight Zone* was television's moment of great art.

The Twilight Zone, however, disrupts the ordinary expectations of art. Human beings create art and seek it through our efforts to transform space (including imagined ones) into place and alien surroundings into familiar ones, the most hoped-for of which is home. Every work of art echoes human activity and points, as with Ariadne's thread, to paths that may lead us out of a maze. (It's no accident, for instance, that art galleries and museums resemble labyrinths, and I suspect much fruit can be found in analyses of the role of "exits" in or of such institutions.) It is we who bring art into being through our transformation of signs – objects we "read" in the world – into symbols or meaningful realities. The former are things we understand how to negotiate, but they are not necessarily things available to us in our terms. We share the negotiation of signs, as Ernst Cassirer pointed out in his *Essay on Man*, with animals. Symbols, however, are meaningful only *for us*; they are the forms by which we live uniquely *human* understandings of reality, including our hopes, fears, and anxieties. Art, in this sense, is symbolic. It reverberates human presence and symbolic life, and in so doing, tells us that we (each individual) are not alone. Even the most abstract art, e.g. a dot on a white canvass, echoes a sense of human presence in a vast universe. And more, even *misanthropic*, art created by human beings to alienate human beings, to be anti-human, to be inhuman, ultimately points to a human origin. It is a performative contradiction. Serling's aims, however, are not misanthropic. The disruptions he offers are more instances of what Jean-Paul Sartre calls, in *Being and Nothingness*, "metastability," the kinds of displacements that remind us of the incompleteness of existence. This existential dimension, which returns to the question of the "where" of twilight zones, signals a phenomenological consideration as well. Phenomenology offers acts of ontological suspension often referred to as parenthesizing or bracketing the natural attitude. By this is meant the ordinary world of naive experience, where we take for granted the world available to us. When we no longer take that world for granted and begin to question each stage of assumptions or presumptions we may have about it, we move into another realm, the realm of theoretical reflection on a path to thematized, idealized, or (a rather ugly expression) eidetic understanding of the objects of our reflection or phenomena at hand. This "zone," if we will, enables us to explore truth outside of our pragmatic interests at hand. These deeper truths, because no longer in the flux of things and everyday presumptions, are always available to us. They wait, out "there," in the realm of reflective possibility. It is with these extraordinary considerations that the ordinary is revealed as capable of being studied, and the realization of how extraordinary our ordinary, naive assumptions are comes to the fore. Disruptions, displacements, enable us to see what we may not have seen before. *The Twilight Zone* as art offers itself from the ideas of its writers, but the narrative movement, contextual framing, and content of ideas such as those found in "The Big Tall Wish" and "To Serve Man," phenomenologically understood, stimulate reasoning that disrupts a centered human universe. What is "art," e.g., for the Kanamits? What are the signs and symbols that make them at "home"? In which version of reality does Jackson really belong? And blacks?

Let us turn here to the work of Frantz Fanon, particularly his first book, *Black Skin, White Masks*. Fanon argued that any serious exploration of race and racism suffers from the problem of its intended audiences' wish to avoid it. Really to discuss race and racism means confronting social situations that are difficult to bear because of not only what they reveal about others but also of the self. Such a claim meant that Fanon had to confront himself through the text, which created a split reflective narrative. Thus, the author *of* the text found himself not only in conflict with himself in the text but also about the text, that is, at the level of the metatext. In this struggle, a part of him wins only if another part loses. The internal author, naive and sincere, attempts to work through the system as a believer in the universal messages of man offered by the modern world. The metatextual author challenges this belief by pointing to the social genesis of symbolically mediated appearance in the face of the demand for human agency, for the transformation of society by those on whom it depends. The realization of the social genesis of the situation of antiblack racism suggests its contingency and changeability. But the absence of necessity is not identical with accident, and so an understanding of the investments in the maintenance of such relationships must be developed. Fanon proceeds in this exploration, much like the protagonist from Dante's *Inferno*, but with himself also serving as the guide Virgil. He takes the reader through layers of failures – of the limitations of language as a reconfiguration of social roles; of the limitations of a transformed value of the self through the love of another; of the limitations of escape even in the life of dreams; of the limitations of rationality alone on the one hand, humor and affect on the other – to the point of tears by which self-delusion is washed away so that the tragic dimensions of reality can be faced: Modern society has no coherent notion of a normal black person or, more specifically, black *adult*. To be well adjusted is to be a happy slave, which is abnormal. To be maladjusted as a condition of normality is perverse. To be well aligned with the system is to be white, which makes such a black person an abnormal black person. To be illicit in the system amounts to being an abnormal person. In other words, there is a "Catch 22" circumstance. Fanon calls such a condition "the zone of nonbeing."

The zone of nonbeing is a form of stillborn status, where one has failed before one has begun. It affects, e.g., dynamics of recognition. One goal of recognition is to be seen as human and valuable. But since the humanity of the seer is presumed, it is his (rarely her) standard of being seen that governs the dialectic. This means that the demand for recognition actually affirms the right of the other to grant it. The project fails from the start. The other movement is at the ethical expectations of recognition or the Self–Other relationship. Fanon argues that the modern world has structured that relationship as properly one between whites and other whites or near-whites or white-like peoples. Blacks are structured as non-Selves and non-Others. It is only in relationship to each other that blacks form a Self–Other dialectic, and from there to whites, asymmetrically, as Others. What this means is that the white world lives without a properly ethical relation to blacks, but blacks always live with a self-recognized ethical obligation to whites. In effect, this means, from the dominant perspective, that blacks cannot "appear" except as illicit. There is always appearance manqué (misapplied or troubled).

Fanon's response was to reassert an existential thesis to accompany his revolutionary demand for social change. At the beginning of his book, he argued that there are people whose lives are exceptions to his thesis. This is because the subject matter is a human one, and human beings are fundamentally incomplete realities. Fanon, in other words, was not a structuralist. His text demonstrated the claustrophobic impositions of a troubled social world, but much of that depended upon the failure to understand that human reality is not only descriptive but also (among other things) interrogative. The expectation of the white world to be a hyper-rational one is as dehumanizing, in his view, as the demand for the black world to be an overly emotional one. He saw both as an attack on reason. He reflected, for instance, that reason often suffered in interracial settings. It had a habit of walking out the room when he, the black, walked in: As he reached out to reason, his overtures took the form in the eyes of others as cannibalistic and bestial. The cauldron and entertainment in the form of the dancing monkey were his lot. The problem was exacerbated, however, by his having to win reason back *reasonably*. He needed to show, for example, that hyperrationality was not identical with reason, or even more: rationality itself, as demanding maximum consistency, *could not be identical with reason*. This is because reason is a meta-reflective activity. It must be able to evaluate itself and everything else, including rationality. Reason, in other words, lives in a (if not "the") twilight zone.

Our short detour through the thought of Frantz Fanon should bring to the fore the insights of "The Big Tall Wish" and "To Serve Man." Those episodes, in stream with many others throughout the series, raised as many questions as they resolved in their cathartic denouement. The boxer Jackson lost much for the sake of ethics. To have won *by the wish* was to have failed ethically. But the episode did not make the ethical situation that easy. Something is lost in the transition from wishful child to, in effect, melancholic adulthood. In *Black Skin, White Masks* an extraordinarily similar situation emerged through Fanon's reflection on Jean-Paul Sartre's identifying Negritude, in his famous foreword "Black Orpheus," as a necessary black anti-racist racism of black superiority over whites for the sake of preparing blacks for more universal revolutionary struggles. Fanon's response? He needed not to know this. Sartre forgot, he lamented, that for the negative moment of the Hegelian dialectic to work, the subject must be lost in the night. In other words, they must believe it. Fanon remained ambivalent to Sartre's deed. It released him from his delusions, but he later reflected, in *Year Five of the Algerian Revolution* or *A Dying Colonialism*, that although whites created "the negro" and "the black," it was the latter who created Negritude. He, along with his former *lycée* teacher Aimé Césaire, took the position that part of the breakdown of delusions required the understanding of white civilization, as well, as barbaric. The atrocities of World War II, for example, were, in their eyes, simply the redirection onto whites brutalities that were considered perfectly ordinary against blacks. There have unfortunately been many instances of undermining the ethical response against those who claim that such instances are proverbial hens coming home to roost. "To Serve Man," in this instance, militates against the comforting denial: "That could never be us." Fanon argued that the building of new concepts and infrastructures that transcended troubled social orders was needed. He, in effect, responded to the collapse of dreams in one generation by demanding imagination and ideals in another. Put differently, Jackson failed to understand that it was necessary for Henry's powers of wishing to last a little longer because Henry, as the next generation, had the future in his hands.

As each episode concludes, these matters continue in the Twilight Zone. We may wish to consider, however, what goes on in that zone that is not appearance and also not absence. The themes considered in *The Twilight Zone*, including the metaphor of the title, are ultimately penumbral. They are both there and here, but they are also not fully here and there. This is because they are at the edge or liminal points of what we are willing to face. Shadows, after all, can occur where there is also light. Unlike fear, where we face something external and independent of us, the disposition here is anxious. It will be useful in today's continued climate of racial anxiety to revisit and think through the spirit of this unusual exploration of imagination and possibility during the tumultuous '60s. In the present, the symbolic and ethical structure of such issues is being challenged daily as political institutions suffer much erosion as effective forces of social change in favor of mostly symbolic representations of change. Claims of civilizations clashing and the rising xenophobia as nations police their borders while their leaders and intellectuals extol cosmopolitanism no doubt have affinities with fears of hungry extraterrestrials seeking exotic cuisine. Serling's efforts in *The Twilight Zone*, albeit in the context of entertainment and drama, sought also to bring to that medium a level of reflection that was more than a thematic hook. This is because we face, in the Twilight Zone, ourselves. The edifying message of each episode of Serling's series lingers as the confusing music accompanies the credits with bongos beating to this intense realization.

SOURCES

Cassirer, Ernst (1962) *An Essay on Man: An Introduction to a Philosophy of Human Culture.* New Haven, CT: Yale University Press.

Cornell, Drucilla (2004) *Defending Ideals: War, Democracy, and Political Struggles.* New York: Routledge.

Dante Alighieri (1982) *The Divine Comedy of Dante Alighieri*, vol. 1, *Inferno*. Trans. Allen Mandelbaum. Toronto, Canada: Bantham Books.

Du Bois, W. E. B. (1898a) *The Conservation of the Races.* Washington, DC: Negro Academy Press.

Du Bois, W. E. B. (1898b) "The Study of Negro Problems," *The Annals of the American Academy of Political and Social Science* XI (January 1898): 1–23. Repr. in *The Annals of the American Academy of Political and Social Science* 56 (March 2000): 13–27.

Du Bois, W. E. B. (1903) *The Souls of Black Folk: Essays and Sketches.* Chicago: A.C. McClurg & Co.

Fanon, Frantz (1967a) *A Dying Colonialism.* Trans. Haakon Chevalier with an introduction by Adolfo Gilly. New York: Grove Weidenfeld.

Fanon, Frantz (1967b) *Black Skin, White Masks.* Trans. Charles Lamm Markman. New York: Grove Press.

Gordon, Jane Anna (2007) "The Gift of Double Consciousness: Some Obstacles to Grasping the Contributions of the Colonized," in Nalini Persram (ed.), *Postcolonialism and Political Theory.* Lanham, MD: Lexington Books, pp. 143–61.

Gordon, Lewis R. (2005) "Through the Zone of Nonbeing: A Reading of *Black Skin, White Masks* in Celebration of Fanon's Eightieth Birthday," *The C.L.R. James Journal* 11, no. 1 (Summer): 1–43.

Nietzsche, Friedrich (1999) *"The Birth of Tragedy" and Other Writings.* Trans. Ronald Speirs and ed. Raymond Geuss and Ronald Speirs, Cambridge Texts in the History of Philosophy. Cambridge, UK: Cambridge University Press.

Sartre, Jean-Paul (1956) *Being and Nothingness: A Phenomenological Essay on Ontology.* Trans. Hazel V. Barnes. New York: Washington Square Press.

Sartre, Jean-Paul (1988) *"What Is Literature?" and Other Essays*, edited by Peter Ungar. Cambridge, MA: Harvard University Press.

Schopenhauer, Arthur (1969) *The World as Will and Representation*, 2 vols. Trans. E. F. Payne. New York: Dover Publications.

Serling, Rod (1960) "The Big Tall Wish." *The Twilight Zone.* Season 1, Episode 27.

Serling, Rod (1962) "To Serve Man." *The Twilight Zone.* Season 3, Episode 89.

West, Cornel (1993) *Race Matters.* Boston: Beacon Press.

8

BLENDING FICTION AND REALITY

"THE ODYSSEY OF FLIGHT 33"

THOMAS E. WARTENBERG

A Global jet airliner, en route from London to New York on an uneventful afternoon in the year 1961, but now reported overdue and missing, and by now, searched for on land, sea, and air by anguished human beings fearful of what they'll find. But you and I know where she is, you and I know what's happened. So if some moment, any moment, you hear the sound of jet engines flying atop the overcast, engines that sound searching and lost, engines that sound desperate, shoot up a flare or do something. That would be Global 33 trying to get home – from the Twilight Zone.

This speech, made in voiceover by Rod Serling, ends *The Twilight Zone* episode called "The Odyssey of Flight 33"[1] and summarizes the essential elements of its narrative. While en route from London to New York – because the episode takes place in 1961, the airport Flight 33 is heading for is still called "Idlewild" – a jet airliner flying above the clouds gets caught by what appears to be a quite literally "in-credible" tailwind that accelerates the plane to a speed so great that it breaks not the sound barrier but what we might call "the time barrier," for the plane is hurtled back in time. When the crew first descends below the clouds, still unaware of their unusual situation, they see a geography that they recognize as New York's – the only problem is that there is no trace of human habitation: no buildings, no people, nothing but undisturbed nature. Suddenly the cabin window reveals a dinosaur below and the crew members realize that they have traveled back tens of millions of years. Captain Farver (John Anderson) decides to take the plane back up over the clouds to see if they can't catch that mysterious wind again in order to reverse their time travel. His plan succeeds and everything seems fine as the plane descends above a then-contemporary Manhattan, complete with the familiar buildings and skyscrapers. But, as Hatch (Sandy Kenyon) talks to the controllers at La Guardia – he can't manage to contact those at Idlewild – it becomes apparent that something is wrong.[2] The controllers don't seem to understand Hatch's aeronautical terminology and are startled by his claim to be flying in a jet plane. What the crew members soon realize is that they have not made it back to their present, but only to 1939, the year of the New York World's Fair whose buildings they spy from the cockpit windows as they head towards La Guardia. As they attempt another ascent to try and find their own present, Serling intones his melodramatic voiceover.

I was 11 years old when I saw the original broadcast of this episode of *The Twilight Zone*, a television series my parents generally did not allow me to watch. German-Jewish refugees from Hitler's Germany, they were overprotective of my brother and me, trying to ensure that we would not be ensnared by what they saw, I think, as the vulgarity of American popular culture. Since they had grown up in Weimar Berlin – itself the site of a thriving avant-garde popular culture – this stance was ironic: as if keeping my brother and me from being contaminated by American mass culture could somehow maintain an awareness of the importance of *Bildung* (culture) that made sense only in the Germany of their youths – if it did even there.

But in the case of "The Odyssey of Flight 33," they may have had a point: For years, afterwards, whenever I heard the sound of a jet plane that I could not see, I was troubled by the thought that maybe it *was* Flight 33 trying to make it home, as Rod Serling's closing words had suggested I should. Although I never sent up a flare, I was really haunted by this episode of *The Twilight Zone* repeatedly triggered in my mind by the sound of jet engines.

What was it about this episode, this story that affected me so deeply?[3] I am still not sure what the complete answer to that question is. In this chapter, though, I will take a stab at providing some elements that help explain it. I will suggest that "The Odyssey of Flight 33" and, more generally, *The Twilight Zone* series as a whole, destabilizes the distinction between fiction and reality, and that this explains at least part of my own reaction to this amazing episode of this outstanding television show.

1

The first thing that now strikes me about my youthful anxiety is that it began with something perfectly real: the sound of an airplane overhead. Living on Long Island – and thus in the path of planes from both La Guardia and Idlewild – this was a frequent occurrence that we mostly didn't think about twice. But after viewing "The Odyssey of Flight 33," my overactive imagination often interpreted that sound as if it signaled that the fictional narrative of the television show actually took place and I was witness to the dire situation of those "poor people" aboard Flight 33, unable to find the world to which they once belonged.

Of course, I was "just a kid." As adults, we "know" that there is a clear line separating fictional truth from reality. We can watch much scarier films and television episodes than the one that freaked me out as a child without actually worrying that what we are watching might be real. We can, to choose a relatively tame example, see King Kong destroying subway trains without worrying that this might happen the next time we board one. This is because we believe in the separation of reality and fiction as distinct realms of existence. Fictional beings and fictional worlds cannot invade the real world.

This line of thought makes it seem plausible to attribute my anxiety from watching "The Odyssey of Flight 33" to a failure to understand what philosophers call "the ontology of fiction," by which they mean things like the absolute line often taken to demarcate the border between reality and fiction. Could it be that, at age 11, I had not yet learned that fictional entities do not really exist so that I could hear the sound of jet engines as the return of Flight 33, although that fictional plane could never enter the real world? Would it make sense to see my anxiety as caused by a mistake in my understanding of the ontology of fictions?

Certainly, there have been events that are to be explained by mistaking a fictional event or entity for a real one. The most famous such mistake occurred on October 30, 1938, during the broadcast by Orson Welles and his Mercury Theater on the Air of a dramatization of H. G.

Wells' *War of the Worlds*, the story of an invasion of the earth by hostile creatures from Mars. Many people in New Jersey, the fictional site of the Mars invasion, panicked when they tuned into the show, thinking that the fictional scenario they were hearing was a real news report. As a result, they sought to evade the Martian threat, which they took to be real, by, among other things, flooding the highways with cars.

But that case is very different from my own youthful one, for it involves a very clear-cut error. The people who panicked in 1938 had tuned in to a realistic-sounding broadcast that was easy to mistake for the real thing. It is a tribute to Welles and his troupe that their re-creation of a radio broadcast in their radio play was so realistic that they could fool so many people so completely. But the adults who made this mistake simply had the false belief that what they were hearing was a real, and not a fictional, broadcast. Of course, the fictional broadcast was presented within a real broadcast, but that does not affect the main point: The mistake they made in regard to *War of the Worlds* was taking a fictional event – a Martian invasion – to be real. Once they learned that what they had heard was only a radio play, their belief in its reality simply disappeared.

Another sort of mistake occurs when a person lacking our concept of fiction is confronted with events that *we* know are to be taken as fictional but that *they* view otherwise. There is, for example, the story of the first viewers of the Lumiere Brothers' film, *Train Arriving at a Station*, who ducked to avoid being hit by the train as it appeared to come straight at them.[4] Or, to take another example, there is an apocryphal story, told by, among others, Stanley Cavell, of a "country bumpkin" who comes to the city and sees a play for the first time.[5] Unfortunately, he has chosen *Othello* and when Othello begins to strangle Desdemona, the astounded bumpkin rushes forward to stop this heinous act, appalled that he alone among so many others is sufficiently moved to undertake this heroic action. Of course, the intended moral of this story is that there is no way for the bumpkin to stop Othello, all he can do is interrupt the performance (i.e. *Othello*), manhandle the actor playing Othello, and upset the rest of the audience who know how to watch plays. What he can't do is save the unfortunate Desdemona from her fate. The characters exist, it is asserted in drawing the lessons from this tale, in a different "space," a different "world," from that occupied by the real people who are its audience and its actors, so that the audience is, in a sense, closed off from the characters' existence just as the characters are from the audience's, even though the audience also, in another sense, witnesses the characters' lives. What the bumpkin has to learn is how the theater functions, how fictional worlds are created, and only then will he be able to appreciate the play in an appropriate manner.

Interesting as these considerations are, they don't solve my problem with "The Odyssey of Flight 33." The actual example of *The War of the Worlds* broadcast and the fictional thought experiment involving the country bumpkin both include a misunderstanding of a fiction, a reaction to a fictional event that takes it to be a real one, although the specifics of the two cases are quite different. And, in both cases, all that was required to rectify the error was some knowledge: of fact in the case of *The War of the Worlds* and of theatrical conventions in the case of the bumpkin and *Othello*. But my case was different, first because it was a *real* event in the *real* world that I was misinterpreting when I took the actual sound of a jet engine that I did really hear to be caused by a *fictional* plane, Flight 33. But also because knowledge was not what I lacked.

Like the listeners to Welles' broadcast, I did not have the general problem distinguishing fiction from reality that afflicted the country bumpkin. For example, I loved Winnie the Pooh and had both heard and read the *Pooh* stories over and over. But I never really believed that I might encounter Pooh or Piglet or Eeyore when I went for a walk in our much less than one-hundred-acre woods. It had to be something specific about the *Twilight Zone* episode that caused me to take a real sound to be evidence for a fictional entity, just as it was the uncanny realism of the radio broadcast that caused so many people to panic at a fiction. But what was it about the show that caused my reaction?

2

So let's consider whether there are specific features of "The Odyssey of Flight 33" that caused my youthful confusion. In pursuing this idea, it will prove helpful to consider what the television show meant by the "Twilight Zone," for the show's title functioned as more than simply a name for the series.

The Twilight Zone television series revolved around narratives in which real people were suddenly immersed in a world that no longer made sense in the ways they expected. That world it called, "the Twilight Zone." The show attempted to unnerve its viewers by showing them stories of individuals who found themselves transported from their accustomed world into this other world. The predicament the show's characters faced was that of somehow making sense of these inexplicable experiences.

Serling gives us a partial explanation of the nature of the twilight zone in his first speech during "The Odyssey of Flight 33" with which I began this chapter. He characterizes it as a realm in which occurrences happen that "nothing within the realm of knowledge or at least logic" can explain.[6] So the twilight zone is a region that somehow "borders" the world of our everyday experience in a way that allows people to seamlessly pass into it without immediately knowing that they have. Their only clue is the odd nature of what happens to them. What's different about the Twilight Zone is that things happen there in ways that radically confound our expectations and are not able to be explained by our normal assumptions about how things take place.

We might think of *The Twilight Zone* as taking up a claim made by David Hume.[7] In attacking the notion that we could actually perceive causality, Hume claimed that we are not justified in assuming that the future would resemble the past, for we possessed no insight into what things *had* to be like. So, on Hume's account, it might just turn out that things started to behave in a radically different manner than they had previously for no reason that we could make out. So, for example, he tells us that we have no good reason to assume that the sun will rise tomorrow just as it did today and had every previous day of our lives. The unusual worlds that different episodes of *The Twilight Zone* describe are all examples of the "Twilight Zone," a place where things behave according to regularities that are radically different from those we are used to and that require the positing of fundamentally different forces for their explanation.

Bearing in mind this general characterization of the nature of the twilight zone, we can turn to "The Odyssey of Flight 33" to see if there is anything special about the specific Twilight Zone posited by this episode. Like every episode, this one involves something happening that is contrary to our normal expectations. This show employs a popular device that is often found in science fiction stories: time travel. But there's a difference in how the show depicts time travel and the usual way it is imagined in other works of science fiction. Generally, time travel is presented as made possible by an invention of a (mad) scientist, as in H. G. Wells' classic novel, *The Time Machine* or the *Back to the Future* films. But in "The Odyssey of Flight 33," time travel happens through an unusual physical occurrence that takes place without the intervention of human beings. What I earlier referred to as an incredible tail wind is an unexplained natural phenomenon that causes the plane to travel in time. So it is not the hubris of a mad scientist or some other human foible that makes time travel a reality in "The Odyssey of Flight 33," but a (super)natural event that lies outside of human control.

Noticing that the time travel in "The Odyssey of Flight 33" is the result of a natural process and not a specifically human intervention, let us characterize the world posited by this episode of *The Twilight Zone* more specifically than we have done to this point. For the Twilight Zone of this episode is not a reality that is completely discontinuous with our own. Rather, it is governed by processes – we might call them "natural" so long as we recognize that they are different from the natural laws of our own reality – that govern what occurs in that world, only we have no idea of what these mechanisms could be, for they are different than those that govern our world. Time travel is, after all, not possible in our world – though some philosophers have debated whether this is really so. But in the Twilight Zone, it is as natural an occurrence as the setting of the sun.

Its portrayal of time travel as happening through an inexplicable yet natural process allows this episode to present the Twilight Zone in a manner that distinguishes it from a great deal of science fiction. Most science fiction creates an imaginary world that stands at a distance from the real world either spatially or temporally or both. Consider, for example, the classic television series *Star Trek*. Although the world of *Star Trek* shares with the world of "The Odyssey of Flight 33" physical processes that appear impossible in our world – transporters are as impossible as time travel – Kirk, Scottie, Spock, and the rest are fictional if for no other reason than they exist in the future. But "The Odyssey of Flight 33" takes place in roughly the present of its viewers, so that they cannot distance themselves from it, as *Star Trek*'s viewers can, by seeing it as something that takes place far in the future. Furthermore, "The Odyssey of Flight 33" presents the Twilight Zone as something into which a person can slip unawares, so that the Twilight Zone is not only temporally but also spatially contiguous with the real world. It is as if there were holes in our world into which someone could fall, much as Alice did into the rabbit hole, only one would wind up, in this case, in the distressing place called the Twilight Zone rather than Alice's Wonderland.

This explains one of the features of "The Odyssey of Flight 33" that made it so unsettling to me: the permeable border between the Twilight Zone and the real world. Viewers of the show were made to see their own world as bordering a twilight zone in which time travel was a reality. Given that air travel was still relatively new and a source of some anxiety for many people, the show tapped that anxiety and enhanced it by suggesting that there were more dangers to flying than were dreamt of by the average anxious passenger. We all were aware of the possibility of a plane crash, but only viewers of *The Twilight Zone* might worry that their flight might temporally displace them from their own world.

3

But this still doesn't really explain my anxiety as an 11-year-old at hearing a jet overhead, for I was not on a plane but securely on the ground. So let me explore another feature of "The Odyssey of Flight 33," this time one that is shared by almost all the other episodes of *The Twilight Zone*. What I have in mind is Rod Serling's intrusion into the fictional world presented by the episode.

Like nearly every episode of the series,[8] "The Odyssey of Flight 33" contains a clear transgression of the separation of the fictional world from the real world when we see Rod Serling himself appear on the screen early in the episode and address the television audience directly:

> You're riding on a jet airliner en route from London to New York. You're at 35,000 feet atop an overcast and roughly fifty-five minutes from Idlewild Airport [now, Kennedy Airport]. . . . Unbeknownst to passengers and crew, this airplane is heading into an unchartered [sic.] region well off the track of commercial travelers – it's moving into the Twilight Zone. What you're about to see we call "The Odyssey of Flight 33."[9]

Serling's practice here is similar to that of Alfred Hitchcock in his highly successful television show, *Alfred Hitchcock Presents* (another show that I had to watch on the sly). Like Hitchcock, Serling appears on the screen and comments on the story we are watching. But there's a difference in Serling's presence, for he generally appears on the set of the episode he introduces.

To understand why this is significant, we need to move beyond a consideration of the content of what Serling *says* and include an awareness of the manner in which he is *filmed*. Serling's speech begins in voiceover, as we see a long shot of the plane taken from the side that shows it flying above the clouds. There is then a cut to a shot taken directly into the cockpit from a camera located roughly where the nose of the plane would be that shows the pilot and co-pilot with some clouds between them and the camera while the voiceover continues. Next, there is a fade to a shot of Janie, the head stewardess, entering the cabin from a door leading to the cockpit. The camera does a slight pan to the left, showing a half-shot of Serling, as if entering the cabin from outside, continuing his narration, now looking directly into the camera – and, hence, at us – as he speaks and explains that the plane has entered the Twilight Zone. He tells us the title of the show and there is a cut to commercial.

But what is unusual about Serling's presence as the narrator of the episode? After all, we are accustomed to the presence of narrators in many films and television shows. We can even categorize some of the different ways that narrators are presented in audio-visual works.

1. Many documentaries have narrators and these narrators often appear on the screen. When a filmmaker appears in a documentary – Michael Moore is one example of a filmmaker whose documentaries are filled with his presence – we take him to exist in the same, really existing world as the events that are being depicted by his film. He might actually be present at the events he describes or they might have happened at some other time, but we take both the filmmaker and the events he describes to exist in the same world as we do, though at times and places distinct from those in which we are located as we watch the film.

2. Some audio-visual fictions have narrators who are characters within their fictions. If a character narrates the events – as does the Jimmy Steward character for most of John Ford's *The Man Who Shot Liberty Valance* (1962) – then we know that he is located firmly within the fictional world that he is describing, even if the events he describes took place at an earlier time than the one of the narration itself.

3. We sometimes see real people introducing audio-visual fictions on television. One example is when an actor introduces a fiction film in which she starred for a television broadcast. Although she plays a character within the fiction that we are going to watch, we realize that it is the real person who is introducing the film in which she once acted. So this constitutes a distinctive type of relationship between a narrator and an audio-visual fiction, for her narration is not of the fiction itself.

At first blush, we might think that Serling's narration of "The Odyssey of Flight 33" fits the third type of audio-visual narration. We might think that Serling, like Hitchcock before him, is presented in a documentary-like manner talking about the fiction he has created. But this would be a mistake, for Serling's narration violates the assumption about the metaphysics of fiction that we saw earlier: that the fictional world of the episode and the real world in which it is filmed are completely disjunct.

We can see this if we consider what happens when we first see Serling on the screen, for what occurs is that, when the camera pans, we see Rod Serling apparently *on board the plane*.

Figure 8.1   Rod Serling enters Flight 303

Although, at a literal level, what we are seeing is simply Serling on the same set as the actors being filmed along with them, this does not fit our actual experience of what we see and hear. Although Serling and the stewardess do not both appear in one frame, when Serling appears on the screen we see him partially covered in the stewardess' shadow. The shadow that covers the lower portion of his body and that also appears on the wall in Figure 8.1 is not his, but that of the stewardess who has just walked out of the frame and farther down the aisle. When we see the stewardess again after the commercial, she continues to proceeds down the aisle in a manner continuous with her movement before Serling entered the scene.

What is disconcerting about this shot is that it seems to frustrate any attempt we make to interpret it consistently, for the visual shots of Serling appear to put him into the space of the fiction, something that his speech clearly rules out. After all, his speech places him *outside* of the fiction, much as the actress in case 3 above was outside of the fictional world of the film she once appeared in, for he comments on what is taking place from the point of view of an observer, saying things that are outside the epistemic reach of the characters. Serling's narration is recorded so as to create a tension between its visual and audio elements.

Ever since the writings of the French film critic and theorist Andre Bazin, film scholars have made a distinction between two ways of looking at the shots of a fiction film. On the one hand, we normally take the shots to be about the fictional world of the film. For most of "The Odyssey of Flight 33," we can view the film this way, seeing it as telling us the story about this fictional flight and the people aboard the plane. But, on the other hand, it is also possible to view those shots as documents that tell us about the shooting of the film. For example, we could look at a shot of the flight's captain and say it shows us what John Anderson, the actor who played him, looked like in 1961, the year of the episode's filming. On Bazin's view, we can attend to the film in either of these ways, but not both simultaneously.

But in the scene in which Serling appears, something very interesting happens: The soundtrack presents its speaker – Rod Serling – in a documentary manner making a comment about the fiction from within the real world, while the image-track presents him as part of the fictional world. A careful viewer of "The Odyssey of Flight 33" is thus caught in a bind. He is given a set of audio-visual cues that cannot be consistently deciphered – except on the assumption that our everyday reality and that of the fiction posited by the episode are not separate realms but rather coexist within a single broader framework of being.

The television show here is employing techniques that were first used in filmmaking by the French avant-garde filmmakers known collectively as the New Wave. In assaulting what they saw as the sterility of their contemporary French films, the New Wave directors used a variety of techniques which violated the conventions that had become standard in fiction films and that attempt to make the act of filming transparent, i.e. not perceptible to viewers. So, to use an example relevant to our purposes, continuity editing required that the sound-track and image-track be synchronized so that, when a person was seen opening their mouth to speak, the sound-track would present their words simultaneously with the image-track showing them speaking. To revitalize the cinema, the New Wave directors believed it was necessary to break such conventions by doing things such as having the sound-track be out of synch with the image-track. Their idea was that this would call attention to the artificial nature of the film medium.

It is just such a "transgression" that we can see at work in "The Odyssey of Flight 33," but to different effect. The episode plays with the fact that television is both an audio and a visual medium, so that it is possible to record a sound- and an image-track that require different and contradictory assumptions about how its content should be interpreted, what the relationship between a narrator and its fictional world is. By including a soundtrack that presents Serling's words as coming from outside of the fiction and an image-track that presumes that he exists within the fictional world, "The Odyssey of Flight 33" presents its audience with a world that makes sense only if it is taken to allow for the interpenetration of real and fictional persons and things, a clear violation of the normal assumptions at work in fiction film and television.

4

I began this chapter with a puzzle: What exactly was going on when, as an 11-year-old boy, I thought I heard Flight 33 flying overhead? What I have tried to show is that there are specific features of "The Odyssey of Flight 33" and general features of *The Twilight Zone* that undermine the assumption that reality and fiction are distinct ontological realms. The unusual feature of this series – and this is especially true, I think, of this one episode – is that its viewer is required to see the real and the fictional as interpenetrating one another.

This interpenetration of distinct realms is established in two ways. In the series as a whole, Serling's presence in the same physical space as the fictions he describes causes a rupture in how we experience them. We are more or less forced to think of the real Rod Serling as present within the fictional world the episode has created, for only on this odd assumption can we make sense of the tension between the audio- and visual-tracks the show includes.

In addition, "The Odyssey of Flight 33" emphasizes this interpenetration of realms through its specific depiction of time travel as a natural phenomenon. The real world and the Twilight Zone are brought into intimate contact because the film presents a radical violation of the natural order as itself a natural phenomenon, albeit one that we have never experienced. For this reason, there is a temptation to see the world of the Twilight Zone as one whose possibility we cannot rule out.

So rather than seeing myself as having made the mistake long ago of taking reality for a fiction, I prefer to think of my younger self as already being an astute viewer of audio-visual fictions who internalized the unusual stance required for viewing "The Odyssey of Flight 33." That is, I was able to see that the usual way of taking a fictional world to be completely isolated from the real world was simply the result of accepting a set of conventions that had become customary for the making of fiction films and, following their lead, television shows. What this *Twilight Zone* episode brought home to me was the artificiality of these conventions, the possibility of creating shows that undermined the stability of the distinction between reality and fiction. But rather than simply accepting these as new ways of creating fictions, fictions that could call attention to the conventions of their own creation, I took them to signal a new way of thinking about the world, one in which fiction and reality would not remain quietly in the places we assigned them, but interpenetrated each other in ways that unsettled at least one young viewer.

ACKNOWLEDGMENT

I want to thank Lester Hunt for his encouragement and assistance in clarifying my ideas for this chapter.

NOTES

1. "The Odyssey of Flight 33," originally broadcast on February 24, 1961, Rod Serling, writer, Justus Addiss, director.
2. The problem is that Idlewild was not built until the early 1940s.
3. One possible explanation is that it triggered an unconscious fear, perhaps of death. While I do not deny this possibility, I shall explore alternative accounts of the trigger that refer more specifically to the nature of this fictional work.
4. There is some debate about whether this was their actual reaction.
5. Stanley Cavell, *Must We Mean What We Say: A Book of Essays* (Scrivners, 1969).
6. Ibid.
7. See, for example, David Hume, *An Enquiry Concerning Human Understanding*, section 7.
8. Lester Hunt tells me, in response to a query, that Serling "was the voice narrator on all episodes, except for an early cut of the pilot episode, and always appears on-screen after the first few episodes, usually on the same set as the actors, at the beginning of the episode." (e-mail)
9. Marc Scott Zicree, *The Twilight Zone Companion* (Silman-Jones Press, 1992), p. 177.

9

EPISTEMOLOGY AT 20,000 FEET

SHEILA LINTOTT

You unlock this door with the key of imagination. Beyond it is another dimension – a dimension of sound, a dimension of sight, a dimension of mind. You're moving into a land of both shadow and substance, of things and ideas. You've just crossed over into the Twilight Zone!

Opening Introduction to "Nightmare at 20,000 Feet"

Epistemology is the branch of philosophy concerned with theories of knowledge and related questions of truth and justification. Although in everyday life we are accustomed to making many knowledge claims, we tend to be very poor epistemologists. We claim to know all sorts of things for which our evidence, in all honesty, is dubious and rarely considered. Some knowledge claims we make explicitly. For example, when boarding an airplane, I might make a series of explicit knowledge claims about the destination of the plane or how long the trip will take. Other of our knowledge claims are made more tacitly. For example, when trying to find my seat on a plane, I make a whole host of implicit assumptions: that I exist, that the plane exists, that the windows look out onto the real world (and aren't television sets or the like), that my perception is trustworthy, and so on. Although all such claims rest on conceptions of truth and knowledge, very few of us have coherent and clear conceptions of what it really means for a belief to be true or when it is accurate to claim to have knowledge. In everyday life we don't bother ourselves much with such abstract issues as *What is truth?* or *What is knowledge?* We assume we know what truth is and then we go about attempting to discern the true from the false; we assert that we know lots of things and we never give a second thought to the justification of these knowledge claims. And we certainly don't spend much time considering whether the claims that seem obviously true to us are actually known to us. For example, before taking my seat on an airplane I don't entertain the possibility that it is a hologram. Of course it seems to be real, but things aren't always as they seem. Maybe my senses are deceiving me into thinking that there is a seat in front of me. How do I *know* that it isn't an illusion? Isn't it *possible* that it doesn't really exist? No, we don't bother ourselves with such matters; it seems that only an insane person would spend time pondering veracity and justification in such straightforward situations, well, an insane person or a philosopher. To ponder such things, to sincerely wonder if you can trust your senses, to consider whether your most basic assumptions are true, to look for justification where others find self-evident truths, this is a feat that requires imagination, for it requires the ability to imagine that you may be wrong regarding some basic assumption about the nature of the world and your place in it.

The episode of *The Twilight Zone* called "Nightmare at 20,000 Feet" encourages us to imagine that possibility. In "Nightmare at 20,000 Feet," based on a short story of the same name by Richard Matheson, we meet Robert Wilson (played by William Shatner). Wilson is a leery and weary traveler, who is boarding a plane with his wife. Wilson's leeriness is understandable as he is on his way home after being released from a mental hospital where he received treatment for a mental breakdown. We learn that his breakdown occurred on the last flight he ventured to board, so we empathize with his struggle to remain calm as he nervously boards the airplane and takes his seat. Things get worse for Wilson after take-off when, during a threatening storm, he spots what appears to be a large gremlin on the wing of the plane. Soon, the gremlin seems to begin tampering with one of the engines. Undetected by every other passenger and crew member, the gremlin appears very real to Wilson. The internal conflict raging in Wilson is obvious; he can't believe what he sees, yet he really does seem to see it. He looks and looks again. He doesn't want to believe it, yet, despite the darkness and the rain and regardless of how many times he looks and looks again, the gremlin truly seems to be there. The consequences here are serious, for if he is right and there is indeed a mischievous gremlin tampering with the engine, all of their lives are at stake. He knows how extremely unlikely it is that there is indeed a gremlin on the wing of the plane. In vain he attempts to share his conviction, but given the frailty of his mental health and the outrageousness of his claim, no one believes him. Finally, he takes matters into his own hands, and, it seems, saves the day.

This episode is one of my favorites in the *Twilight Zone* series for several reasons, including Shatner's signature performance, the unlikely look of the gremlin (you might think that a creature that appears to deny the laws of physics would be more streamlined), and the sheer implausibility of the story. However, I enjoy the episode most for its ability to confront the unsuspecting viewer with a significant philosophical and practical question. This question is, *What is truth?* "Nightmare" leads audience members on a voyage from doubt to belief and perhaps to the realm of knowledge. In what follows, I discuss Bertrand Russell's views on truth in order to trace Wilson's journey into the Twilight Zone, a journey that begins with perception and doubt, proceeds to belief, and perhaps ends in truth.

TRUTH AND FALSITY

Won't you even allow the possibility?
        Robert Wilson to his wife in "Nightmare"

Bertrand Russell once said that he would never die for his beliefs because he knew he might be wrong. In other words, despite the fact that one must believe in order to know, no matter how sincerely, intently, and strongly one believes something, it may be false. So, in considering the difference between knowledge and belief, between, for example, Wilson's belief that there is a gremlin on the wing of the plane and his knowing that there is a gremlin on the wing, one crucial element to consider is the whether the belief is true, for to know something, not only must you believe it, but it must also be true. This, in fact, is the way we distinguish belief from knowledge. Think of the many beliefs you've held in your life that have subsequently been exposed as false. Or think of the many beliefs past cultures have held that we now know were never true. A favorite example here is the belief at one time held by the greatest minds that the earth was flat. Despite the fact that they had evidence supporting their belief and (almost) everyone agreed that it was true, we now know that they were mistaken. Thus, although they thought they knew something, they merely strongly maintained a false belief.

In a chapter of *Problems of Philosophy* called "Truth and Falsehood" Russell attempts to discern what it means to say that something is true. This quest to define truth must be clearly distinguished from attempts to determine which of our beliefs are true. Of course, understanding the meaning of truth does not entail believing all and only true claims any more than understanding the meaning of happiness entails acting in all and only ways conducive to one's happiness. Life is messy, after all, and having a sound theory does not guarantee flawless practice in any human endeavor. The truth or falsity of one's beliefs is independent of one's understanding of what truth is; most of us do not have a clear conception of truth and yet we have many true (and false) beliefs.

Russell argues that for any theory of truth to be at all satisfactory, it must accomplish three things. First, it must draw a clear distinction between truth and falsity such that these two terms are opposite. If a theory defines truth in such a way that falsity is not its opposite, then the meaning of truth, and for that matter, the meaning of falsity, become vacuous. Consider Wilson's belief that there is a gremlin on the wing of the plane. He is the only one who holds that belief on the flight, not even his wife shares it. She believes quite the opposite, namely, that it is not the case that there is a gremlin on the wing of the plane. So, it seems that if Wilson's belief is true, those who believe he is wrong must hold a false belief. Notice that whether he is correct is irrelevant, for the point holds in either case. If he is wrong, his belief is then false and, by definition, those who thought he was wrong hold a true belief.

Some theories of truth fail to meet this very basic requirement. One such theory, a rather popular one in some circles, we can call the "Personal Truth" view of truth. The Personal Truth theory of truth reduces truth to a matter of personal belief and seems to claim that if someone has a belief to which they resolutely subscribe, then in some sense that makes the belief true, at least for that individual. You may have heard people say things like: "Well, if he believes it, it is true *for him*" or "This is my truth, you don't have to believe it" or "I believe it and that is good enough for me." These sentiments disclose the workings of the Personal Truth view of truth in the mindset of the person who asserts them. But what do these claims actually amount to? If Wilson's Personal Truth is that there is gremlin on the wing of the plane and his wife's Personal

Truth is that her husband is mistaken in his belief that there is a gremlin on the wing of the plane, then, as we saw above, only one of them is correct. The Personal Truth view of truth is actually just a complicated and convoluted way of talking about beliefs. Belief is not the same as truth, however, and we can easily amass countless examples to illustrate this point.

TRUTH AND BELIEF

> *I didn't tell you before because I wasn't sure if it was real or not, but I am sure now. It is real. There's a man out there or a gremlin, whatever it is. If I described him to you, you'd really think I was gone.*
>
> Robert Wilson to his wife in "Nightmare"

In order to distinguish between truth and falsity, it is essential that we distinguish between truth and belief, for very frequently our strongly held beliefs turn out to be false. Yet, although belief is not sufficient for truth, it, or something like it, seems to be necessary. The second qualification that Russell insists on for any adequate theory of truth is that the theory must make truth a property of beliefs or propositions. Beliefs, statements, and propositions are things that can be true or false. For example, the following are candidates for truth and falsity:

- There is a large furry gremlin on the wing of the plane.
- It is not the case that there is a gremlin on the wing of the plane.
- Robert Wilson is hallucinating.
- It is not the case that Robert Wilson is hallucinating.
- Robert Wilson is married.
- Robert Wilson is a human being.

Contrast the above statements with the following, which are not candidates for truth and falsity:

- A large furry gremlin
- A wing of an airplane
- Robert Wilson and a gremlin
- Robert Wilson
- A threatening storm
- Julia Wilson

This second group of examples is a list of things that may or may not exist, but as they exist they are not true (or false). "A large furry gremlin" is neither true nor false, but it is either true or false that "There is a large furry gremlin on the wing of the plane." The matter, that is, the stuff of the world, exists as it does and in a manner entirely independent of truth and falsity. It takes a mind with ideas and attitudes to accurately or inaccurately apprehend the stuff of the world. Without minds, and thus without thoughts, ideas, beliefs, and so on, there would be no such thing as truth and falsity. In our quest to understand the world we inhabit, truth, and even more frequently, falsehood, are born. Russell sums this up when he says: "If there were no beliefs, there could be no falsehood, and no truth either. . . . If we imagine a world of mere matter, there would be no room for falsehood in such a world. . . . Truths and falsehoods are properties of beliefs and statements" (*Problems of Philosophy*, pp. 120–1).

So, the world as it is in itself is neither true nor false, it just is; rather, our understanding of the nature of the world is correct or incorrect. Your beliefs are true or false, the objects of your beliefs just are what they are. Think of it this way: the gremlin tampering with the plane is not true or false, but Wilson's belief that the gremlin is tampering with the plane is true or false. The gremlin is not true; rather, it is true *that the gremlin is on the wing of the plane*. The gremlin is not dependent upon a mind for its existence, however, the truth about the gremlin can be considered only by a mind able to entertain beliefs and ideas. It is in this way, but importantly not in every way, that truth is mind dependent, that is, truth depends upon a human mind.

TRUTH AND CORRESPONDENCE

ROBERT WILSON: *It's all right now, darling.*

JULIA WILSON: *I know, but I am the only one who does know . . . right now.*

Exchange between Robert Wilson and his wife at the end of "Nightmare at 20,000 feet"

The final qualification for a theory of truth that Russell presents is that it must recognize that the property of truth that is attributed necessarily to beliefs or statements is conditional on something independent of the belief itself. If Wilson's belief is true, it is true not because he believes it, not because he believes it strongly, and not because he believes it despite wishing it were false. Instead, it is true because of some relationship the belief has with something outside itself. What that something else is posited to be is a distinguishing mark between various theories of truth. For example, some hold the relationship maintains between the belief and facts, while some hold that the key relationship is found between the belief and other beliefs, and there are other contenders as well.

Russell argues that the meaning of truth is found in a correspondence between a belief and a fact. That is, what it means to say that Robert Wilson's belief that there is a gremlin tampering with the wing of the plane is true is that his belief corresponds to a fact of the matter: that indeed there is gremlin tampering with the wing of the plane. This sounds straightforward enough; the correspondence theory tells us what might have seemed obvious to us. It tells us that:

"There is a gremlin tampering with the wing of the plane" is true *if and only if* it is a fact that there is a gremlin tampering with the wing of the plane.

The correspondence theory of truth seems commonsensical; a given claim is true provided that it corresponds to the facts. However, there are problems with the theory. To see the major reason why many find the theory unsatisfying, we should remind ourselves of the role that truth plays in our attempts to know the world. We believe that knowing something entails its being true. Wilson knows that the gremlin is there if and only if the gremlin is there. If he is hallucinating, then regardless of how strongly he believes it, his belief is false and his claim to knowledge fails. Obviously, we want to know things, so we want to apprehend the facts of the matter. We are motivated by a desire to have knowledge of all sorts of matters, from the trivial to the profound. One of the more ubiquitous desires we have is to know *that we know* something. We may find ourselves absolutely reveling in the knowledge that we know something is the case, especially when others disagree. It is one thing to know some truth or another, knowing that we know that truth can be the source of even greater satisfaction.

Wilson's case is drastic because he is aware that someone has to do something if his belief is true. Someone has to stop the gremlin or the plane will crash due to engine failure as a result of the gremlin's tampering. Thus, he has a belief and he believes that it is true and while Russell's theory tells him that it is true if it corresponds to reality, the correspondence theory gives him no way to tell whether it is true. The belief is true if and only if it corresponds to reality. But how can we know *that*?

He knows it if his belief corresponds to a fact, but the correspondence theory offers no way of determining whether his belief does correspond to a fact. As Russell explains: "if truth consists in a correspondence of thought with something outside thought, thought can never know when truth as been attained" (*Problems of Philosophy*, p. 121). Help, in the form of a test for truth, can be found in another theory of truth: the coherence theory.

TRUTH AND COHERENCE

I'm not imagining it. I am not imagining it. He's out there. – Don't look. He's not there now. He, he jumps away whenever anyone might see him, except me. Honey, he's there. I realize what this sounds like. Do I look insane? . . . I know I had a mental breakdown and I know I had it in an airplane. I know it looks to you as if the same thing is happening again, but it isn't. I'm sure it isn't.

Robert Wilson to his wife in "Nightmare"

Over the course of "Nightmare at 20,000 Feet," Robert Wilson grows increasingly confident that there is a gremlin tampering with the engine on the wing of the plane. At first, he can't seem to believe it, but time and again, he sees it. Eventually his confidence is high enough that he tries to warn the others, but no one believes him. Of course, they won't believe him; his claim is wildly implausible, he is visibly agitated, and some know his history and thus have the reasonable suspicion that he may be mentally unstable. Under the circumstances, who would believe him? To make matters worse, when he does succeed in getting someone else to entertain the remote possibility that he is correct, whenever that person looks out the window to investigate whether there is someone or something on the wing of the plane, the gremlin disappears, floating upward to avoid detection. The gremlin, it turns out, is considerably more mischievous than he first appeared. Wilson realizes this and realizes that he will have to take matters into his own hands. With the intensity of a man confident in his convictions, he quickly conceives a plan. For her safety and so she doesn't try to stop him, Wilson sends his wife Julia for a glass a water. He then acts very quickly and purposefully, stealing the air marshal's gun, breaking open the emergency window, and, heroically, while hanging precariously out the window of the plane, he shoots and kills the dangerous gremlin.

The coherence theory of truth defines truth in a way similar to the correspondence theory, with two very significant differences. On the coherence theory of truth, a belief is true just in case it coheres with the set of beliefs that we believe to be true. Thus, both the correspondence and the coherence theories insist that truth has its opposite in falsehood, that truth is a property of beliefs, and that the property of truth is attributable to a belief in virtue of a relationship between that belief and something else. The difference between the two theories can be seen in the nature of the relationship involved, coherence versus correspondence, and the objects that are related, beliefs and facts versus beliefs and beliefs. The coherence theory of truth maintains that the meaning of truth is found in coherence between a belief and other beliefs. F. H. Bradley, a proponent of the coherence theory of truth explains that his "object is to have a world as comprehensive and coherent as possible" (*Essays on Truth and Reality*, p. 210). In other words, Wilson's belief that there is a gremlin on the wing of the plane is true, according to the coherence theory of truth, if and only if that belief is consistent with the set of beliefs that we take to be true; if and only if, that is, it helps round out the system of our beliefs about the world. Bradley recommends accepting claims as true only "because and as far as, while taking them as real, I am better able to deal with the incoming new 'facts' and in general to make my world wider and more harmonious" (*Essays on Truth and Reality*, p. 211).

Russell argues against the coherence theory as an adequate definition of truth. He finds it lacking as a theory because there may be more than one set of coherent beliefs which contradict one another, but are wholly consistent as sets in themselves. Russell uses the example of an imaginative novelist to explain this problem: "With sufficient imagination, a novelist might invent a past for the world that would perfectly fit on to what we know, and yet be quite different from our real past. In more scientific matters, it is certain that there are often two or more hypotheses which account for all the known facts on some subject" (*Problems of Philosophy*, p. 122). So truth cannot, according to Russell, be defined by the notion of coherence. He insists that correspondence remains the best definition of the meaning of truth, even though the correspondence theory of truth fails to give us any test for truth. The coherence theory fails where the correspondence theory succeeds, for it does not offer an acceptable meaning for truth. However, the coherence theory also succeeds where the correspondence theory fails by giving us a good test for truth. Thus, the best overall theory of truth may be found by merging the correspondence and the coherence theories and using correspondence as a definition with coherence as the test.

DEFINING AND TESTING FOR TRUTH: CORRESPONDENCE AND COHERENCE

The flight of Mr. Robert Wilson has ended now. A flight not only from point A to point B, but also from the fear of recurring mental breakdown. Mr. Wilson has that fear no longer, though for the moment he is as he has said, alone in this assurance. Happily, his conviction will not remain isolated too much longer, for happily, tangible manifestation is often left as evidence of trespass, even from so intangible a quarter as The Twilight Zone.

Voice-over ending of "Nightmare at 20,000 Feet"

The situation on the flight of Robert Wilson is quite problematic, for while he is sure that there is a gremlin tampering with the plane, others are sure that if he is seeing anything at all, it is a result of his mental anxiety and instability coupled with the torrential storm they are flying through and he is not seeing a gremlin because there is *not* a gremlin on the wing of the plane. The two different interpretations can't be simultaneously true. Either the gremlin is there or it isn't. There seems to be some agreement on the fact that Wilson believes that he sees a gremlin, the question is whether he believes it because there *is* a gremlin or because he is hallucinating that there is a gremlin; that is, the question is whether what he believes to be true *is* true. The correspondence theory tells us that his belief is true if it corresponds to the facts of the matter, yet it gives us no way to access those facts.

The gremlin and the hallucination stories are each seemingly consistent with the evidence. Although both stories (of the gremlin and of the storm plus Wilson's mental instability creating a gremlin appearance) are consistent with the evidence, one seems more plausible for its fit with the rest of what we believe to be true. We have certain beliefs about physics, gravity, and so on that seem to rule out the possibility that there is a gremlin on the wing of the plane. Wilson is in the uncomfortable position of believing something that does not seem to cohere with the set of beliefs most people on the plane hold as true. The other passengers, and Wilson as well, have the following beliefs: This plane is flying at an approximate elevation of 20,000 feet. This plane is flying at least as fast as 150 miles per hour. The claim that there is a person or person-like creature tampering with the wing of the plane just doesn't fit. In other words, it doesn't cohere with other beliefs we know to be true; it seems to contradict them. Initially at least, the hallucination story has the added benefit of not contradicting the set of beliefs we generally take to be true.

The episode ends with Wilson on a stretcher after being carried off the plane, which appears to have landed safely on the ground. In the background we see evidence of the gremlin's tampering and the voice-over assures us that this evidence will lead others to come to believe that Wilson was indeed correct. But the correspondence theory can only tell us that Wilson was correct provided that he was correct, i.e. his belief was true if it corresponds to a fact of the matter. However, what we want to know is if he was correct! The coherence theory of truth offers us a method of discerning truth from falsity. No claim is taken as infallible and each claim is tested for the extent to which it coheres with the rest of our beliefs. Although a belief may look on first pass to contradict our system of beliefs, we may learn, on closer inspection, that it fits. This may be due to the unearthing of some new evidence and/or to learning that some of our previously held beliefs were actually mistakenly assumed to be true. For example, the evidence of trespass left by the gremlin will introduce new beliefs into our system and we may find room to fit the possibility that Robert Wilson was correct into our system of the world.

Robert Wilson was right that there was in fact a gremlin tampering with the wing of the plan if and only if there was. This we learn from the correspondence theory of truth. However, what the correspondence theory is completely silent about is whether Robert Wilson was in fact correct. In order to gain some insight into that issue we will need to utilize the test of truth articulated by the coherence theory of truth. We test his claims for the extent to which they cohere with all of the other claims and evidence we can amass. Although his story was outlandish, there is evidence to suggest it was true, for, indeed, "happily, tangible manifestation is often left as evidence of trespass, even from so intangible a quarter as *The Twilight Zone*" ("Nightmare at 20,000 Feet").

SOURCES

F. H. Bradley, *Essays on Truth and Reality* (New York: Oxford University Press, 1962).
Bertrand Russell, *Problems of Philosophy* (Buffalo: Prometheus Books, 1988).

10

RATIONALITY AND CHOICE IN "NICK OF TIME"

AEON J. SKOBLE

The *Twilight Zone* episode "Nick of Time" is a fascinating psychological thriller, a case study in choice making, rationality, and irrationality. It is a compelling and eerie drama, as we expect *Twilight Zone* episodes to be, but it is unusual also: it does not use the famous "twist" ending which is the hallmark of so many classic episodes, and it also does not depend in any way on the reality of supernatural forces. When we think of the greatest episodes, we typically think of one of these two devices: Henry Bemis breaks his glasses, "To Serve Man" is a cookbook, Nan Adams is already dead, Talky Tina really talks. "Nick of Time," by contrast, on close examination is actually entirely realistic, yet the viewer is nevertheless propelled into the Twilight Zone.[1]

A young married couple on a honeymoon drive, Don and Pat Carter (William Shatner and Patricia Breslin), have car trouble near Ridgeview, Ohio. While waiting for their car to be repaired, they decide to pass the time in a diner, and start playing with a novelty fortune-telling machine. The fortune-telling machine has a little devil's head bobbing on top, so it looks mildly sinister or mysterious. They insert a penny, ask a yes/no question, and receive answers which are extremely vague, yet which coincidentally seem congruent with how things come to pass. For example, Don has been wondering the entire trip whether he has received a promotion at work, and when he asks the machine, it seems to say yes. A phone call to the office reveals that he has indeed received the promotion. Given the vagueness of the responses ("what do you think?", "it has been decided in your favor," "if that's what you really want," and so on), the machine had a better than even chance of being right, but Don starts to think the machine really *can* tell the future. This raises interesting philosophical questions about the nature of decision making, the phenomenon of the "self-fulfilling prophecy," and what it means to be rational, as well as what it means to be free.

The viewers have seen that Don is prone to superstitious beliefs in the first place, a believer in rabbits feet and the like.[2] So it's not a surprise to Pat when Don starts taking the machine a little too seriously. But Pat does find it alarming when Don starts becoming obsessed with the machine. Pat is more level-headed and rational, and while she has hitherto indulged Don's superstitions, regarding them as relatively harmless eccentricities, she sees that in this case, Don is letting the machine tell him what to do.

FREEDOM AND CONSTRAINT

One way to understand freedom is to think of it in terms of the freedom to act on one's decisions. If I am unconstrained by others, then I am free. But this needs qualification: even if I am unconstrained by other people, I am always "constrained" by the laws of nature. For instance, my "decision" to fly like a bird is one I cannot act on, so it's correct to say that I am not free to fly like a bird, even though it would be odd to conclude that I am thereby oppressed or coerced. So we might modify our conception so that we say we are free when we are constrained *only* by natural laws, or that only the constraints *of others* can rob us of our freedom. But what happens when we are self-constrained? A heroin addict is often said to be in thrall to his addiction. Many philosophers as far back as Plato have noted the possibility of our being "enslaved" to our desires or fears. We can thus curtail our own freedom. This can contain an element of self-fulfilling prophecy: as long as Don continues to *think* that he is not free to leave the diner, there's a sense in which he is not free to leave the diner. In a larger sense, of course, he *is* free to leave – the machine doesn't literally have any power over him – a point which Pat's level-headedness helps him to realize, and the significance of which is underscored by an eerie coda to the episode in which we see another couple begging the machine to release them, not realizing that, like Don and Pat, they could leave whenever they wanted to.

Is it in fact irrational to believe that the fortune-telling machine has real power? Despite the appearance of accuracy regarding Don's promotion, it is in fact at odds with science and reason to think that coin-operated novelty machines can predict the future or know what one's boss has decided. Like astrology, the machine only *seems* accurate, and is in fact speaking in the broadest and vaguest terms, such that almost anything could be seen as confirmation. At worst, it has a 50–50 chance of being right. When Don asked whether he was going to receive the promotion, he was told "it has been decided in your favor," which turned out to be true. (If the machine had said "no," one suspects that Don would have concluded immediately that it does not predict the future, and not gotten involved with it.) This encourages him to take the most charitable interpretations of even the vaguest predictions. Even "what do *you* think?" is taken by Don to be an example of accurate prediction of the future. To the objective observer, it is plain that this is irrational. Pat certainly sees it as such, and she knows that Don's credulity about the machine stems from the same superstitious nature that makes him "believe in" a lucky rabbit's foot, and so on. Superstitions are, by definition, irrational beliefs. Suspension of one's rational faculties robs one of one's autonomy. If you cannot leave a diner because a robber is holding you hostage, you have lost autonomy because it has been taken from you. In Don's case, he has lost autonomy because of his own irrationality, and regains it when he resumes being rational. Indeed, part of what enables him to give up his commitment to superstition is his realization (prompted by Pat) that he is losing autonomy. It is his desire to be in charge of his own life which makes him give up his fears and superstitions.

WHAT WERE YOU THINKING?

What makes people irrational in this way? It's practically a truism of cognitive psychology that people are prone to "fall for" several types of irrationality.[3] One example is our tendency to notice things that happen as opposed to things that do not happen. This is often known as "confirmation bias." For instance, if the phone rings while one is in the bath tub on two or three occasions, one might start thinking "this *always* happens to me," while not noticing the many times the phone rang while *not* bathing. So, if we start with the hypothesis that the rabbit's foot brings good luck, and we rub it every day, and one day something lucky does happen, that's taken as confirmation of the hypothesis, while the many other days on which nothing happened are ignored.

The vague prediction presents a different invitation to irrationality. Since the predictor cannot be wrong, it must have been the interpretation that was wrong, but this proves the accuracy of the predictor. A famous example recounted by Herodotus[4] in the fifth century BC is the Delphic oracle telling King Croesus that if he made war against the Persians, a great empire would be brought down. The oracle would have been "right" no matter what the outcome, so Croesus' dismay at losing his own empire does not cause him to conclude that the oracle doesn't have special powers.

Granted that there are a variety of common failings of reason, we should respond with a conscious and cautious approach. If we know we must drive on a hazardous road, we drive a little more carefully. If we know that our rational faculties are prone to certain patterns of error, we should make an effort to be aware of them. This means making a conscious effort to avoid confirmation-bias effects. For instance, Don's lucky rabbit's foot did *not* prevent the car from breaking down in the first place, so why should he continue to look to it for luck? Don would more easily see the "good luck" as coincidental if he made a point of noticing the times when the rabbit's foot doesn't work. Pat's "level-headedness" or "common sense" is in fact better science. Pat seems to have an implicit understanding of Don's confirmation-bias problems when she points out that the machine's predictions are too vague to be impressive, and that a lot of what is going on is coincidence. Don isn't swayed by these observations, of course – that's a symptom of confirmation bias – although he is affected by Pat's later observation that by holding superstitious beliefs he is giving up his own autonomy.

Since we all lack perfect, complete information, are we all unfree? That would be to overstate the case. It is not the mere presence of occasional irrationality that robs one of autonomy. But by the time we see a wholesale abandonment of rationality, in Don's case exemplified by his broadly superstitious attitudes, especially the willingness to believe that the machine controls him, it's clear that one is no longer autonomous. Don is unfree to the extent that his entire worldview is governed by superstitious beliefs, which inhibit his decision-making process, and he takes back his freedom at just the point when he deliberately gives up his superstitions. After realizing that Pat is correct, he tells her (and from the way the scene is acted, we infer that he is also reminding himself, and perhaps informing the machine as well) that henceforth he will go where he wants to go, be his own master. It would be wrong to characterize this as "defying the machine," as the machine never really had any power over him to begin with. Perhaps Don's earlier sense that it did was encouraged by the devil-head on the machine, implying malevolence, but even in a theological context, the devil only has power over the sinner to the extent that the sinner gives it to him.[5] If Don is "letting" the machine control him, then he can take back that control. More specifically, it is Don's recognition of a more rational worldview, and his announcement of it, that produces the freedom to act on his own will. He is now free in the sense that his will is bounded only by laws of nature. Just as he is not a prisoner of some person, neither is he a prisoner of a supernatural, malevolent napkin dispenser, and neither is he a prisoner of his false beliefs about supernatural, malevolent napkin dispensers.

The distinction between being "imprisoned" by a supernatural, malevolent napkin dispenser and being "imprisoned" by one's false beliefs about supernatural, malevolent napkin dispensers is an important one. If there really *were* such a thing, one would be hard pressed to avoid its power. But in the latter case, all that is necessary to break free is to realize the falsehood of the belief. One does this through the application of rationality, which entails first of all the recognition of rationality. Aristotle notes that while some people make mistakes in the application of reason, others are so confused as to deny the very reality of reason. He even claims that their refusal to engage their rational faculties makes them unfree in much the same way that plants are.[6] While Don is not quite at plant level, his widespread embrace of a host of superstitions is a failure of rationality, a failure to recognize that the universe is governed by a set of physical laws which rule out the sorts of magical powers he attributes to rabbits' feet and four-leaf clovers. Operating under this mindset makes it easy for him to come to think that the fortune-teller has magical powers also, and only his acceptance of a more rational worldview liberates him.

STYLE AND SUBSTANCE

Why is this such an effective episode? As I noted earlier, "Nick of Time" doesn't actually fit into the more familiar *Twilight Zone* patterns. Departing from a pattern or formula isn't by itself a virtue (sometimes it can be a flaw). So the departure from pattern in this episode has to be something that relates to the ideas the story is trying to convey: we fear the unexplainable and we fear loss of autonomy, yet we can trap ourselves through irrationality. As the story arcs, we actually see a progression of ideas, from the scary (being trapped by a machine, losing autonomy) to the positive, even life-affirming notion that freedom, at least in the sense of autonomy, is available to those who would embrace it (with the help of reason). The true cause of Don's lack of freedom turns out to be a feature of the natural world under his control. That makes this episode an optimistic one, despite its eerie feel. The ideas make the story a good one, and the departures from formula enhance this by showing that the machine is powerless, and that Don can be in control of his life simply by choosing to be.

Contrast, for example, the episode "The Fever" in which a man's obsession with a sinister slot machine leads to his death. But here, the slot machine really *was* trying to kill him! That episode takes place in a world where machines have intentions and can pursue people and so on. Part of what makes "The Fever" effective is that the viewer isn't sure whether the machine is actually malevolent, or if this is mere obsession, and the "twist" is that it is the former. We don't know we're in the presence of the supernatural until the end. Similarly, in "The Hitch-Hiker," the last-minute revelation of the supernatural element defines the twist ending. In other episodes, we know we're in the presence of the supernatural earlier – for instance in "The Purple Testament," Lt. Fitzgerald (William Reynolds) can tell which of his men will die. This episode's effectiveness comes not from the revelation of supernatural forces afoot, but from how Fitzgerald deals with it. In Shatner's other appearance on *The Twilight Zone*, "Nightmare at 20,000 Feet," we know the gremlin is real all along, so the drama comes from the fact that no one *else* believes there's a gremlin. "Living Doll" is like this also: we know all along that Talky Tina really talks; the surprise is that she kills Erich (Telly Savalas).

But "Nick of Time" doesn't have a twist ending, and it doesn't have a supernatural element, the two most recognizable features of *Twilight Zone* stories. This episode is actually an instance of a tiny sub-genre of episodes the eeriness of which is entirely psychological. There are really only a handful of episodes which rely neither on the "twist" ending nor on the supernatural. In "The Lonely," Corry (James Warden) comes to *regard* his android companion (Jean Marsh) as a person, but we know she is not. The episode's effect comes from our seeing Corry's self-delusion and its effect on his emotions. In "Two," it is the gradual overcoming of distrust (and a language barrier) over the course of the episode which is used to explore human nature.[7]

It isn't the negative characteristics of *not* having a "twist" and *not* having a supernatural element that makes these stories good ones. Rather, they share with "Nick of Time" a common *theme*: it is the protagonists' irrational thinking that is the real problem.[8] The ideas are the source of the quality of the story, the stylistic moves (whether in terms of sticking to formula or departing from it) enhance the conveying of the ideas. What puts the viewer into the Twilight Zone in "Nick of Time," partly, is our vicarious experience of the protagonist's fear. Don is afraid of cracks in the sidewalk and so forth, and later he comes to be afraid of becoming a prisoner of the machine. Overcoming his fear turns out to be the key to avoiding the object of his fears, and this is done through rationality.

We also see fear in the other couple (Walter Reed and Dee Carroll), who really are imprisoned by their superstitions. They seem to have been "trapped" in Ridgeview for a long time, and they appear haggard, beaten. They plead with the machine to tell them it would be all right to leave, but are rebuffed. What is really imprisoning them, of course, is the same fear which Don has overcome, and our parting glimpse of the other couple is a sad picture indeed, especially when contrasted with Don and Patricia happily driving away. The second couple's loss of autonomy, of self-control, is something that the viewer (even the non-superstitious viewer) can empathize with, thus giving the episode real emotional power, and effective Twilight-Zone eeriness despite (or perhaps because of) its departure from our expectations.

ACKNOWLEDGMENT

I am grateful to Lester H. Hunt for many helpful comments on earlier drafts of this chapter.

NOTES

1. "Nick of Time" (November 18, 1960), written by Richard Matheson and directed by Richard L. Bare.
2. Don's propensity to be superstitious about the machine might also be exacerbated by the devil-head swaying back and forth on top of the machine.
3. This is also well-known to teachers of logic.

4. Herodotus, *The Histories*, I, 53.
5. Indeed, another name for the devil in folklore is "Old Nick," which makes a delightful double-entendre in the episode title (although Don wouldn't know this, of course). I am grateful to Lester H. Hunt for reminding me of this.
6. For instance, in *Metaphysics* IV, 4.
7. "The Shelter" is arguably another example, but some might object that it does have a twist in that there is no nuclear attack. Either way, my main point stands, that episodes with neither a "twist" nor a supernatural element are rare. In these cases, an examination of human emotion, or rationality lost and regained, makes for the suspense and dramatic impact.
8. Arguably, "The Monsters Are Due on Maple Street" is another example of this, as the citizens' fears aren't well-justified. But this episode does have a twist: there really are Martians at work. The townspeople are acting irrationally because they have no justification for their beliefs, even though it turns out that their beliefs are true.

II

"THE LITTLE PEOPLE"

POWER AND THE WORSHIPABLE

AARON SMUTS

INTRODUCTION

The array of idols that humans have at one time or another worshiped is bewildering. It is fairly obvious that there is no end to what people are willing to worship. But can they be wrong? That is, can people mistakenly worship something that is unworthy of veneration? Although members of tolerant, liberal democracies may be uncomfortable in suggesting that others are mistakenly worshiping some gods, it is fairly clear that not everything should be worshiped. This opens the possibility for mistakes. What may be less clear is what exactly makes something worthy of worship.

Unfortunately, the history of philosophy provides fairly little help.[1] Although philosophers and social scientists have explored religious rituals and the phenomenology of worship, there has been very little discussion of what makes something worthy of worship.[2] Fortunately, we find a sophisticated examination of the issue by Rod Serling in the *Twilight Zone* episode "The Little People" (third Season, March 30, 1962). In this episode, Serling presents a powerful argument to the effect that people can indeed be wrong about their choice in objects of worship – that is, people can worship things that do not warrant the response. More particularly, the episode supports the claim that power is not sufficient to make something worthy of worship, or what we can call "worshipable."

"The Little People" opens on a planet where two spacemen, Peter Craig (Joe Maross) and William Fletcher (Claude Akins), have made an emergency landing in hopes of repairing their ship. The required repairs are extensive and the spacemen have been toiling away on the planet for days, if not weeks. During the interval, Craig discovers a race of tiny people, perhaps $1/100^{th}$ his size. By waging a campaign of terror, the immoral psychopath, Craig, demands that the natives worship him and him alone. Through what we can only imagine would be a tremendous effort, the natives erect a life-size effigy of their jealous god. Drunk on power, the self-declared deity refuses to leave when the ship is finally repaired. While forcing his partner off at gunpoint, Craig declares that there is only enough room for one god on the planet. Luckily for the natives, Craig's reign is short. A second group of spacemen, 100 times the size of the previous, arrives on the planet. While looking around, one of the giants accidentally crushes Craig between his fingers. The little people celebrate by tearing down the idol of their fallen god.

To determine what would make something worthy of worship would be to say what makes the complex set of emotions, attitudes, and desires fitting, or appropriate, to an object. Rather than attempt to provide a complete answer to the question of what makes something worthy of worship, I will confine my examination to the relationship between power and the worshipable – the topic of Serling's screenplay. By considering the example of "The Little People" and a few variations, we can clarify the role power plays in making something worthy of worship. The episode presents a scenario where a relative, although great, advantage in strength is not sufficient to make something worshipable. But what of far greater powers, such as that of creating the universe – is such power sufficient? Alternatively, is great power necessary for something to be worthy of worship? Furthermore, we must ask if something could have the power to make others properly worship it.

In order to answer these questions we must first achieve greater clarity about what it means to worship something. When one thinks about worship, images of chanting monks, prostrating practitioners, and incense waving devotees immediately come to mind – that is, one thinks of people engaged in ritual practices. But by "worship" I do not have in mind the act of engaging in a ritualistic practice of paying tribute. One can pay tribute to fallen soldiers, elders, or benefactors without thereby worshiping them. By "worship" I mean a complex of attitudes, desires, and emotions directed toward something, not a devotional act. The act of acknowledging this complex is an act of worship. An act of worship is different from a mere ritual; an act of worship must be sincere. One may behave as if one worships something by engaging in ritual acts that are typically expressive of feelings of worship. But it is not an act of worship unless one genuinely worships the object.

To genuinely worship is not simply to fear, respect, admire, or feel gratitude and love. It is beyond these, but most plausibly includes them all. On most accounts, to worship is to venerate, to honor, and to love, perhaps unquestioningly – to feel unworthy in the presence of awe-inspiring greatness.[3] Of course, this notion of worship is characteristic of the Christian ideal of the proper attitude one should hold towards God. It is a perfectly acceptable consequence, that if this is not the attitude that Hindus adopt towards gods such as Ganesh, then it would follow that they do not worship Ganesh – despite the fact that they may honor, revere, and pay tribute to him. However, there are clearly other Hindu gods, such as Krishna, that inspire the emotion complex and attitudes that are worship – this is certainly Arjuna's response to Krishna after the theophany in the eleventh teaching of the *Bhagavad Gita*. Although a Christian paradigm, the notion of worship under consideration is widespread enough for this discussion to have general significance.

Given this rough characterization of worship, we can proceed to explore the three questions I introduced above concerning the relationship between power and the worshipable. 1. Is power sufficient to make something worthy of worship? 2. How much power is necessary for something to be worthy of worship? 3. Does omnipotence impart the holder with the power to make others worship it properly?

IS POWER SUFFICIENT?

The first question about the relationship between power and worship that "The Little People" encourages us to explore is whether power is sufficient to make something worthy of worship. To restate the question: Could power, irrespective of other facts, ever be enough to make something worshipable? This does not to ask if power is necessary – that is, whether to be worshipable something would have to have great power – but whether power, on its own, is ever enough. This question is of crucial importance, because in a prereflective state, many if not most people might be inclined to answer incorrectly – in the affirmative. Indeed, much like spaceman Craig, there is good reason to believe that we are erroneously encouraged to worship the God of the Old Testament principally for his tremendous power.

In the book of Exodus, God instructs Moses to ask Pharaoh to free the Israeli slaves held captive in Egypt. Seemingly working at cross-purposes, God tells Moses that "I will harden [Pharaoh's] heart, so that he will not let the people go" (4:21). Fulfilling his promise, God hardens Pharaoh's heart repeatedly through the next several chapters. In response to each hardening, God punishes Pharaoh's defiant stubbornness by afflicting a plague on the Egyptian people. Finally, after God slaughters the firstborn child in every Egyptian household, Pharaoh is beaten into submission. But not yet finished with Pharaoh, God hardens Pharaoh's heart one last time so that he will pursue the Children of Israel into the desert, thereby setting up the Egyptian army for total destruction in the Red Sea.

The principal interpretive puzzle raised by this passage is this: Why does God seemingly work at cross-purposes? If he wants to free the Israeli people, it certainly does not help to make the Pharaoh stubborn and defiant. Rather than harden, why not simply soften his heart and avoid all the bloodshed? God explains that "I will harden Pharaoh's heart, and he will pursue them, so that I will gain glory for myself over Pharaoh and all his army; and the Egyptians will know that I am the Lord" (14:4). As this passage indicates, the ultimate purpose is a display of power, to both the Egyptians and the Israelites. The plagues send a message: Let there be no doubt, the God of the Israelites is capable of conquering the armies of the strongest earthly empire.

But so what? What is the appropriate reaction to such a powerful deity? It is not at all obvious that such power warrants worship. The question we must ask – the question raised by "The Little People" – is whether such powers are enough to make something worthy of worship. Putting aside the contentious question of whether the God of the Old Testament is worthy of worship, the question we need to answer is whether power, however vast, could ever be sufficient to make something worshipable. "The Little People" shows fairly clearly that having powers like ours – even if they exceed our most fanciful exaggerations – is not sufficient to make something worthy of worship.

This is not to say that it would be inadvisable to capitulate to great power. If the options are to either suffer a fate far worse than the Melians at the hands of the Athenian hoplites or to feign worship of a powerful giant such as spaceman Craig, we would all be well advised to fall to our knees and sing his praises. Clearly, if something is far stronger than you, it might be prudent to obey its commands. Periodically, you might even want to publicly acknowledge that you know it is stronger – that is, if it likes this kind of thing. But an advantage in strength would not make a bully worthy of worship, no matter its province – earthly, extraterrestrial, or heavenly.

Spaceman Craig towers over the little people, much like the giant in Goya's painting "The Colossus" (1808). Similarly, most of the Greek gods are formidable forces, much stronger and often smarter than their subjects. From the point of view of mere mortals, the powers of the gods of Olympus are nothing less than awe-inspiring. Certainly it would be prudent to court their favor and to take measures to avoid their wrath, but no Greek god is worshipable. To the last one, they are extremely flawed, if not petty, deities, just like spaceman Craig. Neither are worthy of the special kind of love, admiration, reverence, and respect that is worship. But what if spaceman Craig had powers dwarfing that of a thousand Zeuses – the power to create and destroy universes, the power to create life?

Again, "The Little People" provides an answer. It clearly shows that something with unlimited powers, including power to create and destroy universes, would not necessarily be worthy of worship. No amount of power could make something worthy of worship if it had the moral character of a megalomaniac spaceman. Imagine a demon that created us for the purpose of torture – not to torture us, but to torture others. He might treat us well, but at the same time use us as a means of inflicting even greater torment on others whom he tortures. Perhaps he has secretly placed us on the far side of a one-way mirror of sorts, dividing our opulent suite from the chamber of horrors where our counterparts suffer unspeakable agonies. Despite its vast powers, such a being would not be worthy of worship. If power alone were sufficient to make something worthy of worship, this hypothetical demon would deserve our most sincere love, admiration, and respect. But it should be clear that it would be inappropriate to feel anything but disgust at such arrant evil, no matter how powerful it might be. Hence, not even the powers of a creator god are sufficient to make something worshipable. So, in answer to our first question, we can safely reply: Power is not sufficient to make something worthy of worship.

IS POWER NECESSARY?

Although power is not sufficient to make something worthy of worship, we need to ask if power is necessary. It is fairly easy to see that to be worshipable something does indeed need power, and lots of it. The real question is how much.

A simple thought experiment shows that great power is necessary for something to be worthy of worship. Imagine that a child gives you a cricket in a jar as a present. You admire the cricket's coloration and do not want to offend the kid, so you decide to take it home and keep it on your desk until it dies a natural cricket death. When you get it home, you discover that the cricket can talk, and not only can it talk, you find that the cricket is by far the wisest and kindest creature that you have ever encountered. You quickly come to realize that the cricket is perfect in many respects. It is perfectly benevolent and, as it turns out, it is also omniscient. It knows your thoughts, all of history, and can foretell the future. Puzzled by its captivity, you become uneasy having such a creature trapped in a jar on your desk. So, you take the jar outside and offer to let it go, assuming that it could probably free itself, but that the gesture is nonetheless proper. Horrified, the cricket begs to be taken back inside for fear of being eaten by a bird. In conversation you discover that the cricket has been reduced to its ignoble state by another god, who was jealous of the cricket's omniscience.

As to whether the cricket is worthy of worship, our intuitions are clear. It is hard to imagine worshiping something as vulnerable as a cricket, even a talking cricket that is perfectly benevolent and omniscient. No matter if we change the scenario and make the cricket humanoid, it is still hard to imagine worshiping a creature that is so weak. If we further alter the scenario and make the creature ten times as strong as a normal person, it does not make a difference. A creature with such limited powers is not worthy of worship. Worship requires something close to awe, and, simply put, the small and weak are not awe-inspiring. Hence, it should be clear that to be a proper object of worship something must have powers far exceeding our own. But how much and what kind of power is necessary?

A testament to Serling's brilliance, "The Little People" suggests an answer to this question as well. The arrival of a second group of even more powerful spacemen at the end of the episode forces us to ask whether the powers and other attributes that might make something worshipable are relational or intrinsic properties. In other words, is the amount of power necessary for something to be worthy of worship simply a matter of how powerful the subject is in comparison to us, or is there a certain amount of power necessary, regardless of our own abilities?

For the sake of argument, assume that a morally perfected version of spaceman Craig is worthy of the worship of the little people. But this would not mean that he is worthy of the worship of his partner, nor would he be worthy of the worship of the second group of giants that land on the planet. Likewise, although many of the lesser gods of Olympus might fear Zeus, their attitude towards him is not one of worship. Hence, it is fairly clear that a relative advantage in power is required for something to be worthy of worship. Although it may seem that to be worthy of worship something would only have to have powers far in excess of our own, or perhaps have powers of a kind that we do not possess, the relational view runs into a serious problem. To introduce the problem, we will need to consider an important issue in the philosophy of love.

Although no one should ever ask this question, imagine that your lover – never one to avoid a horribly awkward situation – turns to you and says, "Why do you love me?" If you are willing to humor such unreasonable requests, you might begin by listing a variety of attractive qualities, such as: great sense of humor, sparkly eyes, sharp wit, kind and forgiving nature, cute ears, insightful, well read, lovely toes, and so on. The problem is that if these properties are what rationally justify your love, it seems that you should "trade up" if given the chance. That is, if someone else comes along with an even better sense of humor, with an even brighter sparkle in their eyes, with an even sharper wit, etc., then you should trade in your lover for the new, improved model. But we do not think that the objects of our love are fungible; they simply cannot be exchanged like old coats. Recognizing this, if one answers the question "why do you love me?" by saying something along the lines of, "there is just something special about you," then one has given up trying to rationally justify their love. This problem has led many philosophers to conclude that although we might be able to explain how we came to love some particular person, we cannot rationally justify our love. Such a conclusion may make us uncomfortable at first, but it is not altogether intolerable.[4] This contrasts sharply with worship.

Although we may think it is plausible that we might not be able to rationally justify our love for another person – we do say that we "fall" in love, as if it is somehow out of our control – this is not at all the case with worship. We do not fall in love with God. No, we think that worship can be justified by appeal to the properties of the object of worship, such as its goodness, knowledge, and power. So, to repeat the question: Is the amount of power necessary for something to be worthy of worship relationally or intrinsically determined? As should now be apparent, the problem for any relational standard of power is that it would allow you to trade up. A more powerful god might come along, as do the giant spacemen who accidentally crush Craig at the end of "The Little People."

The significance of the possibility of trading up is partly a matter of whether or not the objects of our worship are fungible. Unfortunately, intuitions are unclear. It certainly seems that most monotheists do not think that the object of their worship can be exchanged, but this is likely because they believe that their god is omnipotent, so the prospect of a more powerful god coming along is not possible. But then again, the thought of abandoning a god for a more powerful deity smacks of disloyalty worthy only of a mercenary. Hence, one cannot help but think that the objects of worship are very much like the objects of love. If monotheism is not just polytheism with a more powerful god that demands exclusive worship, the objects of worship are not fungible. In any case, if the objects of worship are, as I suggest, not exchangeable without loss of value, then a relational standard will not suffice, at least for monotheists. Polytheists need not rationally trade in one god for another, since they can likely just add new deities to their existing panoply. But for monotheists, something more is necessary to prevent the problem of trading up.

If the objects of worship are not fungible, the monotheist has two options: stick to a relational standard and deny that we can rationally justify our worship, or appeal to intrinsic properties of the object of worship. As noted above, it would be highly counterintuitive to suggest that we cannot justify our worship. We do not just find that we are forming the desire to worship some god or another. Worship must be rationally justifiable. Hence, the first option is a nonstarter. As for the second option, if one appeals to intrinsic properties, they would have to be absolute, else the problem of trading up again arises, since a greater god could be just around the corner.

Earlier, I concluded that great power is one of the necessary conditions for what makes something worthy of worship. The cricket example shows that in order for something to be worshipable it must possess power far greater than our own. The arrival of the second group of spacemen at the end of "The Little People" presents the problem of trading up, which shows that an even greater advantage in power is not enough. An even greater group of spacemen might crash-land tomorrow. Hence, to be worshipable something must possess absolute power – that is, if our worship is not promiscuous. So, in answer to the second question, we can conclude that to be worthy of exclusive worship, something must be omnipotent. However, to merely be worthy of non-exclusive worship – assuming that it is psychologically possible to worship more than one thing at the same time – some lesser degree of power may suffice.

THE POWER TO MAKE OTHERS WORSHIP

So far we have explored two questions about the relationship between power and the worshipable. We have concluded that power is not sufficient and that unlimited power would be necessary to make something worthy of exclusive worship. Spaceman Craig's reign of terror over the tiny natives raises an additional question: Can we be made to worship? More specifically, the question I now want to consider is whether something could have the power to make others *properly* worship it? Admittedly, this question is a bit cumbersome, but the "properly" is important. To understand why I have qualified the question in this manner, we will first need to explore an unqualified version of the same question: Can something have the power to make others worship it?

Among philosophers of religion, there has been some discussion of whether God can command our worship. Many if not most theists believe that we are obligated to worship God, precisely because he demands it. Depending on the demarcation scheme, the first, or the first two, of the Ten Commandments explicitly command worship:

> You shall have no other gods before me. You shall not make for yourself an idol, whether in the form of anything that is in heaven, or that is on the earth beneath or that is in the water under the earth. You shall not bow down to them or worship them, for I the Lord your God am a jealous God, punishing children for the iniquity of parents, to the third and forth generation of those who reject me. (Exodus 20:3–5)

Similarly, from the second page until the page before the last, the Koran repeatedly warns of the dismal fate – "grievous punishment" (2:5) of "the Destroying Fire" (104:4) – in store for unbelievers who fail to worship Allah. The Koran could not be more emphatic: "They have incurred God's most inexorable wrath. Ignominious punishment awaits the unbelievers" (2:90).[5]

In every major monotheistic religion, God demands faith – that is, he commands our worship.[6] Of course, one could take issue with the claim that faith and worship are identical. Perhaps, one might argue, the kind of faith that God demands is mere belief, not the emotion complex that I have described as worship.[7] This minimal interpretation might save the traditions from absurdities, but I do not think that it is even slightly plausible. It simply does not make sense to think that God would be jealous if we merely believed in other gods. Although I might not be able to devote myself to multiple gods, I could certainly believe in hundreds without diminishing my affections for my favorite. Jealousy is only appropriate if the text is referring to something akin to the attitude of worship, roughly, as I describe it. Mere belief does not fit God's jealous response. Regardless, I have no intention of engaging in a three-front exegetical battle, since the actual doctrines of any given religion are largely irrelevant to our more abstract question: Can one be made to worship (in the sense described earlier)? Whether or not the God of the Jews, Christians, or Muslims commands this kind of attitude has no bearing on our issue. However, since it is highly plausible to think that the major monotheistic traditions hold that God demands worship, our third question has significant implications.

Spaceman Craig's familiar demand that he be worshipped by the little people forces us to ask the question, can one coherently command worship? Clearly, one can be intimidated into supplication by a bully, but it is not so clear that one can force the sincere attitudes and desires that are worship. It seems that the attitudes and emotions that compose worship can only arise voluntarily. At least, philosophers Campbell Brown and Yujin Nagasawa think so. They argue that,

> Worship is, just like love or admiration, always voluntary. It is logically impossible for one reluctantly or unwillingly to worship anything. One might *pretend* to worship God by following certain religious rituals, but that does not mean that one actually worships God.[8]

Brown and Nagasawa are primarily concerned with whether one could sincerely worship something because it commands our worship. And they seem right to conclude that we cannot love or worship something out of mere compliance to a demand.[9] However, the statement of their conclusion may be a bit too strong.

To better see the possible problem with the formulation of Brown and Nagasawa's conclusion, consider the last stanza of Sappho's poem "Hymn to Aphrodite." In this poem Sappho invokes the goddess Aphrodite to help her win the affections of a young woman. In a fantasy of optimism, Sappho imagines the arrival of the goddess, willing to grant her every wish. Aphrodite speaks: "Who, O / Sappho, is wronging you? / For if she flees, soon she will pursue. / If she refuses gifts, rather she will give them. / If she does not love, soon she will love / even unwilling."[10] Perhaps not in the sense that Brown and Nagasawa have in mind, but it is perfectly coherent to think that one can be made to love unwillingly – that is, one could be made willing. It is not at all logically contradictory to think that one could be made to love, and perhaps worship, as well.

Although one might not have the power to make oneself worship another out of mere compliance with a command, it is perfectly conceivable that like fabled love potions or the will of Aphrodite, something could have the power to impart the attitudes, emotions, and desires that constitute worship to another. By having the ability to affect another's psychological states, one could have the power to make oneself the object of another's worship. Certainly a god with the power to create the universe could have the power to make mere mortals feel awe, admiration, respect, love, and most anything else.

We should conclude that it is logically possible that something could have the powers to make others love or even worship it. But one might object that there is something perverse in this kind of love. Perverse or not, the way one comes to love another does not change the ultimate response. Imagine meeting Sappho's lover, who exhibits all the symptoms of being in love and frequently announces her feelings. We would conclude that Sappho and her lover are very much in love. It is not clear why we would need to revise our claim if we later came to find out that Aphrodite's interventions are what caused the girl to fall for the tenth muse. No, the way one falls in love does not change the fact that one is in love. Hence, it is safe to say that one could have the power to make others love.

Nevertheless, the above discussion reveals that something is not quite right about love gained through incantations or heavenly machinations. The difficulty is in saying just where the problem lies. Perhaps what seems suspect about love garnered from potions is that it is not freely chosen by the lover. Although this is likely close to the correct answer, it is not a completely satisfactory solution. Assuming that people have free will, we do not think that unwilled actions could be freely chosen. The problem is that love does not appear to be the product of will. One symptom of this, as we noted above, is that it is extremely difficult, if not impossible, to offer a clear account of how our love for another is rationally justified. We typically say that we "fall" in love, and we do not always choose to fall; typically, it just happens to us. Although we might not be able to say that love should always be freely chosen, we still might want to say that love should be authentic – a genuine outgrowth of one's self, major commitments, and goals. For one's values and commitments to be authentic, they must be, in some important sense, one's own. They would have to be autonomous. Regardless of our precise notion of authenticity, it is clear that love earned through potions and spells would be inauthentic.[11]

One does not have to be a Kantian moral theorist to recognize the value of authenticity; one merely needs to be a value pluralist. Consider two worlds. The first world is much like our own. People fall in love and decide to pursue the objects of their love without divine intervention. The second world differs in one crucial way: Rather than allowing people to fall in love with whomever they please, a panel of cupids makes the decision for them. Immediately following the verdict of the cupids, a love-laced arrow is fired, making the target fall in love with whomever the cupids decide. Overall, the amount of happiness in the two worlds is the same. Perhaps the second world is even more joyful, since the wise cupids might make better match-makers than the normal mechanism of our fallible human hearts. Nevertheless, my intuitions are clear: The first world is a far better place to live. It is a better world. Even if the cupids always make the same decision, deciding on the same object of love that their first-world counterparts would have selected, the second world is less desirable. The fact that we judge the first-world, the world absent of paternalistic cupidian interference, as better than the second, shows that we value authenticity in love. And the value of authenticity arises for worship just as it does for love.[12]

Although something could have the power to make others worship it, it is clear that forced worship is not as desirable as authentic worship. This brings us back to the question I asked at the beginning of this section: Can one have the power to make others properly worship it? The notion of "proper" worship is ambiguous. There are two senses in which one might say that worship could be improper. First, by improper one might mean that the worship could have been caused by suspect means. Second, one might mean that worship would be improper if the object worshiped were not worthy of worship. I have in mind this second sense, that the worship would be unfitting of its object. Certainly, worship caused by the mind-altering abilities of a powerful agent might be less desirable than voluntary, authentic worship, but this does not show that such worship would be improper in the sense of unfitting.

In order to determine if something could ever make someone worship it properly, in the fitting sense, we need to try to consider all of the possibilities. Something with the power to do so might make others worship it for two different types of reasons. First, it might make others worship it primarily out of a desire to be worshiped. Alternatively, something might make someone worship it because worshiping benefits the person or others affected by that person. The options are roughly that one could coerce worship either for one's own benefit or for the benefit of the person who is doing the worshiping.[13]

It is fairly clear that the first case – where one is made to worship for the benefit of the object of worship – could never be fitting. It is never worth denying a person's autonomy for the sake of a god's self image. To see why, we merely need to ask, what kind of being would want to be worshiped by coercion? It is clear. If something has and acts on the desire to make others worship it, then it has a moral character equivalent of that of the megalomaniac spaceman Craig. But power-hungry tyrants are not worthy of worship, no matter how strong they might be. Necessarily, the act of making someone worship you for *your* benefit would make you unworthy of worship. Hence, nothing can have the power to make others worship it properly for its own sake.

The second case is more complicated. For the sake of argument, we should assume that it might sometimes be permissible to deny people their autonomy in such an otherwise egregious way, if the benefits are clear and compelling.[14] In order to see if one could be made to worship something for the benefit of the one doing the worshiping, we need to figure out exactly how one could benefit from worship. Perhaps one might be happier, less troubled by existential concerns, and have a greater sense of purpose if one felt genuine worship. But I cannot see why the benefits of worship could not be achieved by other means. If the same goods could be had without worship, then we have no reason to think that the worship is not motivated by a desire to be worshiped. Hence, unless the goods can only be achieved by worship, we have no reason to think that the situation is any different from where one is made to worship for the sake of the object of worship.

The problem is that there is not a single plausible reason why one would have to be made to worship to reap the benefits. Certainly it could not be to prevent eternal damnation, since any god that would torture those whom it did not make worship and reward those that it did make worship would be a twisted sadist, no more worthy of worship than the most wicked devil imaginable. On the other hand, if mere happiness is the intended result, a god could simply administer a divine form of Prozac. If a god could make people worship it, then it could just as easily make them happy. Worship is not necessary for blind happiness, contentment, general life satisfaction, or even a pleasant disposition. Hence, I am simply at a loss for any plausible account of the benefits that could not be had by any means but worship.

Without a clear benefit that would justify coerced worship, I am forced to conclude that any act of imposing worship on another would make the object unworthy of worship. If this is right, then it is logically impossible to make someone appropriately worship you. This is simply not a power the worshipable can posses. Something could have the power to make others worship it, but by exercising that power it would prove itself unworthy of worship. Hence, any such worship would be mistaken or improper. Since it is not clear that one can have a power that logically cannot be exercised, it is safe to say that one cannot have the power to make others properly worship it. Of course, if someone could produce a compelling reason why someone would need to be made to worship for benefits that could not be achieved via other direct means, then my conclusion would need to be revised.

CONCLUSION

I hope to have shown that in Rod Serling's "The Little People" we find a characteristically sophisticated examination of a philosophical issue – in this case, the nature of worship. Much of the philosophical content of this current study must be attributed to the episode itself, since it would be impossible to develop an adequate interpretation of "The Little People" without explaining the position it takes on the role of power in worship. Not only does the episode make philosophical claims, it provides reasons for us to believe these claims. For instance, although spaceman Craig's powers are awe-inspiring to the little people, his moral depravity invalidates any suggestion that he is a worthy object of worship. This gives us a compelling reason to believe that power is not sufficient to make something worthy of worship. The episode does not simply come out and tell us that power is insufficient; it actually leads us to this conclusion via the example of a megalomaniac spaceman. Since Serling provides support for his evident conclusion, I would not hesitate to say that "The Little People" does philosophy, in the most flat-footed sense of what it means to "do philosophy."[15]

With additional reflection on a few related examples we are able to see that no amount of power would be sufficient. Similarly, by considering the role of the second group of spacemen we were able to see that for monotheists, something close to absolute power will be necessary to prevent the problem of trading up. In addition, spaceman Craig's demand to be worshiped allows us to consider the complicated question of whether or not someone could be made to worship properly. No doubt Serling's rich example will reward further scrutiny for those interested in the larger question of what makes something worthy of worship.[16]

NOTES

1. Richard Swinburne presents a fairly standard Christian view of what would make something worthy of worship. In "Holy and Worthy of Worship," the last chapter of *The Coherence of Theism* (Oxford, 1993), Swinburne argues that an omniscient, omnipotent, morally perfect, holy, supreme benefactor would be worthy of worship.

   The question of what makes something worthy of worship is touched upon in some discussions of the problem of evil. Although the amount of evil in the world might not show that God does not exist, it might provide reason to think that God is not worthy of worship. Chapter 4 of *The Brother's Karamozov* is frequently read as an argument to this effect.

2. For example, Rudolph Otto's *The Idea of the Holy: An Inquiry into the Non-Rational Factor in the Idea of the Divine* (1917), describes what it is like to experience the presence of what one takes to be awe-inspiring greatness.

3. Tim Bayne and Yujin Nagasawa provide a more elaborate description of the kind of worship that I have briefly characterized. See Bayne and Nagasawa, "The Grounds of Worship", *Religious Studies* (vol. 42, 2006, pp. 299–313). Rudolph Otto's description of the experience of the "numinous" is similar, but not identical, to what I am calling worship. Otto describes an experience of which he calls a *mysterium tremendum* (a tremendous mystery). The experience is one of fascination and awe directed at an overpowering otherness with tremendous energy. It involves feelings of unease, humility, and fascination. The experience Otto describes is what it might be like to think that you are in the presence of a being worthy of worship. But one can worship something without having such an experience.

4. For a good discussion of the problem, see Laurence Thomas, "Reasons for Loving," in *The Philosophy of Erotic Love*, eds. Robert Solomon and Kathleen Higgins (UP Kansas, 1991). Bennett Helm also provides an excellent summary of the problem in his entry "Love" in the *Stanford Encyclopedia of Philosophy*.

5. *The Koran*, trans. N. J. Dawood (Penguin, 2003).

6. We also find the command to worship in the New Testament: Matthew 4:10 and Revelation 19:10, 22:9.

7. Here I am making reference to Annette Baier's theory of love as an emotion complex. I do not want to endorse this view of love, since I think that love is likely more than a complex of emotions. It also involves a suite of

desires and beliefs that cannot be reduced to the causes or consequences of emotions.

8. Campbell Brown and Yujin Nagasawa, "I Can't Make You Worship Me", *Ratio* (XVIII, 2005, pp. 138–44), p. 142.

9. Martin Blaauw takes issue with Brown and Nagasawa's claim that one could not come to worship something out of compliance with a demand. His counter-argument sometimes seems to confuse the act of worship with the attitude. See, Martin Blaauw, "Worship Me! A Reply to Brown and Nagasawa," *Ratio* (XX, 2005, pp. 236–40).

10. Sappho, "Deathless Aphrodite of the Spangled Mind", trans. Anne Carson, *Norton Anthology of Western* Literature, vol. 1 (Norton; 2006), p. 497.

11. For a clear discussion of the major ways to elucidate the notion of autonomy, see L. W. Sumner, *Welfare, Happiness, and Ethics* (Oxford, 1996), pp. 167–71.

12. James Rachels makes a far different argument against worship based on autonomy. He argues that to worship something would be to acknowledge its absolute authority. This would require giving up one's moral autonomy, which is something we should never do. Hence, we should never worship anything. See James Rachels, "God and Moral Autonomy" in *Can Ethics Provide Answers* (Rowman and Littlefield, 1997).

13. I am ignoring the possibility that some powerful creature might make some people worship some other god, since allowing this to happen – not reversing the results – seems identical in all relevant ways.

14. On Kantian grounds it would likely never be justified, since it is not clear that anyone could consent to being made to worship. At least, post hoc consent is not possible: Even if the person made to worship came to think that it was a good thing, we have no more reason to treat this as autonomously chosen than the typical products of brainwashing.

15. The question of whether film can do philosophy has recently received a good amount of deserved attention. For an introduction to the issue, readers are advised to look at the special issue on film of the *Journal of Aesthetics and Art Criticism*. The essays in this volume have been published as a book: Murray Smith and Thomas E. Wartenberg, eds., *Thinking Through Cinema: Film as Philosophy* (Blackwell, 2006).

16. I would like to thank Heidi Bollich for reading multiple drafts of this chapter and for discussing power, worship, and the *Twilight Zone* during our walks in lovely Prospect Park. Lester Hunt provided helpful comments on a previous version of this chapter. My patient office-mate, Susan Feagin, helped me work through some initial thoughts on the subject. And Noël Carroll forced me to clarify some of the key points of this chapter during a symposium on worship.

12

NOTHING IN THE DARK

DEPRIVATION, DEATH, AND THE GOOD LIFE

———

JAMES S. TAYLOR

INTRODUCTION

Things are different in *The Twilight Zone*. People go about their everyday activities unaware that they are dead, or that they are merely store mannequins that have come to life for a short period of time before having to return to their inanimate existence. People can walk back into their own childhoods, or forward into the future. Robots pitch for baseball teams, or serve as companions to convicted criminals. But, at first sight, *The Twilight Zone* has something importantly in common with our everyday world: the view that to die is to suffer a great misfortune. And so, in *The Twilight Zone*, as in our everyday world, people try to cheat death: a man terrified of dying sells his soul to the Devil in exchange for immortality; a septuagenarian resists his family's attempts to sell his grandfather clock, certain that if they do so he will die; while in "Nothing in the Dark" an old woman hides herself in her tenement apartment, convinced that this is the only way to keep "Mr. Death" from visiting her.

The most poignant of these episodes that focus on the fear of death is perhaps "Nothing in the Dark." At the start of this episode we hear of how when she was much younger, the old woman, Wanda Dunn, who has spent most of her life barricaded in her apartment, saw "Mr. Death" in the person of a nice young man riding a bus, who helpfully picked up a ball of yarn that an old woman riding near to him was knitting with.[1] But, when he handed it to her, his fingers brushed hers – and she was dead before she had either finished the socks that she was knitting, or reached her destination. Subsequently, Wanda has seen Mr. Death come to people in many guises. In each case, he cut their life short, robbing them of satisfying their hopes, dreams, and aspirations. Against this background it is clear why Wanda has barricaded herself into her basement tenement apartment, and refuses to have any contact with the outside world. She has no telephone, and her food is delivered to her each week, in accordance with a list that she leaves outside her door, together with the money to pay for it. And she never collects her purchases until the delivery boy has left, for fear that he might be "Mr. Death" in disguise. And even though Wanda has to make many sacrifices to stay alive, giving up her enjoyment of the outdoors, and of the sun that she loved so much as a young girl, her strategy is working. Just as she is the only person still living in her tenement block, all the other tenants having moved out, as they allowed building contractors in to their homes who served them notices of eviction, so too is she the only person from among her friends who remains alive.

Yet this is *The Twilight Zone*, where nothing is as it first appears. Although at the start of "Nothing in the Dark" we might sympathize with Wanda's fear of death, and her efforts to avoid it, as the episode progresses our assumption that death is a harm to the person who dies is called into question. The episode begins with a gun fight outside Wanda's apartment, in which a young police officer, Harold Beldon, is wounded. He crawls to her door, and asks her for help. She is reluctant to do so, since she suspects that he is simply "Mr. Death," trying to trick her into letting him in so that he can touch her, and rob her of life. However, his plight overcomes her caution and she brings him in. Beldon is pleasant, mild-mannered, and handsome (he is played by a young Robert Redford), and soon Wanda is confiding in him about her fear of death, and how she is living to avoid it. Beldon understands her point of view, but is not persuaded by the arguments that she offers to justify her fear. After all, as he points out, Wanda's fear of death has severely curtailed her life – and she does not really offer any reasons as to why death is so fearful. Beldon obliquely questions why both Wanda, and we, should accept the standard view that death is a harm to the person who dies – and thus is something to be dreaded and feared. Instead, he presses, perhaps we should accept another view: that death is *not* a harm to the person who dies. Beldon is not alone in holding this striking view, for it was first made famous by the ancient Greek philosopher Epicurus. If Beldon and Epicurus are right here, then we are living in a world where death should hold no fear for us. Rather than continue to accept the assumptions that we shared with Wanda at the start of "Nothing in the Dark," then, we should reject them – not to embrace death, but to lose our fear of it. And as I will argue in this chapter, this Epicurean view – and not Wanda Dunn's – is the one that we should accept. There really is nothing in the dark of death that we should fear.

THE EPICUREAN VIEW OF DEATH

In his "Letter to Menoeceus" Epicurus writes:

> Foolish, therefore, is the man who says that he fears death, not because it will pain when it comes, but because it pains in the prospect. Whatsoever causes no annoyance when it is present, causes only a groundless pain in the expectation. Death, therefore, the most awful of all evils, is nothing to us, seeing that, when we are, death is not come, and, when death is come, we are not.[2]

This Epicurean argument for the view that death is not a harm to the one who dies is simple, elegant, and persuasive. Epicurus notes that when we are not dead, our deaths have not harmed us. To be sure, we might be harmed by worrying about our deaths, for such worry will be unpleasant to us and is likely to make our lives go worse than they otherwise would be. This is Wanda's situation in "Nothing in the Dark": she is so terrified of dying that she has given up the pleasures of the outdoors, and the sunlight that she loves, to try to avoid her fatal contact with Mr. Death. A similar fate befell Sam Forstmann, who, in "Ninety Years Without Slumbering," believes that his life will end once his antique grandfather clock stops ticking, and so who spends much of his time tinkering with it to keep it going. But to acknowledge that we might be harmed by the *fear* of death, and hence to accept that death could pain us "in the prospect," is not to accept that our deaths harm us. What causes someone harm if she is in a situation such as Wanda's is not her death itself, but her thinking about it. Accordingly, then, when we are not dead, we are not harmed by our own deaths, for "when we are, death is not come." Furthermore, notes Epicurus, when we are actually dead we will suffer from "no annoyance." This is because, for Epicurus, when we die we cease to exist. To be sure, after our deaths our corpses might continue to exist, moldering in graves, or our ashes might exist, scattered to the four winds, but *we*, understood as individual experiencing beings, will not. Since at death a person will cease to exist as a person, he will be immune from harm, since only things that exist can be subject to harm. It makes no sense, for example, to talk of the characters in *The Twilight Zone* as *really* being harmed by any misfortunes that befall them, since they do not really exist. Once we are dead, then, we cannot be harmed. Putting these two observations together, it seems clear that we cannot be harmed by our own deaths. We cannot be harmed by them when we are alive, for when we are alive our deaths will not yet have occurred. And we will not be harmed by our own deaths when we are dead, for when we are dead we do not exist, and so we are immune from harm. Thus, since we are either dead or alive, and since our own deaths cannot harm us in either case, death cannot be a harm to the person who dies.

Yet despite its simplicity, elegance, and persuasiveness, Epicurus' argument for the view that death is not a harm to the person who dies has been almost universally rejected by philosophers. Steven Luper-Foy, for example, has called the Epicurean view of the harmlessness of death inane, while Christopher Belshaw holds that when taken in its entirety it is "pretty hard to swallow."[3] However, before we defend the Epicurean view of death against its critics it would be sensible first to dispel some of the misunderstandings that might surround it, and then to elaborate and defend the underlying assumptions that it is based on.

ELIMINATING MISUNDERSTANDINGS

It is important to be clear that the Epicurean argument shows only that a person's death is not a harm to the person who dies. It does not show that the thought of death cannot be harmful, or that death cannot be harmful to persons other than the one who dies. Nor does it show that the way in which a person dies cannot be harmful to him. It is clear that thinking about one's own death can be harmful – although that this is so does not show that one's own death is itself a harm to one. It is also clear that a person's death can be harmful to those who loved her when she was alive, for they will be deprived of her company once she is dead.

For example, in "Long Distance Call," Billy was deprived of the company of his much-loved grandmother when she died, and became deeply upset – until he began to talk to her from "the other side" on the telephone. Again, however, even though this is true this does not affect the Epicurean claim that death is not a harm *to the person who dies*. Finally, the Epicurean is not committed to denying that a person can be harmed by the *process* of dying, which might be painful or frightening. But to accept this is not also to accept that the end of this process – the person's death – is also a harm to her.

EPICUREAN ASSUMPTIONS

With these clarifications of the Epicurean view of the harmlessness of death in place we should now elaborate and defend the assumptions on which it is based. The first of these is the view that once a person dies she no longer exists. This assumption is based upon the Epicurean view that a person's death annihilates her, for, according to Epicurus, a person's mind is composed of a group of atoms that disperse upon death. For Epicurus, this was not so much a definition of what it was for a person to die, as a correct physical account of what happened at a person's death. Epicurus, then, would simply reject as physically impossible the view that persons might be posthumously punished for their misdeeds by being made to experience the consequences of them over and over again, as happened to Kapitain Leutnant Lanser on "Judgment Night," or that persons can continue to experience things after their deaths when they do not realize that they have died, as was the fate of Nan Adams in "The Hitch-Hiker," who continued driving to California, unaware that she had been killed in a car accident in Pennsylvania.

The second major assumption that the Epicurean view rests on is that what is harmful or beneficial for a person depends on her experiences. In its crudest form, this hedonist view of human well-being can be captured by the old adage, "What you don't know can't hurt you." At first sight, this might seem plausible. Imagine a man who desires to live in extreme privacy, but who is constantly and covertly watched by his inquisitive neighbors. Even though he would be horrified were he ever to discover that they were watching him, he never even suspects that they are, and he dies believing that his desire for privacy was fulfilled. In this case it seems right that this man was unharmed by his neighbors' violation of his privacy – and that he was because he did not know about it. In other cases, though, it seems that a person has been harmed by an event even though he never experiences the harm that it seems to have caused him. To show this, Joel Feinberg has developed an example in which a woman has devoted 30 years of her life "to the furtherance of certain ideals and ambitions in the form of one vast undertaking." Unfortunately, one month before she dies "the empire of her hopes" collapses and she is disgraced. However, the woman's friends conceal this from her and she dies contented. It seems that in this case Feinberg is right to claim that "it would not be very controversial to say that . . . [this woman] . . . has suffered grievous harm . . . although she never learned the bad news."[4]

But accepting that the woman in Feinberg's example was harmed by the collapse of her enterprise even though she never came to know of this does not undermine the second assumption that the Epicurean view is based upon. This is because the Epicurean is not committed to the form of hedonism outlined above. Rather, given that dead persons have no experiences, the Epicurean who believes that death is not a harm to the person who dies is only committed to the *weaker* claim that for an event to be harmful to a person it must affect her experiences.[5] And this claim is compatible with the view that the woman in Feinberg's example, above, was harmed by the collapse of her enterprises, even though she never came to learn of it. This is because this collapse, together with her friends' deception, leads to this woman behaving in ways that she would not have done were she to know the truth of her situation. Given the reasonable assumption that this woman had an interest in guiding her actions in accord with what was actually the case, rather than guiding them in accord with what others believed she should know about her situation, this woman was harmed insofar as her experiences were different than they would have been were this interest not to have been thwarted.[6] The experiences that this woman has, then, were worse for her than the experiences that she would have had had her friends not kept the collapse of her enterprise from her, since in having these experiences she was deprived of having the experience of responding to her enterprise's collapse. To be sure, were she to know of the collapse of her enterprise and so have the experience of responding to this she might well have experienced more pain and sorrow that she did when this collapse was kept from her. However, acknowledging this is compatible with claiming that in the respect outlined above her actual experiences were worse for her, and so she was harmed by them, even though her friends' actions might have led to her suffering less harm overall.

DEATH AND DEPRIVATION

The major assumptions that underlie the Epicurean view that death is not a harm to the person who dies are thus defensible. But that these assumptions can be defended does not mean that this Epicurean view should be accepted. Both Thomas Nagel and Fred Feldman, for example, believe that the Epicurean view that a person's death is not a harm to her should be rejected. Both Nagel and Feldman argue that a person's death will harm her if it deprives her of the goods of life that she would have otherwise enjoyed. This criticism is certainly plausible. After all, we often think that it would be worse for a person to die sooner rather than later, on the grounds that an earlier death would rob her of more of the goods of life. This was the view of Wanda Dunn, who was terrified that her death would deprive her of the goods of living her life in the light. This view is also the basis for *The Twilight Zone* episode "One for the Angels," in which Lewis J. Bookman, a salesman, convinces Mr. Death to let him make one last big sales pitch before he dies – "one for the angels." Unfortunately for Bookman, Death realizes that he intends to welsh on his agreement – and so decides to take a young girl in his place. Yet although, as these episodes of *The Twilight Zone* illustrate, the deprivation view of the harmfulness of death is plausible, to show that the Epicurean view of the harmlessness of death is false we need to move beyond such an intuitive rejection of it and offer arguments against it.

DID ANTHONY HARM AUNT AMY?

The first argument in favor of the deprivation view of the harmfulness of death to consider is Nagel's. Nagel offers an example of a man who has suffered a fate very similar to that of Aunt Amy, a character in "It's a Good Life." Aunt Amy lived in Peaksville, Ohio, whose inhabitants wake up one morning to discover that the rest of the world has vanished, and their town was on its own.[7] Worse yet, one of the children in Peaksville, Anthony Fremont, can control things with his mind – and has a tendency to destroy things that displease him. Disliking singing, he turned Aunt Amy into a "smiling, vacant thing" when, forgetting this, she started to sing. According to Nagel, in such a case it is plausible to hold that the person who was turned from a normal adult to a "smiling, vacant thing" suffered a great harm. And, claims Nagel, it is plausible to hold this because the change that such a person underwent would deprive her of the goods that she could have otherwise enjoyed.[8]

On the face of it, this sort of example grounds a good case for the view that a person's death can harm her through depriving her of the goods of life that she would have otherwise enjoyed. However, an Epicurean has two possible responses to such a deprivation-based objection to her view that death is harmless to the person who dies.[9] The first is based on the claim that when Anthony changed Aunt Amy into a smiling, vacant thing he killed her, leaving only her (animated) corpse. If this is a correct description of the case, an Epicurean could argue, then, to hold that Aunt Amy was harmed by Anthony is simply to beg the question against the Epicurean position. Alternatively, if an Epicurean thinks that if Aunt Amy was not killed by Anthony but continues to exist as a smiling, vacant thing, then she could simply claim that Aunt Amy, like the woman in Feinberg's example, above, was indeed undergoing a misfortune, albeit one that she was not aware of.[10] If she adopts this approach to examples of the type that Nagel developed, an Epicurean could agree that the person in question was harmed – but refuse to accept that this shows that death is a harm for similar reasons, on the grounds that whereas Aunt Amy existed, and so could be a subject of harm, the dead do *not* exist – and so they *cannot* be harmed. An Epicurean, then, can offer a plausible response to deprivation-based accounts of the harm of death that are based on examples such as Nagel's – and he can do so irrespective of his views concerning whether or not Aunt Amy continues to exist as Aunt Amy after Anthony has lashed out at her with his mind.

WAS WANDA DUNN RIGHT TO BE WORRIED ABOUT DEATH DEPRIVING HER OF THE GOODS OF LIFE?

A more sophisticated deprivation-based objection to the Epicurean view of death has been developed by Fred Feldman. Feldman begins his objection by reconstructing the Epicurean argument in favor of the view that death is not a harm to the person who dies:

1. Each person stops existing at the moment of death.
2. If (1), then no one feels any pain while dead.
3. If no one feels any pain while dead, then death does not lead to anything intrinsically bad for the one who dies.
4. If death does not lead to anything intrinsically bad for the one who is dead, then death is not extrinsically bad for the one who is dead.
5. Therefore, death is not extrinsically bad for the one who is dead.[11]

Feldman notes that according to the proponents of this Epicurean argument only experiences can be good or bad for a person. An experience is intrinsically good or bad for a person if it is an experience that is good or bad in itself.[12] Thus, eating an enjoyable meal would be an intrinsically good thing for a person, while suffering from hunger would be intrinsically bad for her. By contrast, something is extrinsically good or bad for a person if and only if he or she would have been intrinsically worse off at a later point in time (for the thing in question to be extrinsically good), or better off at a later point in time (for it to be extrinsically bad), had it not taken place.[13] Thus, eating an enjoyable meal might be extrinsically bad for a person were it to give her food poisoning at a later point, while being hungry might be extrinsically good for a person if he suffered its pangs while in a foreign city, and in alleviating them discovered a wonderful restaurant that he subsequently visited many times.

If we accept Feldman's account of what makes something extrinsically bad for a person then it seems that the Epicurean argument as outlined above is flawed. This is because even though we can accept that nothing can be *intrinsically* bad for a person once he has died because once a person is dead he can not experience anything (and so nothing is good or bad in itself for him), a person's death might still be *extrinsically* bad for him if it would make him intrinsically worse off. And, claims Feldman, if a person's death would deprive him of things that are intrinsically good for him then it would indeed be extrinsically bad for him. Thus, concludes Feldman, premise (4) of the above Epicurean argument is false. It is not true that something is extrinsically bad for a person *only if* it leads to something that is intrinsically bad for him.[14]

Feldman's argument is, at first sight, persuasive. It explains why we think that certain events are bad for persons "even though they are not themselves painful experiences, and they do not lead to any painful experiences." For example, it explains why we think that the failure to have the opportunity to develop his literary talent would be bad for a mute inglorious Milton, or why never having known the pleasures of being human would be bad for the mannequin in "The After Hours." (In this episode of *The Twilight Zone* a woman buys a thimble in a department store on a floor that turns out not to exist – and she then discovers that she is actually a mannequin who is allowed to enjoy some time as a human but who now must return to her inanimate state.) But closer examination of Feldman's argument shows that we should not accept it as a good reason to reject the Epicurean view of death.

Feldman's account of when something is extrinsically good or bad for someone is certainly plausible in the cases outlined above. Yet all of these cases have something in common: that the persons whose well-being is in question *all exist at the time at which they are said to be better (or worse) off.* It thus makes sense to claim that these persons are better or worse off than they could have been. However, to ask whether or not a person who is now dead would have been better off *had she lived* is to ask whether something that does not exist (i.e., the person who is now dead, and so who does not exist, on the Epicurean understanding of death) would be better off under different circumstances. But this question does *not* make sense, for what could it mean to ask whether something that does not exist would be better off under different circumstances? If the referent of this question does not exist, there is nothing about which one can intelligibly say that it would be better or worse off under different circumstances. There is, quite simply, nothing to *be* better or worse off.[15] Noting that the question of whether something would have been better or worse off under different circumstances requires one to assume that the thing in question exists shows that Feldman's account of what it is for an event to be extrinsically good or bad for something rests on the same assumption: that the subject of the question actually exists. Since this is so, a more explicit version of Feldman's account of what it is for something to be extrinsically good or bad for a person would require that the "he or she" whose well being is in question *exists* at the time at which the comparison is being made. But once this is made explicit, then Feldman's argument against the Epicurean view of death fails. Even though Feldman is correct to note that premise (4) of the Epicurean argument, as he outlines it, should be replaced with his account of what makes something extrinsically good or bad, something can only be extrinsically good or bad for a person if she exists. Since a person ceases to exist upon her death nothing can be extrinsically bad for her – and this is true even on Feldman's account of what it is for an event to be extrinsically good or bad for something. Feldman's deprivation-based account of why death is a harm to the person who dies is thus mistaken.

MUST WE EXIST TO BE HARMED?

Yet although it seems correct to hold that a more explicit version of Feldman's account of what it is for something to be extrinsically good or bad for a person should require that she exist to be so affected, Feldman takes pains to deny that a person must exist for an event to be extrinsically good or bad for him. Feldman holds that "a state of affairs can be extrinsically bad for a person whether it occurs before he exists, while he exists, or after he exists. The only requirement is that the value of the life he leads if it occurs is lower than the value of the life he leads if it does not occur."[16] To illustrate this, he considers an example "in which something bad for a person occurs *before* the person exists": Feldman's father loses his job before Feldman was born.[17] In consequence of this, Feldman "had to move to another town, and I was therefore raised in a bad neighborhood and had to attend worse schools." This was bad for him, he contends, ". . . because the value-for-me of the life I would have led if he had not lost his job is greater than the value-for-me of my actual life." Feldman concludes by claiming that "the same may be true of cases involving things that will happen after I cease to exist."[18]

Unfortunately for Feldman, the intuitive force of this example rests on the very view that he wishes to deny: that for something to be good or bad for a person she must exist to experience the goodness or the badness in question. Given Feldman's stipulation that he would have existed irrespective of whether or not his father lost his job, it seems that his example provides a plausible case for the view that a state of affairs that occurs before a person exists can be bad for him. However, the force of Feldman's example rests on the intuition that because his father lost his job the experiences that he had were worse than those that he would have had had he not done so. As such, it rests on the intuition that a state of affairs can be extrinsically good or bad for a person *depending upon the experiences that it causes him to have.* But since this is so, this does not support Feldman's claim that "the same [i.e., that a state of affairs is extrinsically bad for Feldman] may be true of cases involving things that will happen after I cease to exist." This is because after Feldman ceases to exist he will have no experiences to be affected by any states of affairs that occur. As such, then, Feldman has only shown that an event can be extrinsically bad for a person if it occurs *before* he exists – he has not shown that an event can be extrinsically bad for a person *after* he exists. And it is this latter claim that Feldman needs to establish to support his view that a person's death could harm her by depriving her of the goods of life that she would have otherwise enjoyed.

IT'S A GOOD LIFE . . .

An Epicurean, then, can defend her view that death is not a harm to the person who dies against the criticism that it is a harm since it deprives the person who dies of the goods of life. The Epicurean rejection of this criticism can be further supported through understanding the Epicurean view of the good life. We have already noted that Epicureans are hedonists, believing that the degree to which a person enjoys or lacks well-being depends on her experiences. For Epicureans, there are two types of pleasurable experience: that which a person feels as she experiences the removal of a lack, and that which one experiences after a pain has been removed.[19] For an Epicurean, the highest type of pleasure is *ataraxia*, or mental tranquility, which is simply the state of having no pain.[20] Since this is her conception of what the good life consists in it is clear why an Epicurean won't be persuaded by deprivation-based objections to her view of the harmlessness of death. Such objections will be based upon a very different view of the good life than that which she accepts; they will be based upon the view that the good life consists of the enjoyment of more of that sort of pleasure that one experiences when a perceived lack is removed.[21] But understanding the Epicurean view of the good life is not useful merely to show us why an Epicurean's rejection of deprivation-based objections to her view of death is so deep-seated; it is also useful in that it might help us to make our own lives go better.

To understand this last point, let us turn again to the two *Twilight Zone* episodes "It's a Good Life" and "Nothing in the Dark." It is clear that the inhabitants of Peaksville do not live good lives. They are perpetually terrorized by Anthony, who "took away the automobiles, the electricity, the machines, because they displeased him, and . . . [who] . . . moved . . . [the] . . . entire community back into the dark ages" – and who can effortlessly send any of them "into the cornfield," or turn them into a "grotesque walking horror," if they ever displease him. Yet despite this, we can still learn about how to live a genuinely good life from the experience of Peaksville. To avoid displeasing Anthony the inhabitants of Peaksville curtail their desires to ensure that they do not behave in ways that he does not approve of; the adults have to curtail their desire to express their disapproval of Anthony's choice of television entertainment, Dan has to curtail his desire to play his new Perry Como record, and Aunt Amy should have curtailed her desire to sing. And they have to convince Anthony that it is *good* that their desires are curtailed in this way. Now, even though the inhabitants of Peaksville do not lead good lives as a result of having to curtail their desires in this way, it does not follow that the curtailment of desire is always a bad thing.

In illustration of this let us draw on the work of the social scientist Barry Schwartz. Schwartz distinguished two sorts of people: those whose decisions are guided by their attempts to maximize their satisfaction ("maximizers"), and those whose decisions are guided by their attempts to ensure that they are simply satisfied enough ("satisficers").[22] Schwartz believes that the proliferation of choices that persons have in a modern consumer society is leading them to become maximizers. Faced by a huge range of choices, people become worried that they are not, for example, watching the best episode of *The Twilight Zone*, or that they are not getting the best deal on the goods that they are buying. As such, even though they would have been happy with the episode that they watched or the goods that they bought had they not realized that there were alternatives to them that they had chosen to reject, the knowledge of the existence of these foregone alternatives renders them dissatisfied with what they have. By contrast, since a satisficer would not be engaged in trying to maximize her well-being she would not be constantly comparing what she has with what she could have had. Since this is so, if she was satisfied with what she had the fact that she had foregone alternatives to it would not upset her. Rather than being discontented maximizers, then, Schwartz claims, we should instead work to become contented satisficers. And this view is in accord with the Epicurean view of the good life. We should not strive to remove the perceived lack of the best episode of *The Twilight Zone*, or the best deal on the good we buy. Instead, we should seek a state of having no pain; we should seek to curtail our desires in such a way that we are immune to the maximizer's pains of knowing that what she has might not be the best. Unlike the inhabitants of Peaksville, then, we do not have to curtail our desires simply to live, to avoid being sent to the cornfield by Anthony. But we should try to curtail them so that we can live *well*.

It is, however, important not to misunderstand the Epicurean view that to live well we should curtail our desires. This view is not that we should strive to shrink our desires to nothing, but, rather, that we should live in accordance with our natural desires. For Epicurus, these are simple: "food, drink, shelter, maybe some friendly human company."[23] We should not try to deny ourselves these to try to induce *ataraxia* artificially. Moreover (and more relevant, perhaps, to practical advice concerning how to live life in the twenty-first century), we should not undermine our own happiness by worrying about our deaths, nor (and more generally) should we worry about the possibility of being subject to future harms that might not affect us.[24] This last point about how to live a good life is part of the message of "Nothing in the Dark." At the close of this episode Wanda recognizes that her life has been ruined not by dying – which, in the words of Mr. Death himself, would come to her more as a harmless "whisper" than as a harmful "explosion" – but by the actions she took as a result of her fear of dying. Wanda, then, suffered the same ironic fate as a maximizer, although for different reasons: By behaving in a way that she believed would secure her a good life she actually acts in such a way as to undermine her ability to achieve the very goal that she strives for.

Of course, an anti-Epicurean could claim that he would be able to account for the badness of Wanda's death, too, in that by hiding from Mr. Death she deprived herself of the goods of a life in the sunlight, as a person who dies is deprived of the goods of life. Yet although this might, at first sight, be a plausible claim, it overlooks the fact that Wanda deprived herself of the goods of a life in the sun precisely because she was scared of the deprivation of the goods of life that she believed Mr. Death would inflict on her. It is her fear of being deprived of the goods of life that led her to be deprived of them. As an anti-Epicurean, then, who feared death and considered it to be a harm, Wanda made the crucial mistake of being concerned about what she might lose from a certain course of action, rather than focusing on simply satisfying the simple human desires for "food, drink, shelter, maybe some friendly human company." Her view that she would "Rather live in the dark than not live at all" was a view that an Epicurean would roundly reject – and it was the view that led to her downfall.

CONCLUSION

In both "It's a Good Life" and "Nothing in the Dark" the characters are portrayed as having a perfectly natural human fear – the fear of their own deaths. But, as "Nothing in the Dark" makes clear, this fear is irrational, for, as Mr. Death, personified in the shot policeman noted, death is "Nothing to be afraid of." Despite Wanda's worries – worries shared both by Feldman, and by many of us – death does not harm the person who dies by depriving them of the goods of life, for once she is dead there is no existing person to be the subject of such deprivation. Nor can a person's death harm her when she is still alive, and would be a subject of deprivation – for then she is not dead, and a person cannot be harmed by what has not yet occurred.[25] Indeed, as the title of "Nothing in the Dark" makes clear, the fear of death is not only irrational, but almost childish – it is children whose fears of the unknown at night we comfort by telling them that there is nothing in the dark. And, indeed, for Epicurus, there is literally *nothing* in the dark of death, for death marks the absolute annihilation of the person who could experience the alleged harm of death that she is so afraid of. Rather than adopting the point of view of the characters in these episodes of *The Twilight Zone*, then, we should instead adopt the point of view of their writers, and recognize that death is not a harm to the person who dies.

However, *The Twilight Zone* can not only comfort us in this Epicurean way – it can also help us to live better lives by showing us that we should be satisficers, rather than maximizers. Wanda's life went ill for her because she tried to maximize its length; had she instead only tried to satisfy her desire for the simple pleasure of enjoying the sunlight things would have been better for her. And it will not do for the opponent of Epicurus to claim that the badness of Wanda's self-imposed deprivation supports the anti-Epicurean view that death is a harm as it deprives the person who dies of the goods of life, for it is precisely Wanda's concern to avoid being deprived of these goods that led to her sorry state. Thus, rather than trying to maximize either the good things that we have, or the length of our lives, we should instead simply enjoy what we have. In viewing *The Twilight Zone*, then, we should be led to adopt a more Epicurean – and less fearful – view of both life and death.[26]

NOTES

1. "Nothing in the Dark," written by George Clayton Johnson, directed by Lamont Johnson, original air date January 5, 1962.
2. Epicurus, "Letter to Menoeceus," in Jason L. Saunders, ed., *Greek and Roman Philosophy after Aristotle* (Free Press, 1966), p. 50.
3. Steven Luper-Foy, "Annihilation," in John Martin Fischer, ed., *The Metaphysics of Death* (Stanford University Press, 1993), p. 270. Christopher Belshaw, *10 Good Questions About Life and Death* (Blackwell, 2005), p. 38.
4. Joel Feinberg, "Harm to Others, " in Fischer, ed., *The Metaphysics of Death*, pp. 181–2.
5. See here Harry S. Silverstein, "The Evil of Death," in Fischer, ed., *The Metaphysics of Death*, pp. 106–9, and S. E. Rosenbaum, "How to be Dead and not Care: A Defense of Epicurus," *American Philosophical Quarterly* 23 (1986), p. 124.
6. For further discussion of this see my "The Myth of Posthumous Harm," *American Philosophical Quarterly* 42 (2005): 311–22.
7. "It's a Good Life," written by Rod Sterling, based on the short story "It's a Good Life," by Jerome Bixby, directed by James Sheldon, original air date November 3, 1961.
8. As Nagel puts it, in such a case we should "consider the person he was, and the person he *could* be now." Thomas Nagel, "Death," in Fischer, ed.,

The Metaphysics of Death, p. 66, emphasis in the original. However, Nagel is wrong to hold that what is relevant is the goods that such a person *could* be experiencing, for there are many ways that she could be, some good, and some bad. Rather, what is important is how such a person *would* be were his condition not to have changed. See Jeff McMahan, "Death and the Value of Life," *Ethics* 99 (1988), p. 41.

9. Glenn Braddock, "Epicureanism, Death, and the Good Life," *Philosophical Inquiry* 22 (2000), p. 55.

10. It is also possible to claim that Aunt Amy was not harmed as she did not experience harm, as noted by James Warren, *Facing Death: Epicurus and his Critics* (Oxford University Press, 2004), p. 27. But, as was argued above, this view is implausible.

11. Fred Feldman, *Confrontations with the Reaper: A Philosophical Study of the Nature and Value of Death* (Oxford University Press, 1992), p. 136.

12. Ibid., p. 133.

13. Ibid., p. 138.

14. Although, as the examples above show and as Feldman accepts, something *can* be extrinsically bad for a person in this way.

15. Note that the problem here is not one of reference, but of predication. We can easily refer to objects that do not exist, such as hobbits. However, it is not clear that we can attribute, or predicate, properties to things that do not exist, for if we do so we would be claiming that it is true that the non-existing thing had a certain property – and it is not clear that we can intelligibly do this. See David-Hillel Ruben, "A Puzzle About Posthumous Predication," *The Philosophical Review*, 97 (1988), pp. 211–36. See also Harry S. Silverstein, "The Evil of Death Revisited," *Life and Death: Metaphysics and Ethics, Midwest Studies in Philosophy Volume XXIV* (Blackwell, 2000), p. 122.

16. Feldman, *Confrontations with the Reaper*, p. 152.

17. Ibid.

18. Ibid.

19. Julia Annas, *The Morality of Happiness* (Oxford University Press, 1993), p. 188.

20. Warren, *Facing Death*, p. 17.

21. Braddock, "Epicureanism, Death, and the Good Life," pp. 57–65.

22. Barry Schwartz, *The Paradox of Choice: Why More is Less* (Harper Perennial, 2005).

23. Braddock, "Epicureanism, Death, and the Good Life," p. 58.

24. Although this does not mean that one should not be prudent.

25. See my "The Myth of Posthumous Harm," pp. 311–22.

26. I thank Mary Sirridge for encouraging me to write this chapter and Lester Hunt for his invaluable comments on an earlier draft.

INDEX

INDEX

INDEX

INDEX

Greek philosophy (*cont'd*)
    freedom–reason relation, 151
    poetic justice, 29, 30, 33
Greek tragedy, 33, 116

harm of death, 171–85
hedonism, 175–6, 182
Herodotus, 150
Hinduism, worship, 157
Hitchcock, Alfred, 130
"The Hitch-Hiker" (TZ episode), 152, 175
Hitler's Germany, 70–1, 73–4
hope, existentialism and, 104–9
horror stories, 27, 34–5
Hume, David, 128
humor, 26–7, 32–3, 34, 35
"Hymn to Aphrodite" (poem; Sappho), 164–5
hypercubes, 81–3
hypertesseracts, 83–4

"I Shot an Arrow in the Air" (TZ episode), 30, 36–7n
"I Sing the Body Electric" (TZ episode), 44–5, 48
identity, personal, 101–4, 106
imagination, 39
    endings, 40, 48–55
    reality–fiction boundary, 77–91
    reason, 98–9
    truth, 137–8
"In His Image" (TZ episode), 94, 97, 104–9
incompleteness, 88
"The Invaders" (TZ episode), 37n, 45, 46, 48
irony
    postmodern, 97
    Tales of Dread, 32–4, 37n
Islam, worship, 163
"It's a Good Life" (TZ episode), 177–8, 182, 183, 184–5

"Judgment Night" (TZ episode), 28, 175
"Judgment at Nuremberg" (teleplay), 9
judgments, treachery of the commonplace, 58–74
justice, Tales of Dread, 26–35

Kant, Immanuel, 115
Kaufman, Dave, 12
Knight, Damon, 113, 114
knowledge, 136–46
    of self, 94–5
    treachery of the commonplace, 58–74
Koran, the, 163
Kripke, Saul, 86, 87
Kroll, Martin, 13–14, 21

Langner, Lawrence, 12
language, reality–fiction boundary, 86–7
"The Last Flight" (TZ episode), 37n
"The Last Night of a Jockey" (TZ episode), 7, 36n
Lewis, David, 59, 88–9
"Little Girl Lost" (TZ episode), 79, 83–4
"The Little People" (TZ episode), 99
    power–worshipability relation, 155–69
live television drama, 6, 7, 8–22
"Living Doll" (TZ episode), 152
"The Lonely" (TZ episode), 152
"Long Distance Call" (TZ episode), 175
love, 161–2, 164–6, 169–70n
Luper-Foy, Steven, 174
lynchings, 12–22

machines
    existentialism and, 106–8
    freedom–reason relation, 147–52, 153
    surprise endings, 44–5, 48

INDEX

magic themes
  freedom–reason relation, 147–53
  Tales of Dread, 26–35
Marxist thought, "pleasure" in film, 54
Matheson, Richard, 137
maximizers, 182–3, 185
Meinong, Alexius, 88
mental tranquility (*ataraxia*), 182–4
metaphysics, reality–fiction boundary,
  77–91
"Midnight Sun" (TZ episode), 37n
Miller, Arthur, 7–8
Miller, Nolan, 16
mob violence, 12–22
modal realism, 88–9
monotheism, 162, 163–4, 168–9
moral judgment, 58–9, 70–4

Nagasawa, Yujin, 164, 169n
Nagel, Thomas, 177–8
narrative
  endings, 40, 41–55
  film noir type, 72–3
  Serling's artistic evolution, 7
  Tales of Dread, 26–35
narrators, 130–4
Naturalism, 7–8
Nazi Germany, 70–1, 73–4
Negritude, 120
neo-Brechtian critical thinking, 48–9,
  54
"Nervous Man in a Four Dollar
  Room" (TZ episode), 7
New Wave cinema, 133–4
"A Nice Place to Visit" (TZ episode),
  32
"Nick of Time" (TZ episode)
  ending, 42, 48
  freedom–reason relation, 147–53
  Tales of Dread, 17
Nietzsche, Friedrich, 116
"Night of the Meek" (TZ episode),
  37n

"Nightmare at 20,000 Feet"
  (TZ episode)
  ending, 46–7, 152
  epistemology, 136, 137–46
"Ninety Years Without Slumbering"
  (TZ episode), 173
"No Exit" (play; Sartre), 93, 94, 98,
  107
Northern–Southern state divide,
  12–19
"Nothing in the Dark" (TZ episode)
  ending, 47–8
  fear of death, 171–85
Nussbaum, Martha, 33

"The Odyssey of Flight 33"
  (TZ episode)
  ending, 43, 48
  fiction–reality overlap, 123–35
"Of Late I Think of Cliffordville"
  (TZ episode), 32–3
"One for the Angels" (TZ episode),
  177
ontology of fictions, 125–6, 134–5
open endings, 42–3, 51
optimism, "In His Image," 104–9
Others, race and racism, 119
Otto, Rudolph, 169n
overcoherence, Tales of Dread, 31

paradox of negative affect, 53–4
"The Parallel" (TZ episode), 79–80,
  84
paranoia, 26–7, 31
Perkins, Victor, 54
personal identity, 101–4, 106
perspective taking, 39–40, 48–55
phenomenology, art and, 117
Pirandello, Luigi, 93, 100–1
Playhouse 90, 9, 17–19
pleasure, Frame Shifting text, 54–5
Poe, Edgar Allan, 27
poetic justice, 29–34, 35

INDEX

INDEX